THE NEW NATURAL

A SURVEY OF BRITISH NA

SOUTHERN ENGLAND

THE NEW NATURALIST LIBRARY

SOUTHERN ENGLAND

Looking at the Natural Landscapes

PETER FRIEND

Collins

This edition published in 2008 by Collins,
An imprint of HarperCollins Publishers

HarperCollins Publishers
77-85 Fulham Palace Road
London W6 8JB
www.collins.co.uk

First published 2008

A CIP catalogue record for this book is available
From the British Library.

Set in FF [SC] Nexus by
Martin Brown

Printed in Hong Kong by Printing Express

Hardback
ISBN 978-0-00-724742-4

Paperback
ISBN 978-0-00-724743-1

Contents

Editor's Preface

L DUDLEY STAMP's *Britain's Structure and Scenery* was one if the earliest books of The New Naturalist Library, published in 1946. Repeated later editions in the period to 1986 testified to the success of his approach towards providing a geological framework for understanding Britain's landscapes and natural history. He began his account in these words: 'The wealth of a country's fauna and fauna and flora is not to be measured by numbers of species alone. Its wealth lies rather in variety, and to a naturalist in the British Isles, the fascination of the native fauna and flora is in the great variety to be found in a small space.' This variety has its foundation in the underlying geology and the landscapes which are derived from the geology, as Dudley Stamp described so well. For some time, it has been the ambition of the Editors to approach this subject again, since our understanding of the geology and associated landscape evolution has increased so very significantly in the last few decades. The author, Peter Friend, has had long experience of active field research in geology and landscape in many parts of the world, as well as having an intimate knowledge of the subject in the British Isles. He has been able to take full advantage of modern developments in computer mapping and colour printing, making it possible to present the subject in a novel fashion, with great clarity, following the New Naturalist tradition emphasising the importance of illustration. The individual treatment of regions and areas of Southern England brings to the fore the significance of geology and landscape for naturalists who have local or wider interests at heart, giving a necessary basis for relating biodiversity to geodiversity. These two aspects of natural history have come to be seen to be widely significant in understanding plant and animal distribution as well as the problems of conservation. The book is therefore a very timely addition to the New Naturalist Library.

Author's Foreword and Acknowledgements

MOST PEOPLE ENJOY SCENERY. In my case, an enthusiasm for exploring the countryside was learnt early on from my parents, and my career as a geologist has since allowed me to explore landscapes from the Arctic to tropical deserts and jungles. My hope is that this book will help more people to enjoy the countryside by bringing together some of the exciting recent discoveries about our Earth.

Landscapes are easy to look at, but difficult to describe in words. Recent developments in computer technology offer powerful ways of analysing and presenting landscapes using maps, diagrams and photographs, and it is this imagery that forms the core of this book. Developing the imagery has been the main role of a succession of enthusiastic helpers. Lucinda Edes, Emilie Galley, Liesbeth Renders and Helena Warrington brought their skills and enthusiasm to the early days of the project, working out what could be done best. James Sample has more recently further developed the methods of presentation, and has played a key role in bringing this project to fruition. All have helped to make the project enjoyable as well as productive.

The home for this project has been the Department of Earth Sciences at the University of Cambridge. I walked into the Department as a first-year undergraduate more than 50 years ago and, apart from a period in the Scott Polar Research Institute, I have been based here ever since. I have been teaching and exploring the scenery and geology of many parts of the world, including

multiple visits to Spitsbergen, Greenland, Spain, India and Pakistan. This has
been an exciting period to be working in geology, particularly in Cambridge,
because many key advances have been achieved by the people working here.
Apart from the great benefit of being part of this research environment, I have
enjoyed the support of six successive Heads of Department and many other
colleagues, especially our administrator Margaret Johnston and her team. It has
been invaluable to have access to the excellent library run by Ruth Banger and
Libby Tilley, and the patient computer support of Jun Aizawa, Aidan Foster,
Pete Hill and Pete Wilkins.

I would also like to acknowledge my debt to the Cambridge college system,
particularly my own college, Darwin. The College has provided me with the
congenial friendship of many people from diverse backgrounds, and their skills
have helped me to remain a generalist in my interests.

Any work of this sort on the British Isles owes a fundamental debt to the
British Geological Survey (BGS), now based at Keyworth near Nottingham.
The numerous Survey maps and reports on this country provide a remarkable
source of carefully observed and objective information. The BGS has also readily
provided advice and discussion of this project, and helped to determine the sort
of coverage and level that would be best.

Many other people have made important contributions by providing ideas
and information. These include: John R. L. Allen, Julian Andrews, Muriel Arber,
Steve Boreham, Becky Briant, Keith Clayton, Tony Cox, Alan Dawn, Colin Forbes,
Brian Funnell, Phillip Gibbard, Steve Jones, Gerald Lucy, Dan Mackenzie,
Bob Markham, Charles Notcutt, Bernard O'Connor, Richard Preece, Graham
Ward and Richard West.

This book is dedicated to the **Dr John C. Taylor Foundation**, which has
provided the financial support for the project, allowing me to work with such a
remarkable succession of talented young assistants. More than 40 years ago,
John spent two summers exploring the geology of Spitsbergen with me, and we
have remained friends ever since. I am extremely grateful for the help of his
foundation during the writing of this book.

Picture Credits

T HE PHOTOGRAPHS and other illustrations that form such a key part of this book have come from many sources, and I am grateful to the following organisations and individuals for kindly allowing me to use their material:

Aerofilms (Figs 133, 232, 249, 252, 256, 258, 259, 261, 270, 280, 309, 312)
British Geological Survey (Figs 152, 284)
Cambridge News (Fig. 233)
Cambridge University Collection of Air Photographs (Figs 25, 118, 120, 243, 253, 282, 300, 310)
Cassini Publishing (Figs 26, 27)
Sylvia Cordaiy Photo Library (Fig. 141)
Robert Harding Picture Library (Fig. 313)
English Heritage (Figs 83, 308)
Landform Slides – Ken Gardner (Figs 17, 18, 43, 55, 70, 75, 76, 85, 88, 104, 161, 162, 165, 195)
Landform Slides – John L. Roberts (Fig. 69)
Last Refuge Ltd – Adrian Warren, Dae Sasitorn and Will Brett (Figs 41, 42, 46, 47, 53, 54, 56, 58, 60, 62, 63, 67, 68, 71, 72, 73, 74, 82, 86, 89, 90, 91, 101, 102, 103, 108, 110, 111, 112, 119, 121, 122, 125, 130, 132, 134, 135, 142, 144, 146, 148, 158, 163, 164, 169, 171, 175, 176, 185, 191, 192, 193, 194, 196, 216, 217, 218, 219, 220, 222, 254)
London Aerial Photo Library (Figs 23, 199, 205, 207, 235, 257, 277, 297, 298, 303, 314)

Norfolk Museums and Archaeology Service – Nick Arber (Fig. 16)
Norfolk Museums and Archaeology Service – Derek A. Edwards (Figs 1, 287, 293, 301, 302, 306, 307, 315)
Network Rail (Fig. 145)
Peter Oliver, Herefordshire and Worcestershire Heritage Trust (Fig. 172)
Mike Page (Fig. 311)
Science Photo Library (Fig. 2)
Sedgwick Museum, Cambridge (Fig. 239)
R. C. Selley – Petravin Press (Fig. 202)
Sheila Smart (Fig. 131)
Suffolk County Council (Fig. 255)
Victoria & Albert Museum (Fig. 250)

Illustrations that do not have a source credited in the caption are my own work, or that of the team working with me at the Department of Earth Sciences in Cambridge.

CHAPTER 1

Looking at Southern England's Landscapes

FIRST APPROACHES

T HE WORD **LANDSCAPE** has different meanings for different people, and the best way to illustrate the meaning I have adopted in this book is to look at an example. I have chosen a landscape in the northwest corner of Norfolk, part of our East Anglia Region (Fig. 1).

FIG 1. Landscape of the northwest corner of Norfolk.
(Copyright Norfolk Museums and Archaeology Service & Derek A. Edwards)

My approach is to focus first on the natural features that we can call landforms, because they have distinctive shapes that directly reflect the processes that formed them. In this Norfolk landscape, coastline landforms are clearly defined but are remarkably varied, ranging from sea cliffs to sandy beaches, gravel spits, wind-blown dunes and salt marshes. Inland, the main features in this photo are the groups of buildings that form the villages and the edge of the town of Hunstanton, and the pattern of fields and woods. All of these are man-made features and are best understood by following the work of *landscape historians*. My interest is primarily in the natural topography on which these man-made features have developed, because even in this rather flat landscape – and not clearly visible on the photograph – there are gentle hills, valleys and streams that I want to try to understand.

Scale and size in landscapes are important considerations that we will return to frequently. The landscapes that we shall be discussing are generally kilometres to tens of kilometres across, and they are often best examined from the air, or by using computer-based maps with exaggerated vertical scale.

Southern England contains many famous and well-loved natural landscapes, ranging from the Chalk Downs, with their unique flora and fauna, to the rocky promontories and bays of Cornwall, Devon and Dorset. In total topographic contrast, the Fens of East Anglia are regarded by some as representing an extreme absence of any scenery at all, but their remarkable flatness is of interest because they are the result of recent sea-level rise, and of engineering on a remarkable scale. These different landscapes are produced by a wide variety of events and processes; exploring these is the theme of this book.

As we have already seen, landscapes have often been extensively modified by people. The early clearance of woodland and the construction of field boundaries have profoundly changed the scenery and, more recently, the construction of buildings, roads, railways, canals and airports has almost completely covered some areas of Southern England. Figure 2 shows night-time lighting in cities, towns and oil platforms, giving a vivid impression of the present extent and distribution of the larger settlements. It is surprising how varied the population density is, even in crowded Britain. Using the figures for 2002, the population density of the UK overall is 244 people per square kilometre, but this conceals a huge variation: 8 people per square kilometre in the Highland Region of Scotland, 143 for Cornwall, 149 for Norfolk and an amazing 13,609 for Kensington and Chelsea in London.

The main focus of this book is the pattern of large scenic features that have resulted from natural episodes that predate human influence. It is not usually difficult to distinguish the natural from the man-made, and the study of the

Boundary of Southern England as used in this book

FIG 2. Satellite image over Britain showing artificial lighting at night.
(Copyright Planetary Visions Ltd/Science Photo Library)

natural can often explain many aspects of the way our ancestors lived in the landscape. It is possible to uncover the reasons why people have chosen to settle with their families in certain places, why villages have grown by the clustering of houses in particular locations, and why some villages have then grown further and turned into towns and eventually cities. Even the roads, railways and airfields have clearly grown using the valley floors, river crossings, better-drained slopes and plateaus that are part of the natural scenery.

There is a further enjoyment that people find in landscapes and scenery that is more difficult to understand. Is it just the physical challenge that causes people to walk and climb to the tops of hills, mountains and other viewpoints? Why do people enjoy the work of landscape painters and photographers? Why do so many tourists in cars choose to take 'scenic' excursions rather than the shortest routes, and why is the preservation of 'unspoilt' or wilderness areas now such a popular cause? It is difficult to understand the various emotions involved, and trying too hard to analyse them may be missing the point. So it seems best to hope simply that this book will help to satisfy some people's curiosity, and at the same time add to their enjoyment of our natural landscapes.

MAPPING AND ANALYSING SOUTHERN ENGLAND

The detailed discussions of most of the rest of this book have involved dividing Southern England into a number of Areas that form the 'building blocks' for the coverage of Southern England (Fig. 3). Each Area is based on a double-page spread of the size used in many of the larger road atlases available for Britain. In this case I have used the Collins Road Atlas, Britain. This means that total coverage of Southern England is provided, and it is easy for the reader to navigate from place to place. At the beginning of each Area description, a location map of the Area and its neighbours is provided. Ordnance Survey (OS) National Grid References are provided for the edges of the Area, in km east and north of the arbitrary OS Grid origin some 80 km west of the Scilly Isles.

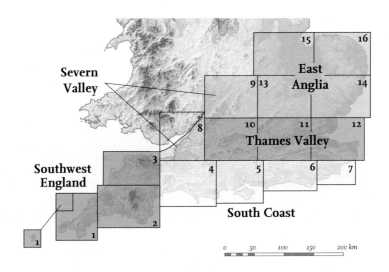

FIG 3. Division of Southern England into Regions and Areas.

For convenient reference the Areas – numbered 1 to 16 – are grouped into five **Regions**. Each Region forms a chapter and starts with a general introduction:

CHAPTER	REGION	AREA
Chapter 4	Southwest	1 West Cornwall 2 East Cornwall and South Devon 3 North Devon and West Somerset
Chapter 5	South Coast	4 East Devon, Somerset and Dorset 5 Hampshire and the Isle of Wight 6 Sussex 7 East Sussex and Southeast Kent
Chapter 6	Severn Valley	8 Bristol 9 The Cotswolds and the Middle Severn
Chapter 7	London and the Thames Valley	10 The Cotswolds to Reading 11 London 12 The Thames Estuary
Chapter 8	East Anglia	13 Northampton to Cambridge 14 Suffolk and North Essex 15 Leicester to the Fens 16 Norfolk

Even the Area building blocks are relatively large, with arbitrary boundaries, and it has generally been helpful to discuss smaller areas within and across these boundaries that are based on natural features of the scenery (Fig. 4). I have called these smaller areas **Landscapes**, because they are characterised by distinctive features, usually reflecting aspects of the bedrock or distinctive events in their evolution.

These Landscapes correspond closely to area divisions of England that were defined by the Government Countryside Agency (www.countryside.gov.uk). This scheme divides England into 159 'character areas' on the basis of natural features of the scenery along with aspects of its human settlement, past and future development, land use and vegetation and wildlife, so they are likely to be familiar divisions to many readers of the New Naturalist series. Other Government agencies (particularly the Department for Environment, Food and

Level 1: *The Region* (e.g. Chapter 8, East Anglia)

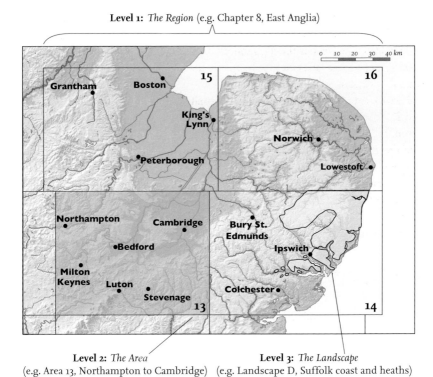

Level 2: *The Area*   Level 3: *The Landscape*
(e.g. Area 13, Northampton to Cambridge)   (e.g. Landscape D, Suffolk coast and heaths)

FIG 4. Examples of the three levels of division adopted in the treatment of
Southern England.

Rural Affairs) that administer the funding of land management use the same
character area division.

Maps displaying patterns of elevation of the countryside above sea level are
an important part of the discussions. The elevation data on the maps in this
book have been compiled and made available as part of the LANDMAP project,
which provides a computer-based digital survey of Britain for research and
educational use. LANDMAP Digital Elevation Maps (DEMs) are based on satellite
radar survey measurements which divide the land surface into a grid of 25 m by
25 m pixels. The average height of each pixel is then measured to produce a
terrain model with a vertical accuracy of about ± 5 m. A standard colour shading
scale is used to represent heights, ranging from greens for the lowest ground,
through yellows and browns, to greys for the highest ground. It is best to use the

full range of colours for each map, no matter what numerical range of heights is involved. This makes it possible to convey the fine detail of slopes etc., whether the map is for the Fens or the high moors. To make it possible to compare between maps using this colour scheme, we have quoted the maximum elevation reached in each Area on each map.

I have used ESRI ARC Geographic Information System (GIS) software in the processing and manipulating of the map data. This software makes it possible to present artificial hill-shading, which makes the topography easier to understand, and to provide maps representing slope patterns in certain areas.

In addition, data on roads, railways, coastlines, town boundaries, rivers, etc. suitable for reproduction at a scale of 1 : 200,000 has been made available by the Collins Bartholomew mapping agency. For any further details of the areas covered, it is recommended that Ordnance Survey *Landranger* (1 : 50,000) maps are consulted.

LANDSCAPE CHANGE

We tend to think of rural landscapes as unchanging features of our surroundings, in contrast to the man-made scenery of cities and towns. Yet we all know of local catastrophes, such as a sea cliff collapsing during a storm, or a flooding river removing its bank and wrecking the nearby buildings, and these are the sorts of local events that do result in change. Despite the excitement, individual changes of this sort are small and can usually be regarded as local modifications. However, over time, the accumulated effects of many such modifications can cause whole landscapes to change.

Size and time clearly both play key parts here. The collapsed cliff or eroded river bank will probably be tens to hundreds of metres long at most, while the larger landscape features picked out in this book are tens or even hundreds of kilometres across. Noting the length scales involved in this way is an important way of keeping such differences clearly in mind.

Moreover, while local events such as the destruction of landforms or buildings may be immediately newsworthy, more long-term patterns of change in the natural scenery are rarely apparent during the life spans of people, and even during the hundreds of years of written records. So it becomes necessary to use indirect and circumstantial evidence – to play the detective – to find out what long-term changes have been going on.

An important step in thinking about the natural landscape is to look at it in terms of modifications to complex surfaces defined by the ground. On land, we tend to be most aware of erosional processes removing material, but it is important to realise that the material removed has to end up somewhere – and this will involve its deposition later, on land or in the sea. How much material was removed from the cliff during the storm or from the banks of the river during the flood? Where did the lost material go, and how did it change the landscape when it was deposited at its new destination? Knowledge of these surface modifications can provide a yardstick that allows us to compare different sorts of changes happening over different periods of time and at different scales, and can help us to work out their relative importance, quoting amounts and rates. For example, a flooding river may remove a hundred metres of river bank, modifying the local landscape a little in the process. However, this modification is unlikely to have much impact on the scenery, unless followed many, many times by similar modifications, over centuries to hundreds of thousands of years. In this way a series of such floods can erode and move material that, in the long run, may be of sufficient volume to significantly change the landscape, for example lowering a hill slope or filling a valley bottom.

The majority of – but not all – surface modification processes act to reduce or flatten topography, mainly by eroding the higher features but also by filling in lower ground with sediment. So logically landscapes might always be regarded as tending towards a flat surface. Our understanding of the processes involved suggests that any land area with mountains or hills will be eroded downwards to an increasingly flat surface as time passes, although the rate of erosion will reduce as the topography becomes more and more smooth. Acting against these flattening processes are periodic movements of the ground surface caused by forces within the Earth, producing new mountains and hills, and so creating new landscapes (Fig. 5).

Continuing research into the processes operating within the Earth shows that movements of the Earth's crust are taking place continuously, even though the rates involved are generally too slow to be noticeable. The discovery that the Earth's surface consists of a large number of tectonic plates in continuous relative movement was one of the major breakthroughs in the earth sciences, and has fundamentally changed our understanding of the planet. More on this topic will be considered in Chapter 3, but at this point it is important to realise just how slow the rates of movement are: at most a few centimetres per year on average (often compared to the rate at which fingernails grow). Occasionally, movements of centimetres or metres occur within seconds along faults during earthquakes, but the average rate of movement is still rather slow. Most of us living in stable areas are totally unconscious of any movement at all because we are, ourselves, moving slowly with the landscape that we live on. Slow though the

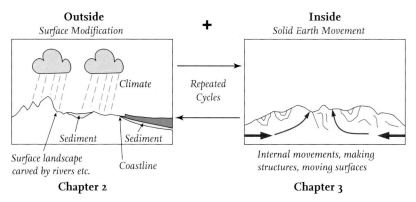

FIG 5. Landscapes are changed by surface modifications (Chapter 2) and solid earth movements (Chapter 3).

movements may be in a particular landscape, so also are the rates of surface modification, and the balance between the two is a delicate one. In much of Southern England modification by surface processes is dominant, but this has not always been the case.

Our next chapter deals with the timescales represented in the landscapes of Southern England and the processes that have been modifying them. Chapter 3 deals with the movements from below – from within the Earth's crust – that are ultimately creating major landscape patterns.

CHAPTER 2

Time, Process Southern England's Landscapes

BEDROCK AND SURFACE BLANKET

W ALK AROUND THE COUNTRY IN SOUTHERN ENGLAND and the
ground beneath your feet is very rarely solid rock. You are walking
over soil made of weathered mineral grains and organic debris,
along with other relatively soft and granular materials that make up the surface
blanket. Beneath the surface blanket lies solid rock, the bedrock of the landscape.

Bedrock forms the bones of the land. From the colour of the soil, to the
elevation of the hills, to the types of vegetation present, the landscape is
profoundly influenced by the bedrock underlying it. For example, in Southern
England the Lower Greensand (a distinctive layer of bedrock of Early Cretaceous
age, see page 26) produces soil water with acidic chemical properties. The Lower
Greensand was originally deposited as sand over a period of a few million years,
more than 100 million years ago. This layer represents a different environment of
deposition from the older sediments on which it lies, and was followed by another
change of environment which produced the deposits that lie on top of it. Both the
preceding and the following bedrock deposits have alkaline chemical properties.
In certain regions the bedrock layers have now been brought to the surface of the
landscape by erosion and movements within the Earth. The Greensand is harder
than the layers above and below it (largely mudstones) and so is generally more
resistant to weathering. In some areas the Lower Greensand lies just below the
surface blanket and has resisted the general landscape erosion to form a distinct
Greensand ridge running across the countryside, characterised by special
vegetation adapted to the acidity of the soils.

It is only in cliffs or at man-made excavations such as quarries that we can see bedrock at the surface in most low-lying areas. By using those areas where the bedrock does outcrop at the surface, and the results of drillings (e.g. for wells), we can discover the types and arrangements of rock below any landscape.

THREE DIFFERENT TIMESCALES

More recent past events tend to be better known and of greater interest than distant past events. Figure 6 is plotted on a logarithmic timescale, so that the most recent times are given more space and greater ages are given less and less space.

FIG 6. Three different timescales, plotted to give more space to more recent events.

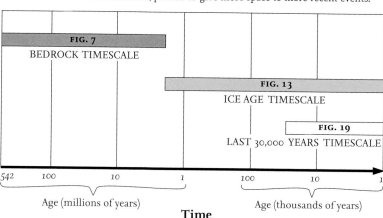

For the purposes of this book, we can distinguish three overlapping timescales to help us to understand the landscapes of Southern England:

The **bedrock timescale** (extending from 542 million years ago to about 2 million years ago)

The **Ice Age timescale** (covering roughly the last 1 million years)

The **last 30,000 years timescale**

We shall now review each of these, commenting on the sorts of episodes in each that are important in our exploration of Southern England.

THE BEDROCK TIMESCALE

Figure 7 is a simplified version of a generally accepted geological timescale relevant to the landscapes of Southern England. The names of the divisions are universally accepted in the geological world and, unlike the previous diagram, the passage of time is represented on a uniform (linear) timescale. The divisions have been selected, and sometimes grouped, to help in our analysis of the situation in Southern England, and these have been colour-coded for use in the rest of the book.

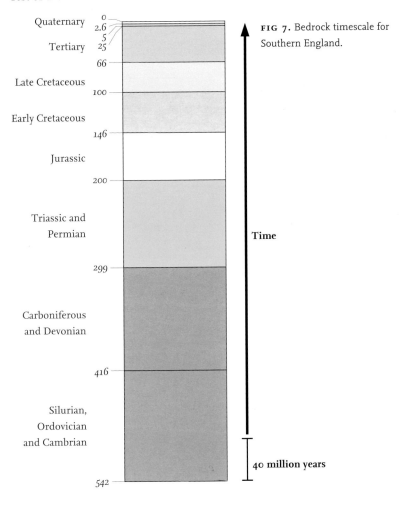

FIG 7. Bedrock timescale for Southern England.

The rocks at, or just below, the surface of Southern England range in age over hundreds of millions of years, and most of them were formed long before the present scenery began to appear. At the time of their origin, these rocks were deposited in a variety of different environments, mostly when mud or sand materials were transported into and/or around the seas that existed where England is now. Most of the bedrock of Southern England was formed in this way and is said to be of *sedimentary* origin. The depositional conditions varied from time to time: the climate varied, the geographical pattern of rising and sinking land movements changed, and the supply of mud and sand brought downstream by rivers changed also. Despite these fluctuations, it is possible to generalise the way that sediment has accumulated over an area the size of Southern England, and to offer a succession of layers of different composition, age and average thickness that can provide a general guide. This is shown in Figure 8.

For each of the Regions (and some of the Areas) discussed in Chapters 4 to 8, a rock column, generalised for that particular area, will show the main bedrock layers. Each column will be coloured using the standard colour codes of this book to represent the ages of the layers.

As an example, we will consider another particularly distinctive layer of bedrock, the Chalk, which ranges between 200 and 400 m in thickness. Chalk is visible quite widely at or just below the surface over perhaps a quarter of the area of Southern England (Fig. 9). Chalk is an easily recognised rock because it is made of very small fragments of lime (calcium carbonate) and is usually brilliant white. It formed from fine-grained limey mud deposited on the sea bed, but through many millions of years of burial below other sediments it has been compressed and altered into the hard rock we recognise today. The Chalk is a result of a unique combination of environmental conditions and the presence of particular algal organisms in the history of evolution. It is only found in northwest Europe, and was only formed in Late Cretaceous times.

The presence of Chalk near the surface in Southern England is almost always linked to the presence of hills and slopes in the scenery, clearly showing that Chalk is a tough material that resists landscape erosion more than most of the other rock types available. The Chalk is also noteworthy because it represents the most recent time when most of Southern England was covered uniformly with soft sediment and a shallow sea: in Late Cretaceous times, except for possible islands in the southwest, there was no emergent land across Southern England.

Like all sedimentary bedrock layers, the Chalk initially formed as flat layers or sheets of sediment, extending widely across the floor of the sea. As will be discussed in the next chapter, these sheets of sediment are generally

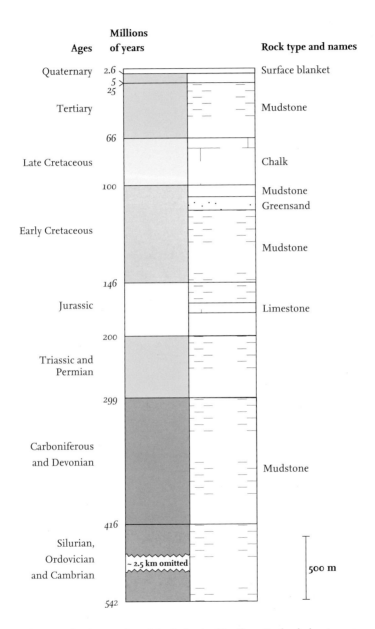

FIG 8. Generalised succession of the bedrock of Southern England, showing a typical thickness for each layer.

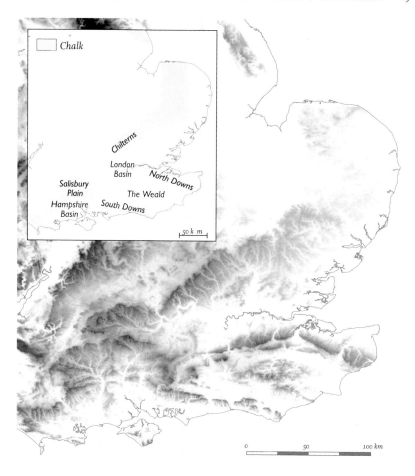

FIG 9. The Chalk and its topography. The darker areas represent the chalk uplands.

characteristic of stretching movement episodes in the Earth's surface. Such movements produce areas of collapsed and low-lying land that can accommodate large volumes of sediment, if it is available.

However, we do not see the Chalk at or near the surface everywhere across Southern England; instead the Chalk forms narrow bands across the land. This is due to later movements affecting the bedrock layers by folding and tilting them, so that some parts were raised (to be later removed by erosion) and other parts were lowered (Fig. 10, A and B). In the millions of years since the sediment layers were laid down, they have been buried, compacted, deformed by various processes, and finally uplifted to form part of the landscape that we know today (deformation processes are treated more fully in Chapter 3). The Chalk layer has been moved and folded as a result of mild compression or convergence, to form a downfold or *syncline* between the Chilterns and the North Downs, and an upfold or *anticline* between the North and South Downs (Fig. 10, C). Later, the central part of the anticline was eroded away to produce the bedrock pattern that we recognise today (Fig. 10, D). The vein-like river valleys visible on the elevated Chalk hills of Figure 9 are evidence of this continuing erosion.

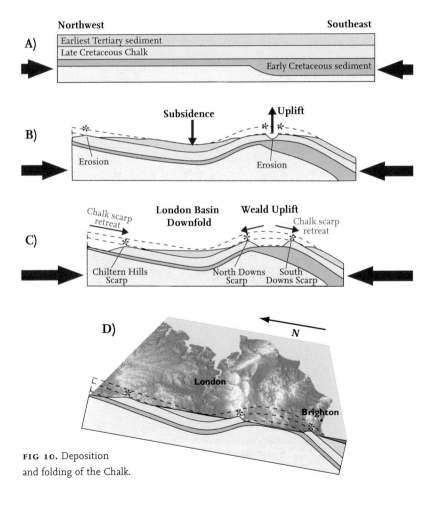

FIG 10. Deposition and folding of the Chalk.

LANDSCAPE MODIFICATION BY RIVERS

Weathering of landscape surfaces and the production of soils by the action of rainwater, air and organisms are important factors in shaping landscapes. These processes affect the bedrock when it is very close to the surface, and most of them weaken the material that they work on. This is particularly so when tough silicate rock minerals are altered to soft clay minerals, which are then easily eroded. Freezing and thawing also works to weaken the bedrock as water in cracks freezes and expands, breaking the rocks into fragments.

Whilst weathering is a widespread and general process, most of the other important landscape processes involve the formation of discrete features that we shall call *landforms*. Rivers result in the formation of a number of important landforms that are described below.

The most important landforms resulting from river processes are the channels of rivers and streams (Fig. 11). When rain falls onto a land surface some of it soaks into the land (forming groundwater), whilst the remainder runs along the surface, collecting in topographical lows and producing stream and river channels. Today, many of Southern England's river channels tend to be relatively narrow and shallow – only metres or tens of metres in width and less in depth – so they occupy an extremely small percentage of the area that they drain. However, they are still the dominant agents of landscape change, causing downwards and/or sideways erosion as well as acting as conduits to transport the eroded material out of their catchments.

Most river channels develop a sinuous course, becoming curved (or *meandering*) to varying degrees, or developing a number of channels separated by islands of sediment (becoming *braided*). The positions of the curves or islands change with time as sediment is shifted downstream, and the position of a river channel will change with time correspondingly.

Because of their ability to erode material and remove the resulting debris, river channels create valleys. The sides of a river valley are referred to as slopes. When a channel cuts downwards the valley sides generally become steeper and slope material (generated by ongoing weathering processes) moves down-slope towards the channel. The material is transported either as small individual fragments or as larger mass flows. Where down-slope movements involve the collapse of large areas of material, the terms *landslip* or *slump* are often used. Slope material is then deposited in the channel and removed downstream by the river.

The simplest valleys result from down-cutting by a river or stream to yield a V-shaped profile in cross-section. The gradient of the valley sides depends on the

FIG 11. Landforms of rivers.

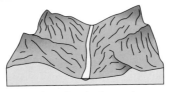

A) Bedrock channel

B) Incised sinuous channel

C) Sinuous channel in floodplain

D) Sinuous channel, floodplain and terraces

strength of the material that the slopes are composed of in the face of erosion. Stronger materials are more difficult to erode and remove, and so can form steeper slopes than weaker materials. In some areas, the river channel is unable to form valley slopes as the material is too weak to form a noticeable gradient. In the Areas we will be investigating, it is clear that some of the slopes are largely the result of a particularly strong layer in the bedrock resisting erosion as the landscape has developed.

As the valley develops, its profile can become more complex. In some cases, slopes appear to have retreated across a landscape some distance from the position in which they were initially created by river down-cutting. A river with a wide valley floor is one of the most obvious examples of this, in which movements of the channel across the floor have caused the slopes to retreat as the valley floor has become wider. In some cases, slopes appear to have retreated over many kilometres from the original valley as numerous collapses of the slope took place.

Overall, therefore, the valley profile and the channel course reflect variations in the strength of the material being eroded, and in the strength and flood pattern of the river. Climate changes are likely to have a major effect on the strength of the river by altering the volume of water flowing through the channels. Additionally, the lowering or raising of the channel by Earth movement effects (see Chapter 3) can affect the evolution of the landscape by river processes. For example, both climate change and the vertical movement of the river channel can initiate the formation of river terraces. Different examples of all these river geometries will be discussed in greater detail in the Area descriptions in Chapters 4–8.

Over millions of years, river down-cutting, slope erosion and material transport tend to smooth and lower landscapes until they approximate plains, unless they are raised up again (*rejuvenated*) by large-scale Earth movements (Chapter 3) or are attacked by a new episode of channel erosion, perhaps due to climate or sea-level change. Southern England generally has a smoothed and lowered landscape, representing hundreds of thousands of years of this river and slope activity.

The branching, map-view patterns of river channels and valleys are an obvious feature of all landscapes. An approach to understanding how this forms is illustrated by a computer-based experiment (Fig. 12) in which a flat surface (plateau or plain) is uplifted along one of its edges, so that it has a uniform slope towards the edge that forms the bottom of the rectangle shown. Rain is then applied uniformly across the surface, causing the formation and down-cutting of channels that erode backwards from the downstream edge. As the experiment

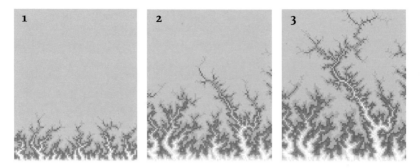

FIG 12. Model showing upstream erosion by tree-like (dendritic) river patterns. (Provided by Dimitri Lague from the work of A. Crave and P. Davy)

continues, the channels and their valleys extend into the uniform sloping surface by *headward* erosion, resulting in longer valleys, more branches and a greater dissection of the surface by those valleys.

As we consider the various Regions and Areas of Southern England, we will summarise the present-day river patterns of each by simplifying the main directions of drainage involved. We will also give an impression of the present-day relative size of the more important rivers by quoting their mean flow rates as estimated in the National River Flow Archive, maintained by the Centre for Ecology and Hydrology at Wallingford.

It seems surprising that today's often sleepy southern English rivers have been the dominant agent in carving the English landscape. However, even today's rivers can become surprisingly violent in what are often described as hundred- or thousand-year floods. Floods in the past were certainly more violent at times than those of today, particularly towards the ends of cold episodes, when melting of ice and snow frequently produced floods that we would now regard as very exceptional.

THE ICE AGE TIMESCALE AND LANDSCAPE MODIFICATION

The most recent Ice Age began about 2 million years ago, and is still continuing in Arctic areas. At various times during this period ice has thickly covered most of northwest Europe. Recent research, particularly measurements of oxygen isotopes in polar icecaps and oceanic sediment drill cores, has revealed much of the detail of how the climate has changed during the current Ice Age. It has been discovered that long cold periods have alternated with short warm periods in a complex but rather regular rhythm. Looking at the last half-million years, this alternation has occurred about every 100,000 years, and this is now known to have been a response to regular changes in the way the Earth has rotated and moved in its orbit around the sun. A closer look at the last million years (Fig. 13) reveals that for more than 90 per cent of the time conditions have been colder than those of today. Warm (*interglacial*) periods, like our present one, have been unusual and short-lived, though they have often left distinctive deposits and organisms.

FIG 13. The last million years of global temperature change.

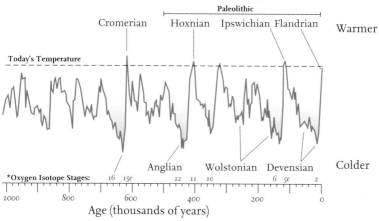

the Oxygen Isotope Stages are an internationally agreed numbering sequence to label the succession of climatic cold (even numbers) and warm (odd numbers) episodes.

One of the most important cold episodes (*glacials*), just under half a million years ago, resulted in the Anglian ice sheet. This was up to several hundreds of metres thick and extended from the north southwards, well into Southern England, covering much of East Anglia and the north London area (Fig. 14). As the ice spread slowly southwards, it was constricted between the Chalk hills of Lincolnshire and those of Norfolk. A wide valley, later to become the Wash and the Fens, was filled with ice to a depth well below that of present sea level. As the ice spread outwards from this valley it dumped the rock material it was carrying, including blocks and boulders up to hundreds of metres across, giving some idea of the tremendous power of the ice sheet. The direct evidence for the presence of an ice sheet is material in the surface blanket called *till*, or boulder clay (Fig. 15). This often rather chaotic mixture of fragments of rock of all sizes (large boulders mixed with sand and mud) lacks the sorting of the fragments by size that would have occurred in flowing water, and so must have been deposited from the melting of ice sheets.

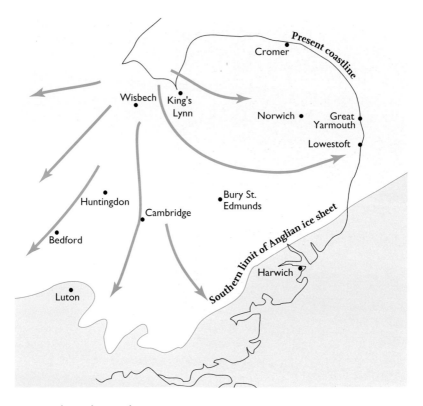

FIG 14. The Anglian ice sheet.

Much of the rest of the surface blanket that accumulated during the last 2 million years was deposited by the rivers that were draining the land or any ice sheets present. As ice sheets have advanced and retreated, so have the rivers changed in their size and in their capacity to carry debris and erode the landscape. Rivers have therefore been much larger in the past as melting winter snow and ice produced torrents of meltwater, laden with sediment, which scoured valleys or dumped large amounts of sediment. The gravel pits scattered along the river valleys and river terraces of Southern England, from which material is removed for building and engineering, are remnants of the beds of old fast-flowing rivers which carried gravel during the cold times.

There are no ice sheets present in the landscape of Figure 16. The scene is typical of most of the Ice Age history (the last 2 million years) of Southern England, in that the ice sheets lie further north. It is summer, snow and ice are

FIG 15. Boulder clay or till,
West Runton, north Norfolk.

lingering, and reindeer, wolves and woolly mammoths are roaming the swampy
ground. The river is full of sand and gravel banks, dumped by the violent floods
caused by springtime snow-melt. The ground shows ridges of gravel pushed up by
freeze–thaw activity, an important process in scenery terms that we discuss below.

The present-day Arctic has much to tell us about conditions and processes in
Southern England during the cold episodes of the Ice Age. Much of the present-
day Arctic is ice-sheet-free, but is often characterised by permanently frozen
ground (*permafrost*). When the ground becomes frozen all the cracks and spaces
in the surface-blanket materials and uppermost bedrock become filled by ice, so
that normal surface drainage cannot occur. In the summer, ice in the very
uppermost material may melt and the landscape surface is likely to be wet and
swampy. Ice expands on freezing, and so the continuous change between
freezing and thawing conditions, both daily and seasonally, can cause the
expansion of cracks and the movement of material, with corresponding
movements in the surface of these landscapes. This movement can cause many

FIG 16. Artist's impression of Southern England, south of the ice sheet, during the Ice Age. (Copyright Norfolk Museums and Archaeology Service & Nick Arber)

problems in the present-day Arctic by disturbing the foundations of buildings and other structures.

Remarkable polygonal patterns, ranging from centimetres to tens of metres across, are distinctive features of flat Arctic landscapes, resulting from volume changes in the surface blanket on freezing and thawing (Fig. 17). In cross-section the polygon cracks and ridges correspond to downward-narrowing wedges (often visible also in the walls of gravel pits in Southern England). Thaw lakes are also a feature of flat areas under conditions of Arctic frozen ground (Fig. 18). They appear to be linked to the formation of the polygonal features, but can amalgamate to become kilometres across and may periodically discharge their muddy soup of disturbed sediments down even very gentle slopes.

Not only can these frozen ground processes be studied in Arctic areas today, but they have left characteristic traces in many of the landscapes of Southern England. Some examples from Norfolk are illustrated in Chapter 8 (Figs 306 and 307), and these provide specific examples of the result of ancient freeze–thaw processes on a small scale. However, the more we examine the wider features of present-day landscapes across Southern England, the more it becomes clear that most have been considerably modified by the general operation of frozen ground processes during the last 2 million years. These processes are likely to have been responsible for the retreat of significant slopes and even for the lowering of surfaces that have almost no perceptible slope.

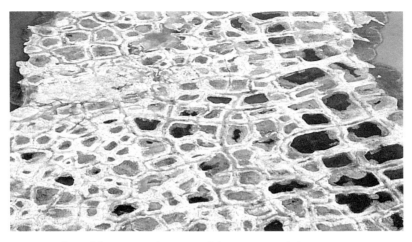

FIG 17. Polygonal frozen ground patterns on the Arctic coastal plain near Barrow, Alaska. (Copyright Landform Slides – Ken Gardner)

FIG 18. Thaw lakes, the larger ones several kilometres long, on the Arctic coastal plain near Barrow, Alaska. (Copyright Landform Slides – Ken Gardner)

THE LAST 30,000 YEARS TIMESCALE
AND RECENT MODIFICATION

The timescale shown in Figure 19 covers a period during which various episodes have changed the landscapes of Southern England, creating our present-day world. These episodes include the dramatic rise in sea level and landward movement of the coastline caused by the warming of the climate following the last cold episode of the Ice Age. They also include the progressive changing of the countryside by people, leading up to the domination of some landscapes by man-made features.

FIG 19. Time divisions for the last 30,000 years (Late Pleistocene to Holocene).

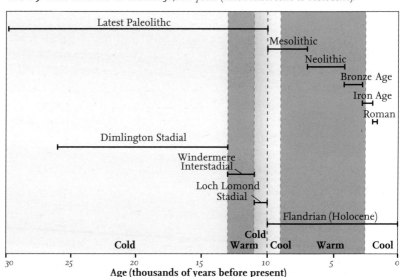

Time Division	Years Before Present
Windermere Interstadial	13,000–11,000
Loch Lomond Stadial	11,000–10,000
Flandrian (Holocene)	10,000–present
Mesolithic	11,000–7,000
Neolithic	7,000–4,150
Bronze Age	4,150–2,750
Iron Age	2,750–1,950
Roman	1,950–1,600

The last 30,000 years have been warm, on average, relative to the previous
2 million years of the Ice Age. However, the higher level of detail available in
this timescale makes it clear that climate change has not been one of uniform
warming during this period. Short periods of colder climate, temporarily
involving ice-sheet growth in the north of Britain (sometimes called *stadials*)
have alternated with short periods of warmer climate (referred to as *interstadials*).

SEA-LEVEL CHANGE

The coastline is the most recently created part of the landscape, and the most
changeable. This is due, in large part, to the rise in sea level over the last 20,000
years, since the last main cold episode of the Ice Age (the Devensian). Twenty
thousand years ago sea level was 120 m lower than it is today because of the great
volumes of water that were locked away on land in the world's ice sheets (Fig. 20).
Land extended tens or hundreds of kilometres beyond the present-day coastline,
and Southern England was linked to northern France by a large area of land
(Fig. 21). Global climate started to warm about 18,000 years ago (Fig. 13) and the
world's ice started to melt, raising global sea level. The North Sea and the
Channel gradually flooded, and Britain became an island between 10,500 and
10,000 years ago. This flooding by the sea is known as the *Flandrian transgression*
and was a worldwide episode.

During the period of most rapid
sea-level rise (between 12,000 and 8,000
years ago), areas of low-lying land were
swamped and some local features of
the coastal scenery moved great
distances geographically towards their
present positions. The sea cliffs, beach
barriers, salt marshes, spits and
estuaries that can be seen today have
only taken up their present positions
over the last few thousand years, as sea-
level rise slowed.

In the treatment of the Regions and
Areas in the rest of this book, maps are
presented that distinguish a *coastal
flooding zone*. This presentation is based
on the simplifying assumption that the

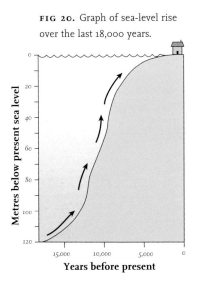

FIG 20. Graph of sea-level rise
over the last 18,000 years.

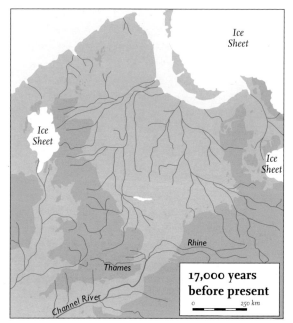

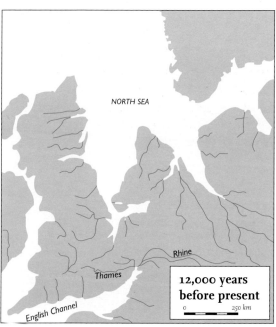

FIG 21. Two episodes (17,000 and 12,000 years ago) in the rise of sea level around the North Sea area. (Redrawn and simplified from *Current Archaeology* **207**, 2006, Gaffney)

solid Earth movement of Southern England (i.e. any uplift or subsidence, see Chapter 3) has been very small compared with global sea-level changes. The coastal flooding zone is defined as extending between the submarine contour 120 m below present sea level and the contour 20 m above present sea level, and it can be used to identify parts of landscapes which are likely to have been areas of coastline activity in the recent past. Areas of land with an elevation between present sea level and 120 m below sea level correspond to the land submerged during the last 18,000 years of sea-level rise. Areas lying at, or up to, 20 m above present sea level may have been subjected to coastal processes during the highest sea levels of earlier interglacial periods, such as the Ipswichian (see Fig. 13). The coastal flooding zone also defines areas of land that are most likely to become submerged during predicted future rises of sea level.

Drowned valleys (Figs 22 and 23) are present on the coastlines of Southern England as a result of recent sea-level rise. Formerly, the rivers draining the majority of these valleys would have transported mud and sand to the sea, where it would have been deposited on the sea bed. However, with the rise in sea level mud and sand are now often deposited in the flooded valleys or estuaries instead, and some have developed carpets of sediment, transported down-valley by rivers or brought up-valley by the sea where tides and storms have been effective.

Coastlines with low seaward slopes and a soft surface blanket and/or bedrock may develop beach barriers when flooded by rising sea level. These barriers are ridges of sand or gravel parallel to the general trend of the coastline (Fig. 24). They are created by the impact of storm waves on the gently sloping and soft landscape. They tend to develop a cap of wind-blown sand which is very vulnerable to storm wave erosion, but may eventually become stabilised by vegetation. Behind the barrier a low-lying area of more sheltered conditions develops and regular flooding at high tide may bring in muddy sediment from the sea that can settle and build up salt marshes.

FIG 22. The drowning of a valley by sea-level rise.

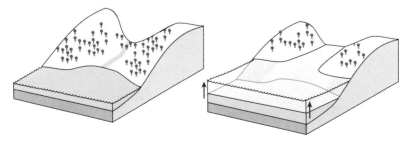

FIG 23. Drowned valley of the Deben, Suffolk, viewed from above the sea off Felixstowe Ferry. (Copyright London Aerial Photo Library)

FIG 24. Cross-section of a beach barrier formed as sea level rises over a very gently sloping landscape.

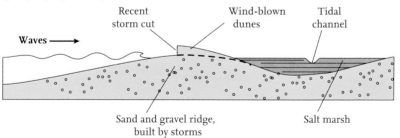

FIG 25. Beach barrier on Scolt Head Island, Norfolk. (Photograph held at Cambridge University Collection of Air Photographs, Unit for Landscape Modelling)

The aerial photograph of part of Scolt Head Island (Fig. 25) in north Norfolk shows the succession of zones parallel to the coastline typical of a recently flooded, gently sloping landscape. On the beach, coast-parallel ridges and hollows (runnels) have been created during recent storms, and are draining water as the photograph was taken at low tide. The crest of the barrier is capped by wind-blown dunes, which have been stabilised by marram grass, but also shows signs of erosion during recent storms. Behind the barrier are salt marshes, generally sheltered from storm waves and developing tidal channels. The salt marshes are forming around the remains of various sand and gravel spits that date from a landscape before the present beach barrier was there. The far side of the salt marsh is marked by a gently curved sea wall built within the last two centuries to reclaim some land by keeping high tides out. Behind that is the boundary between the present flat seaward zone of young sediment and the older terrain, marked by a complex field pattern that is underlain by Chalk bedrock.

DEVELOPMENT BY PEOPLE

My concern in this book is primarily with natural landscapes, and I will tend to comment on the development by people since the Bronze Age only where this relates to the natural features in an interesting way. However, in reviewing the appearance of the whole of Southern England, I have been struck by an intriguing distinction made by some landscape historians: the distinction between ancient and planned countryside (Figs 26–28). I have based my approach on the discussions offered by Oliver Rackham, ecologist and landscape historian, and these are summarised below.

Ancient countryside (Fig. 26) consists of many hamlets, small towns, ancient farms and hedges (of mixed varieties of shrubs and trees), along with roads that are not straight, numerous footpaths and many antiquities.

Planned countryside (Fig. 27) has distinct villages, much larger than the hamlets, along with larger eighteenth- and nineteenth-century farms, hedges of hawthorn and straight roads. Footpaths are less common and the few antiquities that are present are generally prehistoric.

I have re-examined the same areas used by Oliver Rackham as examples of these two countryside types, and compared the early Ordnance Survey maps with maps of the same area generated by me using the data and methods used in this book (see Chapter 1). The shading and 'hachured' patterning used in the earlier maps represents the hills and slopes rather clearly – better than the contour representation used in the present-day Ordnance Survey *Landranger* maps, although these show man-made features much more clearly. My map representation is a compromise in that it represents elevations and slopes using colours and hill-shading, but also allows the patterns of roads and settlements to be seen.

Oliver Rackham's conclusion is that many of the distinctive features of planned countryside were created by the general parliamentary enclosure of land during the eighteenth and nineteenth centuries. This involved the wholesale conversion of commonly held land with open fields into enclosed fields awarded to individuals and institutions. Many landscape historians have claimed earlier origins for the difference between ancient and planned countryside, believing that historical and cultural differences in the people who settled and developed the two areas played an important role. Variations in the bedrock geology also seem to be important here. For example, the ancient countryside shown in Figure 26 is underlain by strongly deformed Variscan bedrock that has been eroded into small hills and valleys (see Chapter 4).

Example of Ancient Countryside

1809

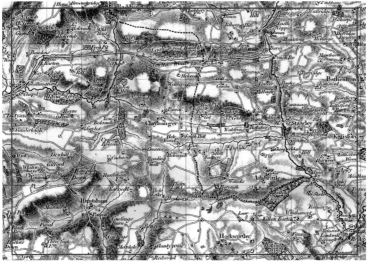

Present day

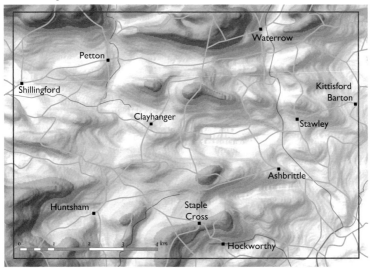

FIG 26. Example of ancient countryside at the Devon–Somerset border, near Tiverton, with 1809 and recent mapping compared. (Upper part from Cassini Old Series map 181, copyright Cassini Publishing 2007/www.cassinimaps.co.uk)

Example of Planned Countryside

1830s

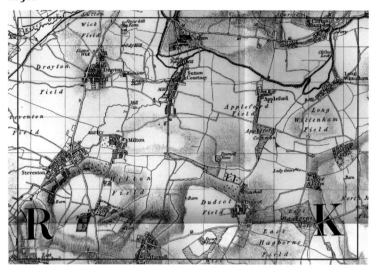

Present day

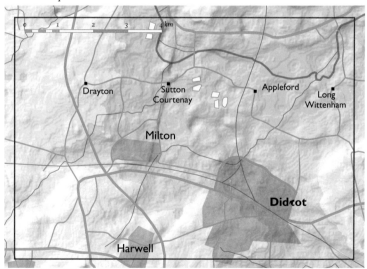

FIG 27. Example of planned countryside at the Berkshire–Oxfordshire border, around Didcot, with 1830s and recent mapping compared. (Upper part taken from Cassini Old Series maps 164 and 174, copyright Cassini Publishing 2007/www.cassinimaps.co.uk)

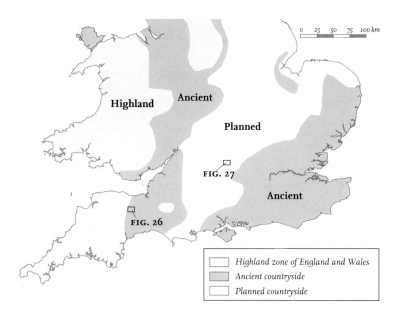

FIG 28. Generalised map distinguishing ancient and planned countryside across Southern England.

In contrast, the planned countryside covered by Figure 27 consists of only gently tilted Mesozoic bedrock that has formed a much flatter and more open landscape.

CHAPTER 3

Movement of the
Earth's Surface from Within

WIDESPREAD MOVEMENTS OF THE EARTH'S SURFACE

TO UNDERSTAND THE CHANGES and movements affecting the appearance
of the landscape on large scales we need to review some geological systems,
especially *plate tectonics*. Many of the large changes that have created
landscapes over long periods of time can now be understood using this discovery.

Knowledge of the processes causing the movement of large (10–1,000 km
length-scale) areas of the Earth's surface has been revolutionised by scientific
advances made over the last 40 years. During this time, scientists have become
convinced that the whole of the Earth's surface consists of a pattern of
interlocking *tectonic plates* (Fig. 29). The word 'tectonic' refers to processes that
have built features of the Earth's crust (Greek: *tektōn*, a builder). The worldwide
plate pattern is confusing – particularly when seen on a flat map – and it is easier
to visualise the plates in terms of an interlocking arrangement of panels on the
Earth's spherical surface, broadly like the panels forming the skin of a football.

Tectonic plates are features of the *lithosphere*, the name given to the ~125 km
thick outer shell of the Earth, distinguished from the material below by the
strength of its materials (Greek: *lithos*, stone). The strength depends upon the
composition of the material and also upon its temperature and pressure, both of
which tend to increase with depth below the Earth's surface. In contrast to the
mechanically strong lithosphere, the underlying material is weaker and known
as the *asthenosphere* (Greek: *asthenos*, no-strength). Note that on figure 30 the
crustal and outer mantle layers are shown with exaggerated thickness, so that
they are visible.

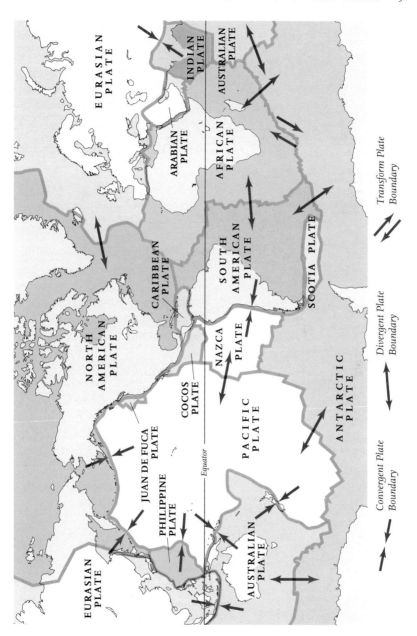

FIG 29. World map showing the present pattern of the largest lithosphere plates.

Most of the strength difference between the lithosphere and the asthenosphere depends on the temperature difference between them. The lithosphere plates are cooler than the underlying material, so they behave in a more rigid way when subjected to the forces generated within the Earth. The asthenosphere is hotter and behaves in a more plastic way, capable of deforming without fracturing and, to some extent, of 'flowing'. Because of this difference in mechanical properties and the complex internal forces present, the lithosphere plates can move relative to the material below. To visualise the motion of the plates, we can use the idea of lithospheric plates floating on top of the asthenosphere.

Looking at the surface of the Earth (Fig. 29), the largest plates show up as relatively rigid areas of the lithosphere, with interiors that do not experience as much disturbance as their edges. Plates move relative to each other along *plate boundaries*, in various ways that will be described below. The plate patterns have been worked out by investigating distinctive markers within the plates and at their edges, allowing the relative rates of movement between neighbouring plates to be calculated. These rates are very slow, rarely exceeding a few centimetres per year, but over the millions of years of geological time they can account for thousands of kilometres of relative movement.

It has proved to be much easier to measure plate movements than to work out what has been causing them. However, the general belief today is that the plates move in response to a number of different forces. Heat-driven

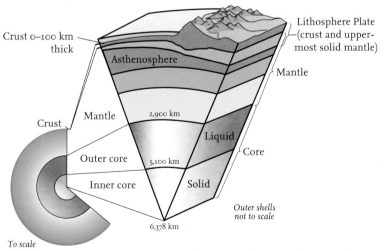

FIG 30. Diagram of the internal structure of the Earth.

circulation (convection) occurs within the mantle, but other forces are also at play. Where plates diverge, warm, new material is formed that is elevated above the rest of the plate, providing a pushing force to move the plate laterally, around the surface of the Earth. At convergent boundaries, cold, older material 'sinks' into the asthenosphere, providing a pulling force which drags the rest of the plate along behind it. Deep within the Earth, the sinking material melts and is ultimately recycled and brought back to the surface to continue the process.

Knowledge of how tectonic plates interact provides the key to understanding the movement history of the Earth's crust. However, most people are much more familiar with the geographical patterns of land and sea, which do not coincide with the distribution of tectonic plates. From the point of view of landscapes and scenery, coastlines are always going to be key features because they define the limits of the land; we make no attempt in this book to consider submarine scenery in detail.

The upper part of the lithosphere is called the *crust*. Whereas the distinction between the lithosphere and the asthenosphere is based upon mechanical properties related to temperature and pressure (see above), the distinction between the crust and the lower part of the lithosphere is based upon composition. Broadly speaking, there are two types of crust that can form the upper part of the lithosphere: continental and oceanic. An individual tectonic plate may include just one or both kinds of crust.

Continental crust underlies land areas and also many of the areas covered by shallow seas. Geophysical work shows that this crust is typically about 35 km thick, but may be 80–90 km thick below some high plateaus and mountain ranges. The highest mountains in Britain are barely noticeable on a scale diagram comparing crustal thicknesses (Fig. 31). Continental crust is made of rather less dense materials than the oceanic crust or the mantle, and this lightness is the reason why land surfaces and shallow sea floors are elevated compared to the deep oceans. Much of the continental crust is very old (up to 3–4 billion years), having formed early in the Earth's life when lighter material separated from denser materials within the Earth and rose to the surface.

Oceanic crust forms the floors of the deep oceans, typically 4 or 5 km below sea level. It is generally 5–10 km thick and is distinctly denser than continental crust. Oceanic crust only forms land where volcanic material has been supplied to it in great quantity (as in the case of Iceland), or where other important local forces in the crust have caused it to rise (as is the case in parts of Cyprus). Oceanic crust is generally relatively young (only 0–200 million years old), because its higher density and lower elevation ensures that it is generally *subducted* and destroyed at plate boundaries that are *convergent* (see below).

Figure 29 shows the major pattern of tectonic plates on the Earth today. The Mercator projection of this map distorts shapes, particularly in polar regions, but we can see that there are seven very large plates, identified by the main landmasses located on their surfaces. The Pacific plate lacks continental crust entirely, whereas the other six main plates each contain a large continent (Eurasia, North America, Australia, South America, Africa and Antarctica) as well as oceanic crust. There are a number of other middle-sized plates (e.g. Arabia and India) and large numbers of micro-plates, not shown on the world map.

Figures 29 and 32 also identify the different types of plate boundary, which are distinguished according to the relative motion between the two plates. *Convergent* plate boundaries involve movement of the plates from each side towards the suture (or central zone) of the boundary. Because the plates are moving towards each other, they become squashed together in the boundary zone. Sometimes one plate is pushed below the other in a process called

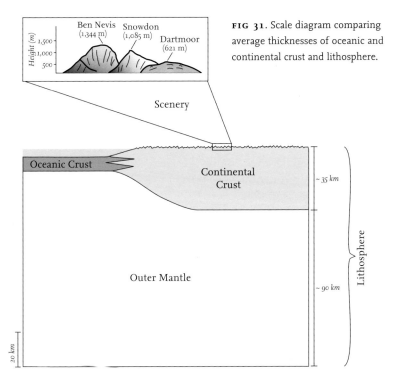

FIG 31. Scale diagram comparing average thicknesses of oceanic and continental crust and lithosphere.

subduction, which often results in a deep ocean trench and a zone of mountains and/or volcanoes, as well as earthquake activity (Fig. 32). The earthquake that happened on the morning of 26 December 2004 under the sea off western Sumatra was the strongest anywhere in the world for some 40 years. It seized world attention particularly because of the horrifying loss of life caused by the tsunami waves that it generated. This earthquake was the result of a sudden lithosphere movement of several metres on a fault in the convergent subduction zone where the Australian plate has been repeatedly moving below the Eurasian plate.

In other cases the plate boundary is *divergent,* where the neighbouring plates move apart and new material from deeper within the Earth rises to fill the space created. The new oceanic crust is created by the arrival and cooling of hot volcanic material from below. The mid-Atlantic ridge running through Iceland, with earthquakes and volcanic activity, is one of the nearest examples to Britain of this sort of plate boundary.

Other plate boundaries mainly involve movement parallel to the plate edges and are sometimes called *transform* boundaries. The Californian coast zone is the classic example but there are many others, such as the transform boundary between the African and Antarctic plates. In some areas, plate movement is at an oblique angle to the suture and there are components of divergence or convergence as well as movement parallel to the boundary.

Britain today sits in the stable interior of the western Eurasian plate, almost equidistant from the divergent mid-Atlantic ridge boundary to the west and the

FIG 32. Diagram illustrating the movement processes of plates (not to scale).

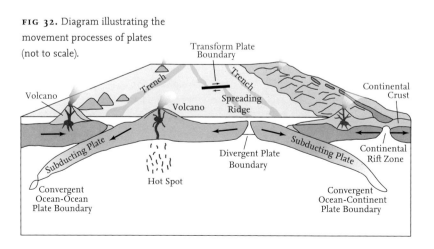

complex convergent boundary to the south where Spain and northwest Africa are colliding. In its earlier history the crust of Britain has been subjected to very direct plate boundary activity: the results of convergent activity in Devonian and Carboniferous times (between 416 and 299 million years ago) are visible at the surface in southwest England, and in Ordovician to Devonian times (between 490 and 360 million years ago) in Wales, northwest England and Scotland.

UNDERSTANDING SURFACE MOVEMENTS

We have been considering the large movement systems that originate within the Earth. There are also more local movement systems operating on the Earth's surface, which are linked to a very variable degree to the large-scale movements of plate tectonics. To explore this complex linkage further, it will be helpful to look now at different processes that may combine to cause particular local movements.

Horizontal movements as part of convergence, divergence or lateral transfer

Tectonic plates are recognised by their rigidity, so there is relatively little horizontal movement between points within the same plate compared to the deformation seen in plate boundary zones. This extreme deformation may involve folding and fracturing of the rock materials, addition of new material from below, or absorption of material into the interior during subduction.

Nonetheless, deformation is not restricted solely to plate boundaries, and does occur to a lesser extent within the plates. In some cases, major structures that originally formed along a plate boundary can become incorporated into the interior of a plate when prolonged collision causes two plates to join. Southern England includes the remains of a former convergent plate boundary and contains many examples of structures of this sort (particularly around Dorset and the Isle of Wight). These structures have often been reactivated long after they first formed in order to accommodate forces along the new plate boundary via deformation within the plate. Conversely, changes of internal stress patterns can sometimes lead to the splitting of a plate into two, forming a new, initially divergent plate boundary. Many of the oil- and gas-containing features of the North Sea floor originated when a belt of divergent rift faults formed across a previously intact plate.

It needs to be stressed that the patterns of deformation (fracturing and folding) due to these plate motions occur at a wide range of different scales, from centimetres to thousands of kilometres. Sometimes they are visible at the scale of

MOVEMENT OF THE EARTH'S SURFACE FROM WITHIN · 57

an entire plate boundary, such as the enormous Himalayan mountain chain that marks the collision of India with Asia.

The effects of features as large as plate boundaries on landscapes persist over hundreds of millions of years, long after the most active movement has ceased. For example, parts of southwestern England, Wales and the Scottish Highlands are underlain by bedrocks that were formed in convergent boundary zones of the past. The tin and lead mines of Cornwall owe their existence to a 300-million-year-old convergent plate boundary, where an ocean was destroyed as two plates converged and continents collided. The convergence released molten rock that rose in the crust and gradually cooled to form granite, while metals were precipitated in the surrounding crust as 'lodes' containing tin and lead (see Chapter 4).

Mapping the patterns of bedrock exposed at the surface often reveals folds and faults that provide key information about the movements that have taken place during the past. Figure 33 provides a key to some of the terms commonly used to classify these structures as a step towards understanding the sorts of movement patterns that they represent. In broad terms, folds tend to indicate some form of local convergent movement, though they may be the result of larger movement patterns of a different kind. Normal faults tend to indicate divergent movements, at least locally, whereas reverse and strike-slip faults tend to indicate convergence. Two broad types of fold are distinguished: synclines are u-shaped downfolds, while anticlines are the opposite – n-shaped upfolds.

Further mapping of folds and faults often reveals complex patterns of changing movements. In the example shown in Figure 34, divergent movements in an area of crust produce plastic deformation in the warmer lower crust, and faulting into a number of discrete blocks in the colder, more brittle, upper crust. This is then followed by an episode of convergent movement that results in closing up the upper crustal blocks and further flow in the plastic lower crust, causing crustal thickening and mountain building at the surface.

Vertical crustal movements as part of other crustal movements
The movement of lithospheric plates is the main cause of convergent and divergent movements affecting thousands of kilometres of the Earth's surface. As shown in Figures 33 and 34, these horizontal movements are generally accompanied by vertical movements that can produce very large scenic features, such as a mountain belt or a rift valley. In this book we are primarily concerned with scenic features at a more local scale, so we now consider various other processes that may be important in creating vertical crustal movements without contributions from large-scale plate interactions.

Folds

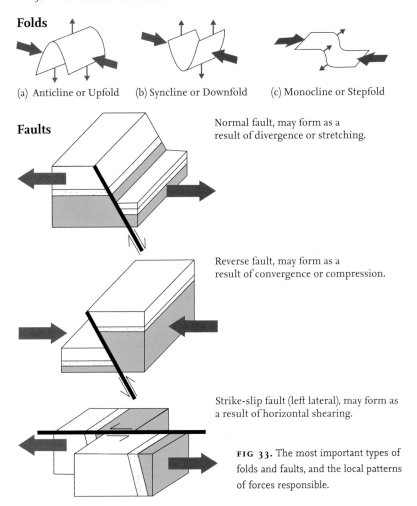

(a) Anticline or Upfold   (b) Syncline or Downfold   (c) Monocline or Stepfold

Faults

Normal fault, may form as a result of divergence or stretching.

Reverse fault, may form as a result of convergence or compression.

Strike-slip fault (left lateral), may form as a result of horizontal shearing.

FIG 33. The most important types of folds and faults, and the local patterns of forces responsible.

Vertical changes by erosion or deposition

Addition or subtraction of material to the surface of the Earth is happening all the time as sediment is deposited or solid material is eroded. The field of *sedimentology* is concerned with the wide range of different processes that are involved in the erosion, transport and deposition of material, whether the primary agent of movement is water, ice, mud or wind. An important point is that few of these sedimentary processes relate directly to the large tectonic movements of the Earth's crust that we have discussed above. Scenery is often

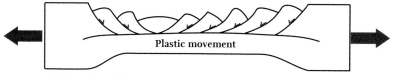

(A) Extension of the crust by normal faulting.

(B) Onset of compression with inversion of normal faults.

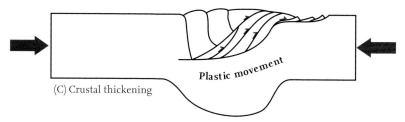

(C) Crustal thickening

FIG 34. Example of a cross-section through the crust, showing how a divergent movement pattern (A) may be modified by later convergent movements (B and C).

produced by erosion of thick deposits that formed in sedimentary basins where material eroded from the surrounding uplands accumulated. One of the characteristic features of these thick deposits is their layered appearance, which is often visible in the scenery. Layering varies from millimetre-scale laminations produced by very small fluctuations in depositional processes, to sheets hundreds of metres thick that extend across an entire sedimentary basin. These thicker sheets are often so distinctive that they are named and mapped as separate geological units representing significant changes in the local environment at the time they were deposited.

Vertical crustal movements resulting from loading or unloading

In addition to the direct raising or lowering of the surface by erosion or deposition, there is a secondary effect due to the unloading or loading of the crust that may take some thousands of years to produce significant effects.

As mentioned above, we can visualise the lithosphere as 'floating' on the asthenosphere like a boat floating in water. Loading or unloading the surface of the Earth by deposition or erosion will therefore lower or raise the scenery, just as a boat will sit lower or higher in the water depending on its load.

An example of this is the lowering of the area around the Mississippi Delta, loaded by sediment eroded from much of the area of the USA. The Delta region, including New Orleans, is doomed to sink continually as the Mississippi river deposits sediment around its mouth, increasing the crustal load there.

A second example of such loading is provided by the build-up of ice sheets during the Ice Age. The weight of these build-ups depressed the Earth's surface in the areas involved, and raised beaches in western Scotland provide evidence of the high local sea-levels due partly to this lowering of the crustal surface.

Unloading of the Earth's surface will cause it to rise. Recent theoretical work on the River Severn suggests that unloading of the crust by erosion may have played a role in raising the Cotswold Hills to the east and an equivalent range of hills in the Welsh Borders (see Chapter 6, Area 9). In western Scotland, as the ice has melted the Earth's surface has been rising again.

Vertical movements by expansion or contraction
Changing the temperature of the crust and lithosphere is an inevitable result of many of the processes active within the Earth, because they often involve the transfer of heat. In particular, rising plumes of hot material in the Earth's mantle, often independent of the plate boundaries, are now widely recognised as an explanation for various areas of intense volcanic activity (for example beneath Iceland today). These plumes are often referred to as 'hot spots' (see Fig. 32). Heating and cooling leads to expansion or contraction of the lithosphere and can cause the surface to rise or sink, at least locally.

An example of this is the way that Southern England was tilted downwards to the east about 60 million years ago. At about this time, eastern North America moved away from western Europe as the North American and Eurasian plates diverged. The divergence resulted in large volumes of hot material from deep within the Earth being brought to the surface and added to the crust of western Southern England. It is believed that the heating and expansion of the crustal rocks in the west has elevated them above the rocks to the east, giving an eastward tilt to the rock layers and exposing the oldest rocks in the west and the youngest ones in the east. This sequence has important implications for the scenery of England's south coast (see Chapter 5).

HOW CAN LOCAL SURFACE MOVEMENTS BE DETECTED?

Having just reviewed some of the processes that cause vertical movements of the Earth's surface, it is useful to consider the practical difficulties of how such movements are measured.

For present-day applications, it seems natural to regard sea level as a datum against which vertical landscape movements can be measured, as long as we remember to allow for tidal and storm variations. However, much work has demonstrated that global sea level has changed rapidly and frequently through time, due to climate fluctuations affecting the size of the polar icecaps and changing the total amount of liquid water present in the oceans and seas. It has also been shown that plate tectonic movements have an important effect on global sea level by changing the size and shape of ocean basins.

Attempts have been made to develop charts showing how sea level, generalised for the whole world, has varied through time. However, it has proved very difficult to distinguish a worldwide signal from local variations, and the dating of the changes is often too uncertain to allow confident correlation between areas.

In sedimentary basins, successful estimates of vertical movements have been made using the thicknesses of sediment layers accumulating over different time intervals in different depths of water. In areas of mountain building, amounts of vertical uplift have been estimated using certain indicator minerals that show the rates of cooling that rocks have experienced as they were brought up to the surface. However, both these approaches are only really possible in areas that have been subjected to movements of the Earth's crust that are large and continuous enough to completely dominate other possible sources of error.

Local horizontal movements are also difficult to estimate, although fold and/or fault patterns may allow a simple measure in some cases. Movement of sediment across the Earth's surface by rivers or sea currents can be estimated if mineral grains in the sediment can be tracked back to the areas from which they have come. In the detailed consideration of landscapes in this book, we have to rely on using the widest possible range of types of evidence, carefully distinguishing the times and scales involved. Even then, we are often left with probable movement suggestions rather than certainties.

CHAPTER 4

The Southwest Region

GENERAL INTRODUCTION

MOST OF THE BEDROCK near the surface in the Southwest Region (Fig. 35) is distinctly older than the near-surface bedrock in the rest of Southern England. It therefore provides us with information about earlier episodes, and this is all the more interesting because these episodes involved movements of the crust that created a mountain belt, the only one fully represented in the bedrock story of Southern England. Not only does this add greatly to the interest of the Southwest, but it has resulted in the presence of valuable minerals that have strongly influenced the human history in the Region.

Bedrock foundations and early history
Sedimentation and surface movement before the mountain building
The Southwest Region consists predominantly of bedrock formed between about 415 and 300 million years ago, during Devonian and Carboniferous times. This bedrock records an episode during which some areas of the Earth's crust rose while others sank, as part of a general buckling of the crust that is the first indication of compression and mountain building (Figs 36 and 37). As the rising areas became significantly elevated they were eroded, shedding sediment into the neighbouring sinking areas that became sedimentary basins. It is these basins that preserve most of the evidence of these events (Fig. 38).

In material that has been further and later deformed, it is difficult to work out the shape of the sinking areas, but many of them were probably elongated or

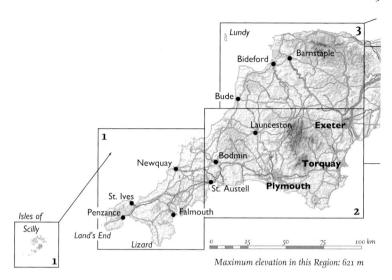

FIG 35. The Southwest Region, showing Areas 1 to 3.

trough-shaped, with the troughs separated by rising ridges that ran roughly east–west, parallel to the general trend of the later mountain belt. The troughs and ridges were caused in the early stages of mountain building by the compression and buckling of the crust. The troughs were generally flooded by the sea, or on the margins of relatively narrow seaways. Muds were the commonest materials to accumulate, although sands were also in plentiful supply. Lime-rich sediments, sometimes with corals and other shelly marine animals, were locally important. There were also periodic episodes of igneous activity that contributed volcanic lavas to the sedimentary successions.

During these episodes of Devonian and Carboniferous basin and ridge activity, the Southwest Region was just one small part of a larger belt of similar activity that extended to the west into Ireland and Canada. Canada was then very much closer, because the Atlantic Ocean is a younger feature that only started to grow (at this latitude) about 100 million years ago, as divergence and spreading occurred along the mid-Atlantic plate boundary. To the south and east, the same belt of activity continued across northern France and into Germany. This broadly east–west trending belt later became the Variscan mountain belt.

Crustal convergence that created the mountain belt
The subsidence and sedimentation were sometimes interrupted by, and generally followed by, episodes of convergence of the Earth's crust. This was

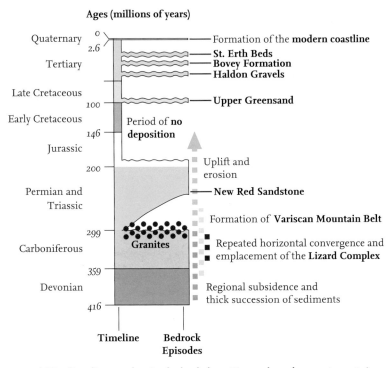

FIG 36. Timeline diagram showing bedrock deposition and emplacement events in the Southwest Region.

caused by compression or squeezing, broadly in a north–south direction, so that areas of bedrock were folded and pushed closer together, making the east–west trending Variscan belt narrower, as if between the jaws of a vice. The map (Fig. 39) and cross-section (Fig. 40) show how the folds and faults of the region vary locally in their pattern, but can be explained generally by convergent movements in this north–south direction. These continued over at least 100 million years, and occurred along thousands of kilometres of the belt. Mountain-building events such as this occur when tectonic plates collide (as described in Chapter 3) and always have a profound effect upon the scenery in the vicinity of the collision. The Variscan mountain belt is just one of the great mountain-building episodes that have occurred periodically, throughout the Earth's history.

Some of the best evidence for the horizontal crustal shortening comes from examining folds that can be seen in the bedrock at many localities (Figs 41 and 42). Folding of the originally flat layers of the bedrock is a spectacular feature of

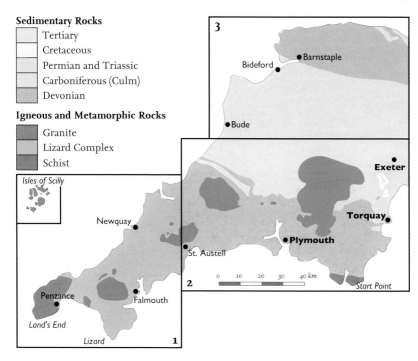

Sedimentary Rocks
- Tertiary
- Cretaceous
- Permian and Triassic
- Carboniferous (Culm)
- Devonian

Igneous and Metamorphic Rocks
- Granite
- Lizard Complex
- Schist

FIG 37. Simplified geological map of the Southwest Region.

FIG 38. Typical Devonian sedimentary basin in the Southwest Region.

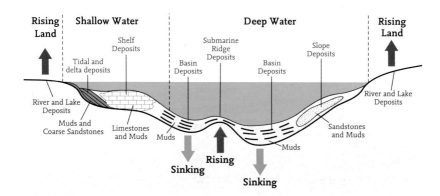

many southwestern sea cliffs, and the direction of the folding gives a clear indication of the direction of the shortening that resulted. Fractures (faults) also frequently cut the bedrock, and careful mapping makes it possible to recognise that, although some of them are very local features, others turn out to have been flat-lying fractures across which many kilometres of movement have taken place.

FIG 39. The major bedrock structures of Southwest England and South Wales.

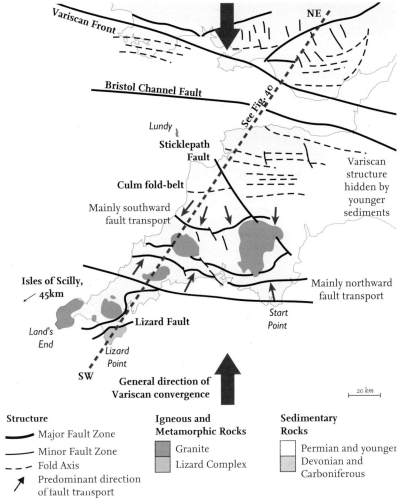

Another feature of the mountain building is that muddy material – the most abundant sediment in the Southwest Region – was often converted into slates that can typically be split into thin sheets and are said to possess a 'slatey cleavage'. These rocks are locally referred to as *killas*, to distinguish them from other rocks with no cleavage, particularly the granites. The conversion into slates took place during the folding and fracturing of the mountain building, when the original muds, rich in clay minerals, were buried deeply below other sediments and then compressed to produce a new layering (or *cleavage*).

One large feature visible in the bedrock is the 'Culm fold belt' or 'synclinorium', a large and complex downfold representing horizontal crustal convergence (Figs 39 and 40). The centre of this feature is a belt of bedrock of Carboniferous age that extends between Bude and Exeter running across the centre and north of the Southwest Region. To the north and south of this, older (Devonian) rocks occur at the bedrock surface, forming the margins of the large downfold or syncline (Fig. 37). *Culm* is an old term much used by miners and European geologists for Carboniferous sediment, and *synclinorium* is a name for a downfold (or syncline) which contains numerous smaller folds.

In the Lizard area, much of the bedrock consists of a distinctive group of igneous rocks (Figs 39 and 40). These rocks cooled and solidified earlier than the main mountain building, and were mostly formed by intrusion of hot molten rock in a way that is typical of the floor of an ocean basin. The Lizard area provides one of the best examples now visible on land in Britain of material

FIG 40. Schematic cross-section representing major structures of the Variscan mountain belt. The deep structure shown is speculative but shows how crustal shortening seen at the surface may be related to deeper, flat-lying fractures (faults). Located on Figure 39.

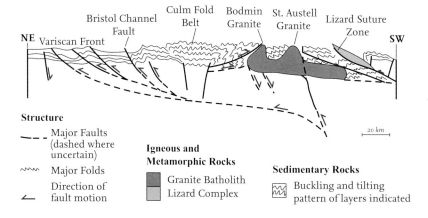

FIG 41. Zigzag folding due to horizontal convergence during the Variscan mountain building is spectacularly exposed at Hartland Quay (Area 3).
(Copyright Will Brett/www.lastrefuge.co.uk)

FIG 42. Zigzag folding due to horizontal convergence during the Variscan mountain building, this time at Bude (Area 2).
(Copyright Dae Sasitorn & Adrian Warren/www.lastrefuge.co.uk)

formed originally as ocean-floor crust. In Late Devonian times, as a result of early Variscan convergence, this large area of oceanic crust was forced northwards over and against sedimentary rocks lying just to the north. This shows how, in a large mountain belt, an area of crust (tens of kilometres across), with a distinctive history as the floor of an ocean basin, can be uplifted and incorporated into a mountain belt as its margins are squeezed together.

Some of the bedrock of this Lizard Complex is called *serpentinite*, after the common occurrence of the green mineral serpentine in sinuous cracks and veins. This gives the rocks an attractive colour patterning, and the absence of quartz makes them surprisingly easy to work with steel tools, giving rise to a local industry of carving serpentinite ornaments.

Granites and valuable minerals

The granites of Southwest England are an important later feature of the Variscan mountain belt. Granites are igneous rocks with coarse (millimetre across) crystals that have grown, interlocking with each other, as the molten material cooled slowly and solidified at some depth in the Earth's crust. The minerals of

FIG 43. Polished slab cut in the Dartmoor granite showing typical granite texture. Crystals of quartz (light grey), feldspar (white) and biotite (black) have interlocked as the magma (molten rock) solidified on cooling. (Copyright Landform Slides – Ken Gardner)

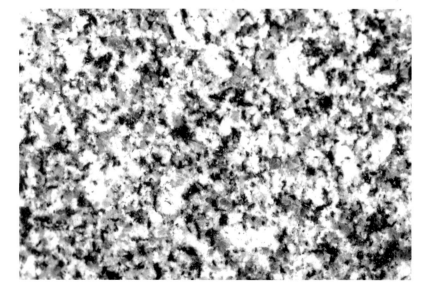

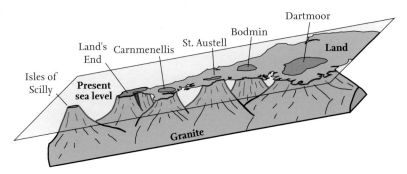

FIG 44. Diagram showing the large granite body below the bedrock of Cornwall and Devon, and the way the granite bosses now visible at the surface are upward extensions of this larger body.

the granite are most commonly quartz (typically about 30 per cent) and feldspar, generally with some other minerals such as mica (Fig. 43). The granite liquid (often called magma) formed as a result of melting deep within the outer layers of the Earth and was then forced upwards, sometimes pushing aside the overlying bedrock and sometimes replacing it by melting. The granites solidified at depths of several hundred metres or more below the surface and are now at, or near, the surface because of landscape erosion. The main granite areas include the Isles of Scilly in the west, followed by Land's End, Carnmenellis, St Austell, Bodmin Moor and Dartmoor in succession to the east. These distinct granite areas at the surface can be visualised as the tops of fingers extending upwards from a single continuous granite body detectable by gravity surveys at greater depth under the spine of Southwest England (Fig. 44). The deep body extends for some 200 km along the length of the mountain belt.

Although there was probably some time range in the arrival of different granite bodies in the upper crust, the main episodes took place at the very end of the Carboniferous and during the earliest Permian, roughly 300 million years ago.

The arrival of the granites from below was only one part of the invasion of the upper levels of the bedrock that took place at this time. Widespread mineralisation around the granites has probably been even more important than the arrival of the granites themselves, in terms of human history. The term mineralisation is used to cover the alteration of the solid granite and the surrounding (older) bedrock that has, in some areas, been caused by the movement of very hot and chemically rich water, using the network of cavities and fractures that existed in the rocks. Because of the chemistry of the rocks

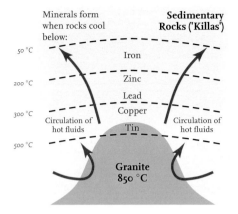

Minerals form when rocks cool below:

50 °C

200 °C

300 °C

500 °C

Sedimentary Rocks ('Killas')

Iron

Zinc

Lead

Copper

Tin

Circulation of hot fluids

Circulation of hot fluids

Granite 850 °C

FIG 45. Simple diagram of a slice through the Earth's upper levels, showing how the temperature patterns around a granite body have been responsible for the distribution of minerals containing the more important chemical elements.

deep down, many different chemical elements were brought to the upper levels and crystallized there to form new and valuable minerals, or caused alterations of the earlier solid rocks.

The granites probably solidified in the Earth at temperatures of about 850 °C, and most of the mineralisation happened at rather lower temperatures as the rocks cooled (Fig. 45). Tin, wolfram, arsenic and copper minerals formed at between 500 and 300 °C, whereas silver, lead, zinc, uranium, nickel and cobalt minerals formed at between 300 and 200 °C, and iron minerals between 200 and 50 °C.

The tin of Cornwall was a major reason why some of the early inhabitants of mainland Europe were interested in Britain. In fact there is evidence that tin minerals were being gathered here more than 3,000 years ago, during the Bronze Age. In those days, much of the material was collected from young sands and gravels derived from the weathering and erosion of the mineral-bearing rock, unlike later times when mining techniques were developed to extract tin directly from the bedrock.

Some granite areas contain much more mineralisation than others, and the range of minerals and chemical elements that are present varies greatly. This depends on the temperature of the granite emplacement and the chemistry of the fluids accompanying and following the granite. The Land's End and Carnmenellis granites are particularly rich in tin, and it is around these granites, in areas near to St Ives, Camborne, Redruth and Helston, that most of the mining has been concentrated. The remains of this mining are often clear to see (Fig. 46), but the presence of the minerals themselves does not generally influence the natural scenery.

FIG 46. Tin mine workings near Cape Cornwall, west Cornwall.
(Copyright Dae Sasitorn & Adrian Warren/www.lastrefuge.co.uk)

   In some of the granites, hot fluids from below altered the mineral feldspar
(one of the dominant granite minerals) and turned it into the soft clay mineral
kaolinite. The china clay industry has developed round the presence of this
mineral, which has usually been extracted from the altered granite by washing it
out with powerful water jets. This process has changed the scenery dramatically,
particularly around the St Austell granite. For every tonne of useable kaolin,
5 tonnes of waste granite material are produced, and heaps of this waste are
obvious scenic features in these areas (Fig. 47). The famous Eden Project at
Bodelva, near St Austell, has been constructed inside a large former china
clay quarry.

FIG 47. China clay excavations at St Austell.
(Copyright Dae Sasitorn & Adrian Warren/www.lastrefuge.co.uk)

The older rocks surrounding each of the granite intrusions generally show evidence of alteration that occurred as the mobile granite worked its way upwards from below. This *contact metamorphism*, often accompanied by the growth of new minerals, is the result of the transfer of heat and introduction of new chemical components from the granite. It has usually resulted in making the rocks more resistant to later erosion at the surface.

Younger episodes
Sedimentary markers
Between 7 and 20 km to the southwest of Exeter, traversed by the A38 and A380 trunk roads, the Great and Little Haldon Hills are capped by a layer of sediments, assigned to the Upper Greensand, and spanning in age the Early/Late

Cretaceous boundary (between about 105 and 95 million years ago). These are the westernmost erosional relics of a continuous sheet of sediment of this age that extended across much of the rest of Southern England. In the Haldon Hills area, the sandy and fossiliferous material seems to have formed near the coastal margin of an extensive Cretaceous sea.

The *Haldon Gravels* are distinctive deposits that occur above these Cretaceous sediments. They consist largely of flint pebbles and contain sand and mud between the pebbles. Some of the gravels appear to be the result of removal by solution of the calcareous Late Cretaceous Chalk that can no longer be found in its unaltered state so far west. The flint nodules in the Chalk were then left as a layer of much less soluble pebbles. Some of the gravel appears to have been carried to its present position by rivers or the sea, perhaps also with the incorporation of kaolinite clay from the Dartmoor granite. The age of these gravels appears to be early Tertiary, perhaps about 55 million years.

A few kilometres west of the Haldon Hills, northwest of Torquay, the Bovey Formation of early Tertiary age (Eocene and Oligocene, about 45 to 30 million years ago) occurs in a distinct, fault-bounded basin. The formation is more than 1 km in thickness and consists primarily of the clay mineral kaolinite, deposited as mud by local streams, and associated with minor amounts of sand, gravel and peat-like organic deposits of lignite. This sediment fill continues to be a very important material for ceramics, pipes, tiles etc. ranging from high-quality china clay to lower-quality materials. Most of the sediment appears to have been carried into the basin from the area of the Dartmoor granite and its surroundings. The Bovey Basin formed as a result of subsidence along the northwest-to-southeast trending Sticklepath Fault Zone (Fig. 39) which cuts across the whole of the Southwest Region. This fault zone seems to have been active during the accumulation of sediment in the basin and so, at least in this phase of its history, it was much younger than the Variscan structures of the Southwest generally. Further to the northwest along the same fault zone is the smaller Petrockstowe Basin near Great Torrington (see Fig. 38), and, offshore, under the Bristol Channel is the larger Stabley Bank Basin, east of Lundy Island.

About 6 km southeast of St Ives (see Area 1), near the small village of St Erth, a small area is underlain by some soft sands and muds. When first exposed by quarrying, these sediments provided a rich assemblage of fossils that are thought to have lived some 3 million years ago, in latest Tertiary times. The fossils suggest sea depths of between 60 and 100 m, and are now about 30 m above sea level, so they provide a fragment of evidence from a period when the sea was more than 100 m higher than it is now, relative to the land of Cornwall. As will be mentioned below, this deposit is rather similar in its elevation to the most obvious plateau recognised in many of the inland areas, which may also relate to an episode when the sea stood at this level.

Drainage patterns
On the scale of the whole Southwest Region, the main upland areas are Exmoor in the north and the zone of distinct granite domes in the south, extending from Dartmoor to Land's End.

The highest point of Exmoor is Dunkery Beacon (519 m). Exmoor has been eroded from Devonian bedrock, and may owe some of its elevation to the greater resistance to erosion of this material compared with the Carboniferous material that forms the bedrock further south. Another possible factor is suggested by the remarkable way that many of the river systems of the southwest drain to the south coast, despite their sources being remarkably close to the north coast (Fig. 48). This is the case for the Exe, flowing from Exmoor southwards via Exeter to Exmouth, and, further west, the Tamar, which begins northeast of Bude and flows southwards past Launceston and Tavistock before discharging into Plymouth Sound. It looks as if this part of the Southwest Region has been tilted southwards as these river systems developed on either side of the high ground of Dartmoor, where the granite resisted erosion. A southerly tilt would also be consistent with a preferential uplift of the Exmoor Hills to the north.

FIG 48. River pathways, mean flow rates (m ^{3}/s) at some river stations, main drainage divide (red line) and main granites of the Southwest Region.

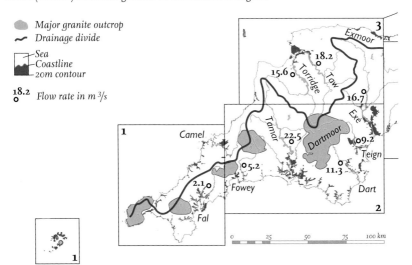

The southern areas of hills correspond so clearly with the areas of granite outcrops that there can be little doubt that the greater resistance to erosion of the granite explains their higher elevations. But how long has this erosion been taking place? Emplacement of the granites was over by the end of Carboniferous times (about 300 million years ago) and there is evidence of pebbles in the New Red Sandstone from the Dartmoor granite and from the altered bedrock close by. Although the precise age of the earliest New Red Sandstone is uncertain, it does not appear to be much younger than the age of granite emplacement. However, it appears that the granites were not being significantly eroded in quantity much before Cretaceous times, 200 million years later and about 100 million years ago. Since then, the granites have been eroded into the present patterns of local hills and valleys, but at very variable rates as climate, coverage by the sea and rates of river erosion changed.

Each of the main granite bodies corresponds closely to an area of high ground, and their maximum heights tend to be greater towards the east (44 m for the Isles of Scilly, 247 m for Land's End, 252 m for Carnmenellis, 312 m for St Austell, 420 m for Bodmin and 621 m for Dartmoor). This gradient is overall only about 3 m per km. The geophysical data on the large, deep granite body (Fig. 44) recognised below the surface granite bodies do not provide independent evidence for a slope of this sort deep down. Some tilting of the landscape downwards towards the west may have occurred, or the slope may simply reflect the greater proximity of the western granite bodies to the sea and repeated episodes of marine erosion.

Ice Age episodes

Ice sheets do not appear to have covered the present land of the Southwest Region to any important extent during any of the major cold episodes of the Ice Age. In the Isles of Scilly, material deposited directly from a grounded ice sheet has been recognised and is thought to be Devensian (last cold phase) in age (Fig. 49). Various giant boulders derived from metamorphic sources are a notable feature of some localities on the North Devon coast, some of which appear to have come from Scotland. However, it is not clear whether they were transported to their present locations by a large ice sheet or by floating ice.

In spite of the lack of an actual ice sheet, the repeated cold episodes of the Ice Age must have had a considerable effect upon the weathering style of the bedrock, for example influencing the granite tors, mobilising material to move down slopes and changing drainage patterns and the surface blanket of soft materials.

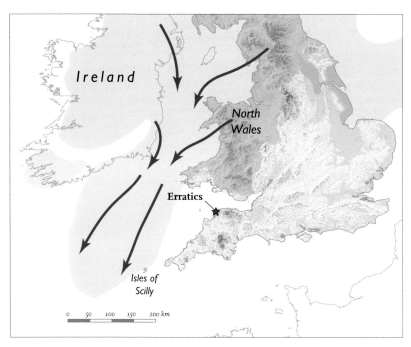

FIG 49. Map showing the greatest extent of the last main (Devensian) ice sheet across England and Wales.

AREA 1: WEST CORNWALL

A remarkable feature of the peninsula of West Cornwall (Figs 50 and 51), as it narrows towards Land's End, is the contrast between the spectacular coastal scenery and the scenery inland. The rocky coastal cliffs and sharply indented coves reflect West Cornwall's exposure to the prevailing Atlantic storms, and contrast starkly with the inland scenery of rolling – though often rocky – hillsides, carved into a network of small valleys and streams.

The main features of the inland landscape appear to have formed over millions of years, and ultimately reflect the bedrock pattern that has been inherited from the Variscan mountain building that ended 300 million years ago. In contrast, the coastal landscape is clearly much younger, and much of it has been produced by changes in sea level that have occurred since the last main cold phase of the Ice Age, some 10,000 years ago. There is some evidence of earlier sea

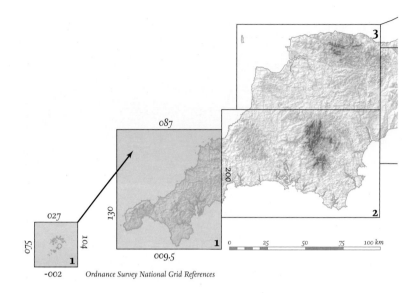

FIG 50. Location map for Area 1.

levels but this is more difficult to evaluate, as it has generally been removed by more recent erosional events.

I have divided West Cornwall into three Landscapes (**A** to **C**), each with distinctive bedrock geology (Fig. 52).

Landscape A: Granite areas

The Isles of Scilly (**A1**; Fig. 53) are formed by the westernmost significant granite bodies of southwestern England. They lie some 45 km southwest of Land's End, scattered over an area approximately 20 km by 15 km. Most of the 150 islands are little more than bare outcrops of granite, sometimes largely submerged at high tide. The landscape is windswept and mainly treeless, with heathlands where the ground has not been cultivated. Historically the islanders eked out a precarious existence from crofting, until the nineteenth century, when shipbuilding and the growing of flowers became economic. Today most of the cultivated land consists of small fields of flowers edged with evergreen hedges, and horticultural work, along with tourism, has become the mainstay of the economy.

The smaller islands are often arranged in rows, separated by 'sounds' (areas of shallow water) that tend to have a northwest–southeast orientation. These sounds must have been valleys before they were drowned by the recent (Flandrian) sea-level rise. Their orientation is similar to that of the valleys and faults of the

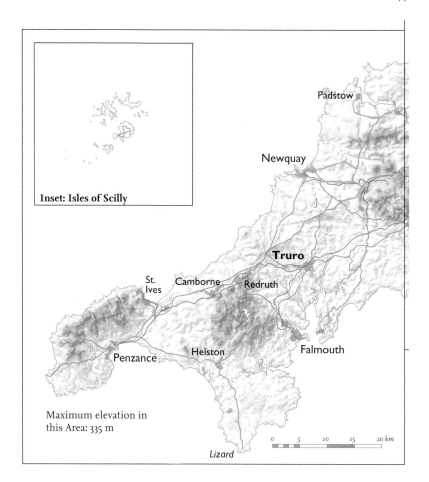

FIG 51. Natural and man-made features of Area 1.

Land's End granite, discussed more fully below. Numerous sandy bays and beaches reflect the granite weathering and the transport of the weathered sediment, by storms and tides, to more sheltered parts of the island landscape.

In the general section of this chapter it has been mentioned that the northern Scillies appear to have been invaded by ice late in the history of the last (Devensian) cold phase of the Ice Age (Fig. 49), and this is surprising in view of their southerly location. It appears that when the Devensian ice sheet had grown to its greatest extent, an elongate tongue of ice, perhaps some 150 km wide, extended for nearly 500 km from the Irish and Welsh ice sheets to the edge of the

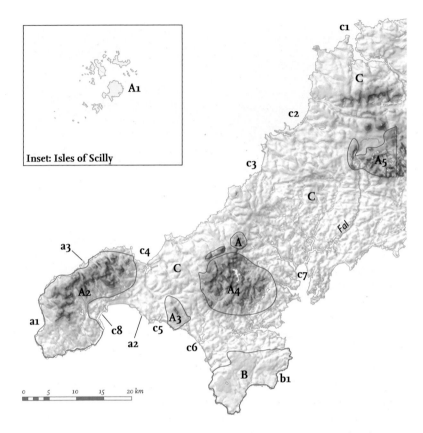

FIG 52. Area 1, showing Landscapes **A** to **C** and specific localities mentioned in the text. Major divisions of Landscape **A** are identified by **A1, A2, A3** etc., and localities are shown as **a1, a2, a3** etc.

Atlantic continental shelf. This tongue became so large because it was vigorously fed by ice from the high ground of Ireland to the west, and the Lake District of England and the mountains of Wales to the east. The ice extended across the mouth of the Bristol Channel, well clear of the present north Cornwall coastline, before leaving ice-laid sediment on the northern fringe of the Isles of Scilly. South of the island areas that were covered by ice, the granite has been weathered locally into tors.

Land's End is the westernmost tip of mainland England. The local cliffs are made of granite and clearly show vertical sets of fractures, probably formed when the granite was cooling and contracting (Figs 54 and 55). Apart from the fractures,

FIG 53. The Isles of Scilly, looking east towards Bryher, Tresco and St Martins. (Copyright Dae Sasitorn & Adrian Warren/www.lastrefuge.co.uk)

the granite is massive compared with the strongly layered and deformed rocks into which the main granites were intruded. Most of the northerly inland areas are exposed and windswept moorland, though arable farming for early vegetables has developed in the valleys to the south. The valleys eroded in the Land's End granite are distinct and often oriented very clearly in a northwest–southeast direction. This orientation is parallel to a large number of faults which appear to have first formed late in the Variscan mountain-building episode. However, they must also have been active much later, after the intrusion of the main granite, because its margin is locally offset by faults with this trend. The movement of superheated water along these fault systems has resulted in mineralisation of the bedrock, altering its resistance to erosion so that valley incision has taken place preferentially in this direction. Tors are largely absent from the Land's End, Godolphin, Carnmenellis and St Austell granite areas, while they are common weathering features on Bodmin Moor and Dartmoor. This probably reflects a difference in the weathering and uplift histories of the different granite bodies.

The Land's End granite (**A2**) forms the bedrock of most of the far southwestern peninsula, which is largely ringed by cliffs. To the east of the granite, St Ives Bay on the north coast and Mount's Bay on the south coast show how much more readily eroded the Devonian killas is in comparison. Along the north coast of the Land's End peninsula, the killas is preserved as a screen of land, rarely more than a kilometre in width, but clearly showing distinctive layering, as seen at Gurnard's

FIG 54. Land's End peninsula from the air, looking eastwards. Note the lack of clear layering in the granite bedrock and the steep fracture surfaces (joints) that have controlled the form of the cliffs. (Copyright Dae Sasitorn & Adrian Warren / www.lastrefuge.co.uk)

Head (**a3**; Fig. 56). Present coastal erosion may have been slowed at this point by the greater strength of the Devonian where it has been altered close to the granite. Just north of Land's End point, Whitesands Bay (**a1**) is one of the only sandy bays to face the open sea to the west. The bay lacks any significant stream system that could have supplied sand to the beach, so it seems most likely that the sand has been carried into this bay by the storms which so often attack this exposed coast.

A distinct, though irregular, platform at 100–150 m above sea level rings the area of the Land's End granite, and tends to be followed by local roads. This may have been formed during an early episode of coastal erosion, when sea level was standing at this height relative to the land (Fig. 57). Some evidence for its age is mentioned below. Its irregularity probably reflects local valley erosion that has taken place since its formation.

FIG 55. Land's End cliffs, looking westwards. Again, note the vertical jointing. (Copyright Landform Slides – Ken Gardner)

FIG 56. Gurnard's Head (Fig. 52, a3), west of St Ives, showing the coastline along the northern edge of the Land's End granite. (Copyright Dae Sasitorn & Adrian Warren/www.lastrefuge.co.uk)

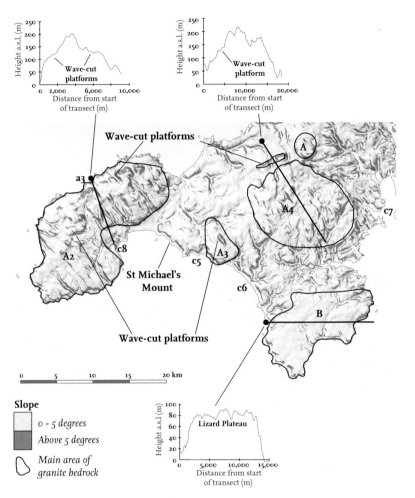

FIG 57. Slope map showing the southwestern part of Area 1. Slopes greater than 5 degrees are coloured red, and the main granite areas and the Lizard Complex are outlined. Topographic cross-sections illustrate wave-cut platforms that are presently inland and show the lack of topography on the Lizard Plateau.

The next main granite bedrock area to the east underlies the Carnmenellis area (**A4**), although there are other smaller granite areas, such as St Michael's Mount (Fig. 58), across the bay from Penzance, and the intermediate-sized Godolphin granite (**A3**), some 8 km to the east. These smaller granite areas show the range in size of 'feeders' that branched off from the major granite body that

FIG 58. St Michael's
Mount. (Copyright Dae
Sasitorn & Adrian
Warren/
www.lastrefuge.co.uk)

underlies the whole Southwest Region (Fig. 44). In all cases the granite bedrock
corresponds to high ground in the landscape – evidence of the greater resistance
of the granite in the face of repeated landscape erosion. Derelict mine engine
houses litter the landscape, especially northwards near Camborne and Redruth,
once prosperous tin-mining centres. To the south, the landscape is more
sheltered and fertile, allowing better farming. Trees are rare because of their past
cutting for fuel for the mining industry, as well as because of the general
exposure of the landscape to the weather.

The same northwest-to-southeast valley pattern that has just been mentioned
in the Land's End granite is also apparent in the area around the Carnmenellis
granite, and appears to be the result of preferential stream erosion parallel to the
faults trending in this direction (Fig. 59).

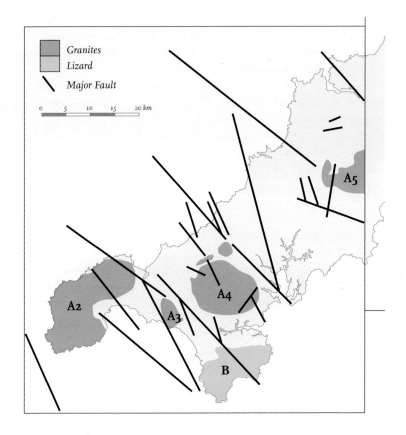

FIG 59. Sketch map showing the orientation of some of the main faults in West Cornwall.

Another similarity to Land's End is the widespread topographic platform at about 140 m above sea level. This platform is particularly clear north of the Carnmenellis granite but is also obvious in the Godolphin granite (Fig. 57). In the Porthmeor and Camborne areas the platform is particularly distinctive, and the continuity of its landward slope is clear on the slope map. It has generally been assumed that these platforms were cut by storm waves when the sea stood at this level about 3 million years ago. At this time, West Cornwall would have consisted of granite islands, like the present Isles of Scilly, while the surrounding Devonian bedrock (killas) was submerged.

The western part of the St Austell granite (**A5**) lies within Area 1, and again its resistance to landscape erosion is shown by the high ground that it occupies. The remarkable feature of this granite is the way it has been altered by the circulation of hot fluids. Much of the feldspar in this granite has been altered to the mineral kaolinite, which is a member of the clay mineral group that is the key component of china clay. The result of this is that the St Austell granite has been quarried, particularly in its western part within Area 1. The kaolinite has been extracted from the rotted granite by high-pressure water jets, which leave large volumes of quartz and feldspar grains that are heaped up in enormous and obvious spoil heaps.

Most of the original heathland and moorland on the St Austell granite has been destroyed by the mining industry. More recently, the Eden project redevelopment of one quarry complex (in Area 2) has brought many visitors to the area.

Landscape B: The Lizard

Lizard Point is the most southerly headland in Britain, part of a wider Lizard landscape comprising a flat heathland plateau bounded by dramatic cliffs and small coves (Fig. 60). Notice how steep many of the sea cliffs are, and that they show little in the way of well-developed, regular layering or fracturing. Unlike the other upland areas of Cornwall, the Lizard is not underlain by granite. As mentioned in the general section of this chapter, some of the area is underlain by serpentinite, a distinctive, decorative rock that was originally part of the Earth's mantle, below the crust and many kilometres below the surface (see Chapter 3). Other parts of the Lizard bedrock were originally basalt lavas and minor sheet-like intrusions along with small amounts of sediments, all similar to successions elsewhere that appear to have formed in or below the Earth's oceanic crust. During the Variscan mountain building, this mixture of distinctive bedrock types appears to have been squeezed up amongst the strongly compressed Devonian killas. Today, the exceptional bedrock chemistry of the unusual Lizard rocks is the reason why the peninsula has such a variety of rare plant habitats. Much of the peninsula is a National Nature Reserve (NNR) or owned by the National Trust.

As in Carnmenellis and Land's End, a wave-cut platform has been identified on the Lizard, although its level is rather lower. In fact, the platform actually forms the Lizard Plateau and is remarkably flat, the ground surface varying between 60 and 100 m above sea level over large areas. This relative flatness probably reflects the rather uniform composition of the rock materials involved, and their uniform resistance to weathering and erosion.

The coast of the Lizard Peninsula is formed almost entirely of steep cliffs, particularly around its southwestern perimeter. A few small beaches do occur in sheltered locations, such as at Coverack (**b1**), and picturesque fishing villages are scattered along the east side of the peninsula around small coves and gullies.

FIG 60. The Lizard coastline. Note the contrast between the jagged coastal cliffs and the flat inland landscape. (Copyright Dae Sasitorn & Adrian Warren/ www.lastrefuge.co.uk)

Landscape C: Cornish killas

Most of the bedrock of West Cornwall is Devonian sediment, folded, faulted and – locally – altered during the Variscan mountain-building episode (see the general section of this chapter). The Devonian sediments, known to miners and quarrymen as *killas*, have been less resistant to landscape weathering and erosion than the granites (**A**) and the Lizard Complex (**B**), and so have been preferentially eroded to form lower landscapes. All the major bays and estuaries of this Area, such as St Ives Bay (**c4**) and the Carrick Roads at Falmouth (**c7**), are situated in killas areas for this reason. The Variscan folding and faulting that deformed the killas has also locally influenced the directions of valleys and their slopes, which have picked out variations in the killas layering, giving an east–west grain to the landscape (Fig. 61).

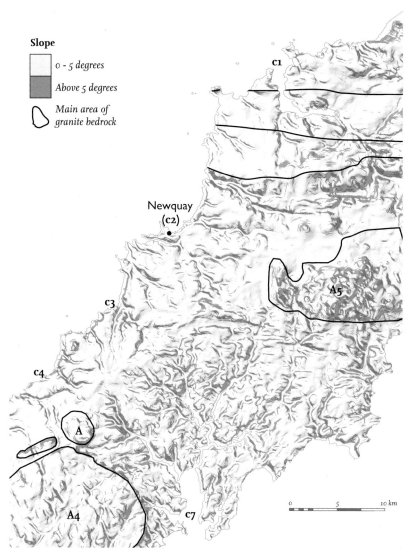

Slope

☐ 0 - 5 degrees

■ Above 5 degrees

⬭ Main area of
granite bedrock

C1

Newquay
(C2)
●

C3

A5

C4

A

0   5   10 km

A4   **C7**

FIG 61. Slope map of the eastern part of West Cornwall. The main granite bedrock
areas are outlined and important boundaries in the Devonian bedrock indicate the
direction of the Variscan folding. Note the circular china-clay workings that are visible
in the St Austell granite (**A5**).

FIG 62. Complex landscape of the North Cornwall coast, looking eastwards from Crantock Beach, over the Pentire Ridge towards Newquay (Fig. 52, **c2**) and Watergate Bay. (Copyright Dae Sasitorn & Adrian Warren/ www.lastrefuge.co.uk)

FIG 63. Headlands, bays and beaches of the Newquay area (Fig. 52, **c2**), looking eastwards from a point 2 km west of Figure 62. Crantock Beach is visible in the middle distance. (Copyright Dae Sasitorn & Adrian Warren/www.lastrefuge.co.uk)

The Flandrian sea-level rise, which ended only 5,000 years ago, has also left its mark on West Cornwall. The most obvious legacy is the extensive array of tidal estuaries at the mouths of the main rivers, which are flooded river valleys or *rias*. The most striking example is the series of branched rias around Falmouth known as the Carrick Roads (**c7**). These extend northwards across half of the width of West Cornwall and have had an obvious major influence on the road and rail transport pattern of the area. Major branch rias to the west, north and east around the Carrick Roads divide this part of the Cornish landscape into numerous isolated peninsulas. The inland valleys of the killas areas tend to be deeply incised with little widening, and the branching patterns of these valleys are very clear on the slope map. The rias are obviously the direct result of the drowning of valleys of this form by the Flandrian sea-level rise.

The coastline of the killas landscape of West Cornwall is extremely varied: small, sandy coves alternating with rocky promontories and high cliffs are typical of this part of the north coast (Figs 62 and 63). This irregular coastline is due to local variation in the type and strength of the killas bedrock, with weaker units (often slates) eroding to small bays while the more resistant rocks (often limestones or quartzites) form the headlands.

The sandy bays of north Cornwall (**c1**, Padstow and the River Camel Estuary; **c2**, Newquay Bay; **c3**, Perranporth and Perran beach; **c4**, St Ives Bay) are famous for surfing, due to the splendid waves that roll in from the Atlantic Ocean. Apart from Padstow Bay (**c1**), at the mouth of the River Camel, most of the north Cornwall beaches are not obviously linked to river sources of sand and so must have been filled by sand transported from offshore sources by storm waves. At many famous surfing beaches, such as Perranporth (**c3**), sand banks built up by winter storms can be eroded in the summer, resulting in dangerous currents sweeping out to sea. The wind-blown dunes of the Penhale Sands, north of Perranporth, are a spectacular example of the way that gales from the west can move beach sand up to 2 km inland. Because of the variation in the killas bedrock, some headlands are long and the inlets are narrow enough to develop fast tidal flows, capable of forming large, regular ripples as seen in the foreground of Figure 62.

On the south coast, storm-built sandy beaches have also formed, for example at Newlyn (**c8**), Praa Sands (**c5**) and at the mouth of Helston valley south of Porthleven (**c6**). Further east, the coastline is much more sheltered and the scenery is dominated by the drowned valleys and quiet inlets of the Carrick Roads (**c7**).

AREA 2: EAST CORNWALL AND SOUTH DEVON

This Area straddles the boundary between Cornwall and Devon (Fig. 64). In terms of the coastlines of the Southwest, it includes a small stretch of the north coast near Tintagel, and a large section of the south coast from St Austell, via Plymouth and Start Point, to Torquay and Exmouth (Fig. 65).

In the general section of this chapter, the early geological history of the Southwest Region as a whole has been outlined, particularly the evolution of the Variscan mountain belt. Younger episodes in the region have also been discussed, involving river and valley erosion of the landscape, the effects of the Ice Age and the changes in the coastline that have resulted from the most recent (Flandrian) rise in sea level.

In the sections below we shall consider more local features of the scenery in this Area, dividing it into four distinct Landscapes (labelled **A** to **D**), each underlain by a different kind of bedrock (Fig. 66).

FIG 64. Location map for Area 2.

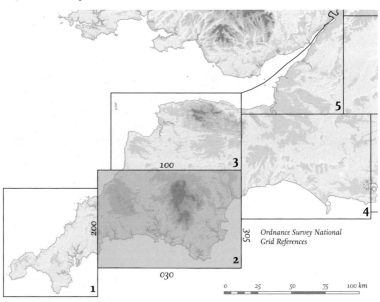

Ordnance Survey National Grid References

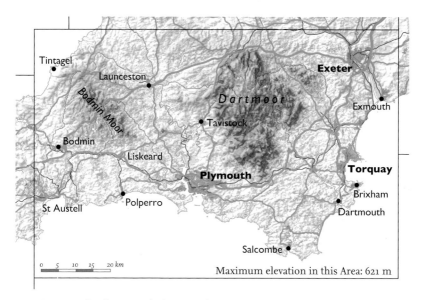

Maximum elevation in this Area: 621 m

FIG 65. Natural and man-made features of Area 2.

FIG 66. Area 2, showing Landscape **A** to **D** and localities (**a1**, **a2** etc.) mentioned in the text.

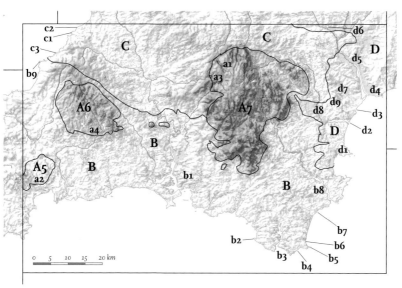

Landscape A: Granite areas

Bodmin Moor (**A6**) and Dartmoor (**A7**) are the most southerly large upland areas in England and, in each case, the granite bedrock has resisted landscape erosion to produce the high ground. The highest point of elevation in this Landscape is High Willhays (**a1**) at 621 m above sea level on Dartmoor. Evidence of the ongoing nature of this landscape erosion is provided by the contrast between the high moorland, with bogs, steep valleys and exposed tors, on one hand, and the surrounding low farmland on the other.

In the general section of this chapter I have outlined some main features of the southwest granites, such as their resistance to erosion and the valuable minerals associated with them. They have also provided excellent strong building stone for the buildings of the Region.

As in the granite areas of West Cornwall (Area 1), mineral mining activities have had a strong impact on the area, and derelict tin mine buildings are scattered over much of the landscape. The china-clay industry has also produced significant changes to the scenery, one of the most remarkable sites being the workings 3 km northeast of St Austell (**a2**). These pits now house the famous Eden Project, an educational charity providing a 'Living Theatre of People and Plants' and attracting over a million visitors each year (Fig. 67).

FIG 67. The Eden Project is situated in a former china-clay pit. (Copyright Dae Sasitorn & Adrian Warren/www.lastrefuge.co.uk)

The present-day pattern of streams and their valleys has evolved from ancestral streams and valleys that carved most of the inland scenery over millions of years. In the general section of this chapter, we have seen the remarkable way that the drainages of the rivers Tamar and Exe flow southwards across most of the Southwest Region to the sea, divided by the high ground of Dartmoor. A general tilt of the Region to the south, and the resistance of the granite domes to stream and valley erosion, appear to have been important factors. Closer examination of the drainage patterns shows that the streams and valleys of the Bodmin Moor granite tend to radiate out from near its centre, but that the distinctly larger Dartmoor granite has eroded down to form two drainage divides, one in the north and one in the south. This may simply be a matter of the different size of these two granite areas, which has allowed a more complex drainage pattern to develop through time over Dartmoor.

The parallel groups of incised valleys that are common in the granites of Area 1 are not clearly developed on Bodmin Moor and not visible at all on Dartmoor. It is intriguing that the fault system that was responsible for the parallel valleys further to the west is not present in these larger eastern granites. This may tell us something about the greater depth of weathering and erosion experienced by the eastern granites.

There are a number of gorges resulting from the deep incision of rivers and streams into the granites and their surrounding materials. Around the Dartmoor granite, the valleys of the River Dart to the east and the Lydford Gorge to the west (a3) are examples of these. South of the Bodmin Moor granite, the River Fowey also has a spectacular and well-known gorge at the Golitha Falls (a4).

Tors are remarkable features of both the Dartmoor and Bodmin Moor granite areas (Fig. 68). They provide a focus for visitors in granite scenery that is often otherwise rather featureless and empty, and there are well over a hundred tors on Dartmoor alone. Tors tend to look like heaps of granite blocks, but a closer inspection shows that they are not jumbled but rather blocks that 'belong' next to their neighbours. These linked blocks are relict volumes of a much larger volume of granite, most of which has disintegrated and been removed by weathering. Tors are very much features of granite weathering, suggesting that the coarse interlocking crystal texture and general lack of layering have caused these remarkable landforms to appear.

Many tors occur on the most elevated parts of the scenery, looking like man-made cairns. Others occur on the slopes of valleys, but it is clear that tors will only form where down-slope processes, driven by gravity, can remove the weathering debris from around them. Cracks in the granite (technically called *joints*) give tors much of their distinctive appearance: near-vertical joints produce

FIG 68. Hay Tor, Dartmoor, looking southeast. (Copyright Dae Sasitorn & Adrian Warren/www.lastrefuge.co.uk)

FIG 69. Hound Tor, Dartmoor. (Copyright Landform Slides – John L. Roberts)

towers and pillars, while roughly horizontal joints give the rocks a layered, blocky appearance (Fig. 69). Most of the joints seem to have formed during the arrival of the granite material from below (intrusion), either due to contraction from cooling of the newly solid material, or due to other stresses acting shortly after solidification. The flat-lying joints (horizontal on hill tops, and parallel to slopes elsewhere) may also be due to the erosion of the present scenery, allowing the granite to expand and fracture as the weight of the overlying material is removed.

The slopes round tors tend to be covered with loose granite blocks (often referred to as *clitter*), generally angular and obviously derived from the tors (Fig. 70). Finer-grained, crystal-size gravel or sand of quartz and feldspar is another weathering product and is locally called *growan* or sometimes *head*. It is clear that much of the alteration of the granite that has resulted in the appearance of the tors must have been strongly influenced by the climate, vegetation and soil-forming conditions existing at different times and in different scenic settings. Much of this has been compared to the weathering and down-slope movement that is seen in high-latitude cold climates today, and so is explained as a result of the cold climate conditions experienced repeatedly during the Ice Age. However, weathering of granites is much faster today in the

FIG 70. Mass-flow terrace, looking westward from Cox Tor, Dartmoor. The terrace is interpreted as being the result of down-slope movement under alternating freeze–thaw conditions. (Copyright Landform Slides – Ken Gardner)

warm, tropical jungle areas of the world, compared to drier, cooler and less vegetated conditions. Early episodes of weathering of the Southwest Region granites may have taken place under the warm, tropical conditions that are indicated by early Tertiary fossil deposits elsewhere in England.

Rock basins are low-lying hollows in the granite topography draped with granite weathering products. Sometimes these are dry and their floors are simply coated with granite weathering materials. In other places the hollows are covered by peat, which is often a feature of the higher and wetter parts of the granite hills. Under very wet conditions, the hollows contain deep bogs or *mires*, with a reputation for being bottomless! How these low hollows were excavated is a puzzle.

Topographic platforms, cut by storm waves during times of high sea level, have been claimed to be present around the Dartmoor and Bodmin granite areas, although they are not as distinctive as those discussed on the Land's End and Carnmenellis granites of Area 1. The Area 2 platforms are at heights of between 200 and 300 m above sea level, but in the absence of dated deposits similar to the St Erth beds of Area 1, their relevance to sea-level changes is open to doubt. Indeed, as mentioned above, terraces have been recognised around the Dartmoor granite that are thought to be the result of down-slope mass movement under freeze–thaw conditions, rather than due to sea-level changes.

Landscape B: *Killas* **and other Devonian bedrock**
Apart from the granites, Devonian sediments make up the bedrock of the southern and central part of Area 2. They consist largely of slates and mudstones with some sandstones, and are known generally as *killas* to distinguish them from the granites and other younger, less altered sediments. In a few localities around Plymouth (**b1**) there are Devonian limestones, similar to the well-known limestones around Torquay (**d1**) and Chudleigh (**d9**). The settings in which these Devonian sediments may have formed are illustrated in Figure 38, in the general section of this chapter.

The youth of the coastal scenery of this Landscape combines with the vigour of many of the processes operating to make it much more distinctive and dramatic than the inland scenery. In the west of Area 2, cliffs characterise the Cornish section of the south coast and often intersect deeply incised valleys that are clearly older features (Fig. 71).

Cornwall and Devon are separated from each other in this Area by the River Tamar, and this meets the south coast in a large drowned valley system around which Plymouth (**b1**) has grown (Fig. 72). Plymouth Sound is one of the best natural harbours in the Southwest and the historical naval importance of this city is the result. Similar, but smaller, valley systems (sometimes called *rias*) are

FIG 71. Polperro, on the south Cornwall coast. (Copyright Dae Sasitorn & Adrian Warren/ www.lastrefuge.co.uk)

FIG 72. The Tamar and Brunel Bridges, between Plymouth (Devon), to the right, and Saltash (Cornwall). (Copyright Dae Sasitorn & Adrian Warren/www.lastrefuge.co.uk)

common all along this stretch of coast, as they are further west in Area 1. Flooded valleys form the estuaries of the River Fowey, east of St Austell, and farther east still at Salcombe (**b3**) and Dartmouth (**b8**).

The headlands from Bolt Tail (**b2**) to Start Point (**b5**) are made of some of the most highly altered and probably oldest bedrock in Devon, although the age of their deposition as sediments is not known. They have been changed locally to mica-rich and hornblende-rich schists that must have been altered (metamorphosed) several kilometres below the surface, before being pushed upwards during the Variscan mountain-building event. The local resistance of these schists to erosion has led to a particularly intricate pattern of small but sharp headlands and tight small bays. The slope map (Fig. 78) reveals a strong east–west orientation of slopes in this area that must be a reflection of folding in the bedrock. Three separate coast platforms, the highest at about 7 m above present sea level, are very clear at Sharpers Head (**b4**). Each platform represents an episode in the retreat and relative lowering of the sea before the latest Flandrian rise.

FIG 73. Slapton Sands (Fig. 66, **b7**). (Copyright Dae Sasitorn & Adrian Warren/www.lastrefuge.co.uk)

Just north of Start Point (**b5**) lies the ruined village of Hallsands (**b6**), which vividly illustrates the damage people can unwittingly do in changing features of the coastal zone. From 1897 to 1902 over half a million tonnes of gravel were removed from the bay off Hallsands to construct an extension to the dockyard at Plymouth. Engineers believed that natural storm currents offshore would replenish the material they had taken, but this did not happen. Instead, the removal of the shingle left the beach open to intense storm erosion, and in January 1917, some 15 years later, the lower part of the village and a sizeable section of coastline were removed by a combination of storm and tide conditions.

Further north, the 3.5 km long barrier beach of Slapton Sands (**b7**) is another shingle barrier kept active by storm waves from the southeast (Fig. 73). The freshwater lagoon behind it, Slapton Ley, is a nature reserve, home to many rare species of plants and animals. It is under threat from erosion and breaching of the shingle barrier, causing flooding by salt water, and from silting up because of ploughing and deforestation of the inland landscape.

This Landscape of Area 2 also includes a short section of the north Cornish coast around Tintagel (**b9**), which was an important trading centre on this difficult coast and became the site of a twelfth-century Norman castle, linked to the legends of King Arthur (Fig. 74). The coastline here is often sheer and rugged, and the bedrock contains sharp folds, fracture surfaces and multiple surfaces of mica-rich cleavage, providing evidence of extreme compression during the Variscan mountain building. Many of the cliffs are flat-topped, because erosion has been controlled by relatively flat-lying surfaces in the bedrock, which contrasts sharply with the hog's-back or whaleback cliffs of other coastal stretches.

Landscape C: The Carboniferous Culm of Devon

The northern landscape of Area 2 is underlain by Carboniferous bedrock (locally known as the Culm) which occupies a complex downfold in this part of the eroded Variscan mountain belt. The coastal bedrock here contains many beautiful examples of folding, for example at Boscastle (**c3**), famous for the flash flood that did so much damage in August 2004. Spectacular folding is also clearly visible at Millook Haven (**c2**; Fig. 75), and at Crackington Haven (**c1**; Fig. 76). In both cases, the convergence directions represented by the folds are near vertical, suggesting that the Variscan folding may have involved a later tilting of an earlier fold set.

FIG 74. Tintagel Head (Fig. 66, **b9**). (Copyright Dae Sasitorn & Adrian Warren/www.lastrefuge.co.uk)

FIG 75. Chevron folding of Carboniferous sandstones and mudstones, Millook Haven (Fig. 66, **c2**). (Copyright Landform Slides – Ken Gardner)

FIG 76. Overturned fold in Crackington Formation, Culm Measures, Crackington Haven (Fig. 66, **c1**). (Copyright Landform Slides – Ken Gardner)

Landscape D: New Red Sandstone and younger bedrock

Along the eastern edge of Area 2, relatively unfolded New Red Sandstone of Permian and Triassic age rests on the folded Devonian and Carboniferous sediments of Landscapes B and C. The junction of the younger material with the older was formed when the younger sediment was deposited on the eroded margins of the Variscan hills. The New Red Sandstone occurs in a wide, north–south trending belt, extending southwards as far as Torquay (**d1**) and Paignton, and with fingers extending westwards to the north of Dartmoor (Fig. 37). Along the coast, from Exmouth (**d4**) southwards via Dawlish (**d3**) and Teignmouth (**d2**), the New Red Sandstone has been quarried and penetrated by the tunnels of the main coastal railway to the Southwest. The sandstone forms dramatic red cliffs, and marks the western edge of the World Heritage Site that extends to the east along the coast of Dorset.

The New Red Sandstone consists of sandstones, gravels and mudstones that formed as alluvial fans, desert dunes and in short-lived lakes along the edge of an irregular hilly landscape of older bedrock. The characteristic red colour so typical of many Devon soils has largely been derived from these New Red Sandstone rocks. In the Exeter area (**d5**), roads have been spectacularly cut through the New Red sediments, and also through some scattered deposits of volcanic rock, mainly lava. These lavas have been highly altered and have not resisted weathering at the surface any more than the sediments of the succession, so they have not had much influence upon the scenery.

An intriguing feature of the New Red Sandstone is the way the original landscape on which it formed is reappearing as the present landscape erodes. For example, the Crediton Basin (**d6**), north of Dartmoor, is now obvious as a remarkably finger-like strip of sediment, only 2–3 km across north to south, but extending almost 40 km west to east (Fig. 37). Detailed examination of the New Red sediment in this basin shows that it was deposited as the fill of a long, narrow valley, with material being derived from north and south as well as along its length from the west. The valley formed parallel to the folds and faults of the earlier Carboniferous bedrock on each side of it, and must have been cut first by river erosion in Permian times, controlled by the earlier folds and faults that were formed during the Variscan mountain convergence. A few kilometres further north, the Tiverton Basin in Area 3 has a similar west-to-east trend, though it is more open and less elongate.

From Exeter (**d5**) to Torquay (**d1**), the base of the New Red Sandstone reveals topography of hollows eroded westwards into a higher ground of Devonian and Carboniferous bedrock. The New Red Sandstone pattern is of alluvial fans radiating downstream, but generally draining towards the east, and it bears a striking general similarity to the present drainage and scenery of the area (Fig. 77).

FIG 77. Reconstruction of the Permian topography and drainage, looking southwards towards the location of present-day Torquay (Fig. 66, **d1**). The current coastline is indicated purely for reference; there is no evidence for a sea in Permian times where the sea now is. ☐ *Permian New Red Sandstone*

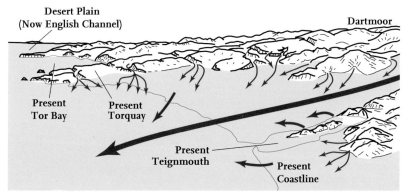

During Variscan convergence, the Devonian limestones were moved into their present pattern by flat-lying faults, and this was then followed by the intrusion of the Dartmoor granite, which may help to explain why the New Red valleys here were shorter than those preserved as the Crediton (**d6**) and Tiverton basins.

I have already described the importance of the Devonian limestones in creating topography in the Torquay area (**d1**) and around Torbay generally. This material is an important part of the bedrock in its own right, and has been quarried widely as a building stone. It was a popular stone for ornaments and furniture, particularly in Victorian times, when cut and polished fossil corals featured in many of the washstands that were produced in the period.

In Torquay the Kent's Cavern complex of caves, formed by solution of Devonian limestones, is an important archeological site, preserving evidence of Heidelberg and Neanderthal man from deposits about 450,000 years old. These were deposited during the Anglian cold phase of the Ice Age, when ice sheets spread across East Anglia and into the Thames valley, though not into the Southwest. The remains of cave bears, hyenas and sabre-tooth cats have also been found in the cave complex, as well as those of modern humans.

The Haldon Hills (**d7**), about 10 km south of Exeter, are clearly erosional relics of the young valley systems of the Rivers Exe and Teign. Their higher ground retains fragments of the Late Cretaceous and Early Tertiary bedrock record and provides information about the history and environments in this key area. The Haldon Hills formed the boundary between the high ground that existed at the time in most of Cornwall and Devon, and the areas of thicker sedimentation that developed since Permian times to the east (Areas 4 to 7). To an extent, the presence of the Late Cretaceous and Early Tertiary material has provided a resistant cap to the Haldon Hills.

The youngest bedrock in Area 2 is the clay, sand and lignite near Bovey (**d8**), between Dartmoor and the New Red Sandstone area. Bovey and Petrockstowe in Area 3 lie on the Sticklepath Fault that runs northwest to southeast across the whole of Devon (Fig. 78). The fault was active about 40 million years ago, at the same time as the Alps were forming as a major mountain belt much further south. It seems likely that this fault formed along the direction of earlier fractures in the bedrock left by the Variscan mountain building and described more fully in Area 1. The Bovey and Petrockstowe basins must have grown as areas of surface subsidence linked to movements of the Sticklepath Fault, and sediment must have been carried into the newly subsiding low ground by streams. The basin sediment is now mined for ball clay, which has been an important source of clay for pottery and many other purposes. There are also layers of lignite and sand which have been used as a fuel and in the making of glass.

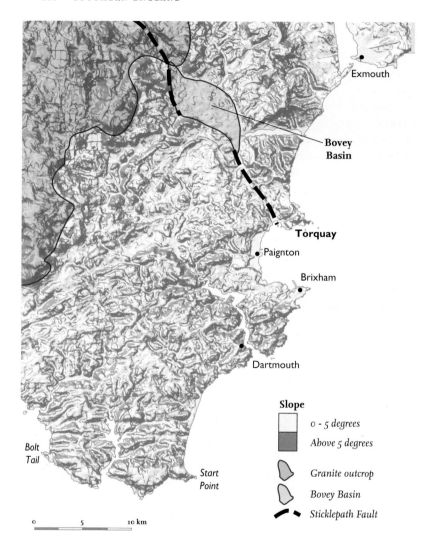

Exmouth

Bovey
Basin

Torquay

Paignton

Brixham

Dartmouth

Bolt
Tail

Start
Point

Slope

0 - 5 degrees

Above 5 degrees

Granite outcrop

Bovey Basin

Sticklepath Fault

0   5   10 km

FIG 78. Slope map of the eastern part of Area 2, showing the distribution of slopes greater than 5 degrees (coloured red) .The Dartmoor granite bedrock area is indicated (orange), as are the Bovey Basin (green) and the Sticklepath Fault (dashed line).

AREA 3: NORTH DEVON AND WEST SOMERSET

This Area (Figs 79 and 80) divides neatly between the high ground of Exmoor in the north, where the bedrock consists of sediments of Devonian age, and an area of Carboniferous bedrock to the south (Fig. 37). The bedding slopes generally southwards, forming the northern part of a large downfold or trough (often called the *Culm synclinorium* or fold-belt in Fig. 39) that forms the central feature of the Variscan mountain belt of the Southwest.

I have selected four Landscapes (**A** to **D**), loosely following the Countryside Commission's character area scheme, with each Landscape being shown in Figure 81.

Landscape A: Exmoor's Devonian bedrock

Exmoor is a hilly plateau ranging in summit elevation between 250 m and about 500 m above sea level. The central parts consist of a treeless, heather- and grass-moorland landscape, which is well seen from the highest point, Dunkery Beacon, at 519 m (**a1**; Fig. 82). Exmoor ponies and red deer roam this landscape.

FIG 79. Location map for Area 3.

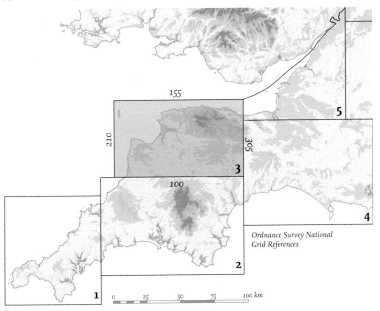

155

5

210

305

3

100

4

Ordnance Survey National
Grid References

2

1

0   25   50   75   100 km

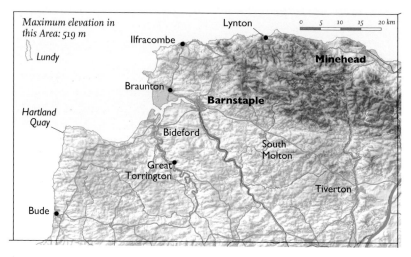

FIG 80. Natural and man-made features of Area 3.

FIG 81. Area 3, showing Landscapes **A** to **D** and localities (**a1**, **a2** etc.)
mentioned in the text.

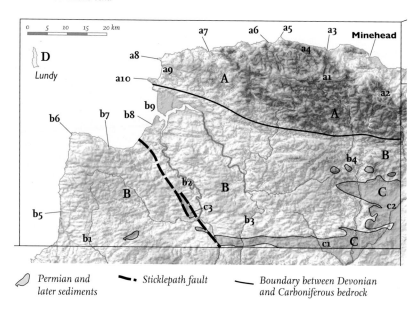

FIG 82. Dunkery Beacon (Fig. 81, a1). (Copyright Dae Sasitorn & Adrian Warren/www.lastrefuge.co.uk)

However, there is much variation in landscape within Exmoor. To the east of the main hilly plateaus and flat-topped ridges are the Brendon Hills (a2), a region of rolling countryside with a large proportion of Exmoor's ancient oak woodland. Though the upper ground of the rest of Exmoor is largely treeless, Exmoor's combes and valleys are quite densely wooded with conifer plantations and broadleaved woodland (Fig. 83). Much of Exmoor is a patchwork of fields claimed from the moor in the nineteenth century. The moorland becomes wetter and more broken into hills and valleys towards the south, approaching Landscape B.

Exmoor is the only large upland area in the Southwest Region that is made of sedimentary bedrock, rather than granite. The bedrock consists of Devonian sediments, folded and altered during the Variscan convergence and of similar composition to the Cornish killas in Areas 1 and 2. Mudstones and sandstones are the commonest types of sedimentary bedrocks in the Exmoor landscape, originally formed in the Devonian basinal setting illustrated in Figure 38.

Exmoor was never glaciated, and the upland plateau surface may be as much as 200 million years old, formed in the Early Jurassic. Gently rounded hillsides and gentle valleys are typical of most of the higher ground, suggesting that the

FIG 83. Heddon's Mouth, Exmoor, 5 km west of Lynton. (Copyright National Monuments Record, English Heritage)

surface was developed over a long period of stream action. A more recent valley incision is also apparent and probably relates to steady upward movement of the ground relative to the sea during Tertiary times.

As the slope map (Fig. 84) shows, local slope patterns in both Exmoor and the Culm area of Landscape **B** have a tendency to run broadly west to east. This is the result of the direction of the folding that formed during the Variscan convergence. Local erosion of tilted sedimentary layers and their fold axes has produced ridges and hillcrests with this orientation. The most obvious east–west slope is the 'Exmoor line', running eastwards from Barnstaple and South Molton (Fig. 80), which marks the join of the more easily eroded Carboniferous sediments (Landscape **B**) and the underlying Devonian sediments.

The coast of Exmoor has some of the highest cliffs in England, formed where the old hilly plateau of Exmoor, with tops locally over 300 m in elevation, has been cut into and removed by young coastal erosion. There is so much interest along this coastline that I will comment on it locality by locality, from east to west (Fig. 81).

Westwards from Minehead, the Bluff is the northernmost point of an isolated hill range that reaches elevations of more than 300 m and runs for some 7 km along the coast. There is a marked change of slope at 200 m, above which the topography is gently hilly, whereas below it descends steeply in numerous

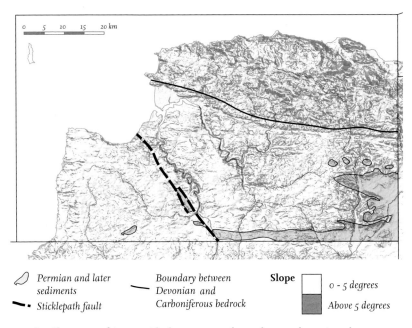

⟋ *Permian and later*
sediments

➤▪ *Sticklepath fault*

── *Boundary between*
Devonian and
Carboniferous bedrock

Slope

☐ *0 - 5 degrees*

▨ *Above 5 degrees*

FIG 84. Slope map of Area 3, with slopes greater than 5 degrees shown in red.

landslides towards small cliffs of bedrock being actively eroded by the sea. There
are many small folds in the bedrock, but generally the coastal slope is of the
hog's-back type (Fig. 85). Views from this hill range extend northwards across the
Bristol Channel and southwestwards across a wide valley, eroded preferentially
in New Red Sandstone and with a capping of Early Jurassic sediment. It is clear
that an early topography of valleys was partially filled with New Red Sandstone
(strictly part of our Landscape **C**), which has later been modified by faulting. The
faulting makes interpretation of this area difficult, so the details of the early
topography are not as clear as they are to the south and north, along this same
important unconformity.

Porlock Bay (**a3**) occupies the mouth of this valley, and has been the site of an
interesting recent planning decision. Until 1996, the bay was protected by a
natural barrier of gravel that had been accumulating under storm conditions and
moving landwards to its present position as the Flandrian sea level rose. Behind
the barrier, farm land had been drained, using tidal gates along with periodic
engineering work to maintain the level of the barrier. In 1996 the barrier was
breached by storm waves at a time of high tide, and it has now been decided to

FIG 85. The typical hog's-back cliff profile of the Devonian bedrock of Exmoor, looking eastwards towards Foreland Point (Fig. 81, a5). (Copyright Landform Slides – Ken Gardner)

let the farmland 'go', returning it to salt marsh. After centuries of attempting to defend the land against the seas, it is difficult to convince people that it is sensible to let some land go, particularly if they have a special interest in it.

The section of the coast from the Culbone Hills (a4) to Foreland Point (a5) illustrates well the contrast between the actively eroding coast and inland areas with an older ground surface. Whereas the coastal slope is wooded and steep, descending from a line of hills some 350 m high, the other side of the hillcrest contains the sinuous and well-developed valley of the East Lyn, flowing parallel to the coast. The mature inland landscape has been transected by vigorous coastal processes of erosion (Fig. 86).

The long coastal section from Foreland Point (a5) to Combe Martin (a7), Ilfracombe and round the corner to Morte Point (a8) and Baggy Point (a10) contains classic examples of different forms of cliff profiles seen in southwest England. The 'corner' at Morte Point (a8) marks a change from bedding-parallel erosion along the north-facing coastline to the east, to erosion that cuts across the folding and layering of the bedrock to the south. This has produced the distinctive finger headlands of Morte and Baggy Points. *Hog's-back* cliffs have small, steep cliffs near sea level that pass upwards into a distinct slope inclined at

FIG 86. Aerial view eastwards from Elwill Bay towards Foreland Point (Fig. 81, a5), showing cliffs with south-dipping strata and hog's-back profiles. (Copyright Dae Sasitorn & Adrian Warren/www.lastrefuge.co.uk)

30–40 degrees towards the sea (Fig. 87). These slopes become gentler towards their summits and may continue into an inland-facing slope, producing a convex-upward, hog's-back form. Contrasting *flat-topped* cliffs are present at Morte Point, further west (a8), and result from horizontal or poorly layered bedrock that produces a near-vertical cliff with a flat top. *Bevelled* cliffs appear to form when rising sea level meets terrain which already has a smooth convex-upwards slope profile.

Lynton and Lynmouth (a6) are twin villages, with Lynton situated on the Exmoor upland some 200 m above Lynmouth, which sits at the head of the deeply incised valley of the Lyn. Lynmouth made headlines in 1952, when heavy rains on Exmoor led to a massive flood, sweeping away many houses in the valley floor and sadly killing 34 people. A similar flash flood at Boscastle (Area 2) in 2004 fortunately did not kill any people, but again illustrates the danger of flooding in the deeply incised young valleys of the northern coast of the Southwest.

The Valley of the Rocks, just west of Lynton, is a further striking example of an old, uplifted landscape under attack from active coastal erosion (Fig. 88). This 'dry valley' contains remarkable weathered Devonian sandstone outcrops, with

(1a) Hog's Back

(1b) Hog's Back

(2) Flat-Topped

(3) Bevelled

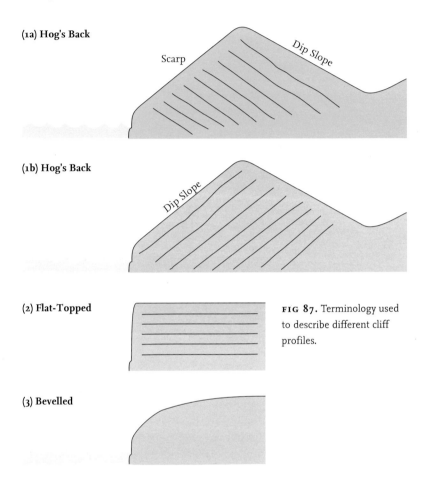

FIG 87. Terminology used to describe different cliff profiles.

names like Castle Rock, Rugged Jack and the Devil's Cheesewring. At its lower (western) end, the valley turns towards the sea, and is then abruptly truncated by the actively eroding coastal cliff. The valley was probably last actively evolving during the last (Devensian) cold phase of the Ice Age, before sea-level rise caused the coast to invade and remove its lower end.

Much of the Exmoor coast consists of inaccessible cliffs with steep wooded slopes, but there is a 3 km long bay (a9) filled by Woolacombe Sand, between Morte Point (a8) and Baggy Point (a10). The bay appears to be the result of a bedrock change from the strong Hangman Grits in the north to weaker Ilfracombe Slates which have been more readily eroded by streams and coastal

FIG 88. The Valley of the Rocks, west of Lynton. (Copyright Landform Slides – Ken Gardner)

processes. Like Croyde Bay, just south of Baggy Point, the beach is popular with surfers since it catches the Atlantic swell waves from the west. Woolacombe Beach is backed by sand dunes which appear to cover an old wave-cut platform eroded during an earlier episode of high sea level.

The raised beaches at Baggy Point (**a10**) and 3 km to the south at Saunton Down provide further evidence of a higher sea level in the past. They are clearly defined and run for about 4 km at a level about 15 m above today's sea. Several deposits of sands and gravels are preserved, cross-cutting the layering of the bedrock beneath. These beaches must have formed before the ice sheet of the last (Devensian) cold phase of the Ice Age reached its maximum extent (Fig. 49). Associated with these beaches is a remarkable range of boulders and pebbles from igneous and metamorphic sources much further north. The growth and decay of ice sheets along with variations in sea level provide an extraordinary range of possible episodes in which these boulders might have been transported.

Landscape B: The Culm (Carboniferous) bedrock area

Culm bedrock underlies the southern part of Area 3 and also the northern part of Area 2. Together these two parts form the Culm fold belt (Fig. 39), which is the Variscan downfold between the older rocks of Exmoor and the Dartmoor–Bodmin Moor uplands. The Culm rocks have not resisted landscape erosion as much as the older rocks to north and south, and so have formed a lower landscape, not exceeding 250 m above sea level. The area is rural and sparsely settled, with an economy relying predominantly upon dairy farming.

FIG 89. The Torridge–Taw Estuary. (Copyright Dae Sasitorn & Adrian Warren/www.lastrefuge.co.uk)

Several large rivers run through this Landscape. In the centre, the valleys of the Torridge (b2) and the Taw (b3) wind northwards from headwaters on the northern margin of Dartmoor, draining the west and northeast before emptying into Bideford Bay (b9, also sometimes called Barnstaple Bay) on the north coast (Fig. 89). It is the rest of the drainage of this Area that is so remarkable, as has been pointed out in the introduction to this chapter. It is extraordinary that the other main rivers – the Tamar (b1) and the Exe (b4) – join the sea along the south coast, yet drain southerly even quite close to the north coast. This has been taken to suggest that the Southwest Region has been tilted southwards, causing the southerly-flowing rivers to erode their headwaters, thus extending their areas to the north.

Landscape erosion of the Variscan folds has picked out sandstone layers to form ridges and valleys, trending west to east, and this is very clearly shown on the slope map (Fig. 84). The southern coastal section of this Landscape runs from Bude (b5) to Hartland Point (b6), and is almost entirely formed of flat-topped

FIG 90. Zigzag folding at Hartland Quay. (Copyright Dae Sasitorn & Adrian Warren/www.lastrefuge.co.uk)

cliffs displaying beautiful zigzag folds, clearly visible at Hartland Quay, 3 km south of the Point (Fig. 90).

From Hartland Point (**b6**) to Clovelly (**b7**), the coast trends parallel to the general direction of the Variscan folding, and many of the cliffs are of bevelled type. This probably reflects the way the coastline runs parallel to the Variscan fold direction, so that a less dramatic cliff is generated. Low cliffs run from Clovelly to Westward Ho! (**b8**), where there is an extensive wave-cut platform which must date from the last episodes of Flandrian transgression (rise in sea level). This platform provides an almost continuous cross-section through the generally steeply dipping bedrock strata which have provided valuable insights into the details of the large deltas in which the Carboniferous rivers deposited sands and muds. At low water mark along this coast, the remains of much younger trees are sometimes visible, providing striking evidence of a much more recent relative rise of sea level.

Landscape C: New Red Sandstone and younger bedrock

The belt of New Red Sandstone and younger sediments that skirts the older deformed Variscan bedrocks of the Southwest Region continues northwards from Area 2 into Area 3 (Fig. 37). In the discussion of Area 2, we saw that this arrangement of the New Red Sandstone marks its contact with the distinct Permian landscape of hills and valleys that formed an edge running across the Variscan mountain belt. The same is true further north in Area 3, where the Crediton (c1) and Tiverton (c2) basins represent remarkably complete relics of this very old landscape. Further north, in the Minehead area, other valleys of this Permian landscape are visible in the present-day landscape.

The present-day landscape that has been eroded in the Permian and younger sediments is generally flatter and lower than that of the older bedrocks, because the younger rocks are relatively weak in the face of stream erosion.

The Early Tertiary Petrockstowe Basin (c3), some 7 km south of Great Torrington, formed along the Sticklepath Fault (Fig. 39) as a result of sinking movements associated with fracturing and movement along the fault. Streams carried clays into this basin, from which they have been extracted commercially, as with the Bovey Basin in Area 2.

Along the north coast for several kilometres from Minehead, southeasterly to Blue Anchor Bay, much of the actual coastline is backed by a flat platform with its upper surface 5–8 m above sea level. Low water reveals a shore of boulder-strewn sand, except in Minehead itself, where the Strand consists of relatively well-sorted sand. This reflects the way that this northeast-facing part of the coast is sheltered from the storm waves that sweep in from the west. Behind the platform, slopes rise abruptly to the main inland hills, and a number of valley mouths and isolated hills were carved during New Red Sandstone times, and perhaps as late as the early Jurassic. This ancient landscape has much more recently been filled with river sediments, which have then, in turn, been covered by seashore deposits, probably reflecting an interglacial high-stand of the sea. This interesting succession of sediments is now being overlain by younger coastal deposits formed during the recent Flandrian (postglacial) rise of sea level.

Landscape D: Lundy Island

I have defined a separate Landscape for this island because it is so distinctive, not only in form, but also in its location.

Lundy Island (Fig. 91) measures approximately 5 km north to south and only about 1 km in width. The highest hill top is 142 m above sea level, but the island is generally flat-topped and surrounded by steep cliffs that provide homes to many seabirds. The northern part of the island comprises desolate heathland, while the main settlement is in the southern part, where the land is divided into small fields and pastures. Most visitors are attracted to Lundy by a natural sense of curiosity, stimulated by its isolated setting.

Most of the island is granite, the same type of igneous rock as many other areas in the Southwest, but the Lundy granite was emplaced in the crust much more recently: about 65 million years ago, compared with some 300 million years ago for the other Southwest granites. The Lundy granite was intruded relatively recently into Devonian sediments that had been deformed into slates during the Variscan mountain-building episode, some of which can be seen in the southeast of the island, near to the landing beach. The Lundy granite formed as the core of a volcano, being the southernmost visible Tertiary volcanic feature in a volcanic province that included Northern Ireland and much of western Scotland. This activity is now understood to have been linked to divergent plate movements that resulted in the growth of the Atlantic Ocean and created important land movements, raising much of the west of Britain.

FIG 91. Lundy Island from the south. (Copyright Dae Sasitorn & Adrian Warren/www.lastrefuge.co.uk)

CHAPTER 5

The South Coast Region

GENERAL INTRODUCTION

A S DESCRIBED IN the previous chapter, the Southwest Region records
the history of part of the Variscan mountain belt, resulting from
movements before 300 million years ago. In contrast, the South
Coast Region records a younger history of episodes largely involving downward
movements and the accumulation of sediment in a Southeast England Basin.

In Areas 2 and 3 of the Southwest Region (Chapter 4), the New Red Sandstone
rests on and against a landscape that had been eroded in the earlier Devonian
and Carboniferous bedrock. This contact is an *unconformity*, created when an area
of hills formed by erosion along the eastern fringe of the folded Variscan
mountains was covered by New Red Sandstone sediments.

The East Devon and West Dorset Area (Area 4) provides valuable information
about the movement between the subsiding Southeast England Basin and the
uplifting crust of the Southwest. Careful tracing of layers within the basin reveals
another, younger unconformity, often called the *Western Unconformity*. This has
resulted from the upward movement of the New Red Sandstone, Jurassic and
Early Cretaceous layers in the west, followed by an episode of erosion before they
were submerged again and covered by the Upper Greensand deposits. The
younger Western Unconformity therefore represents a time gap in the
depositional record of the western part of the basin, equal to the time
represented by the Wealden and Lower Greensand deposits that are missing
here but visible further east (Fig. 94). Note how the Upper Greensand lies
parallel to (*conformable with*) the top of the Lower Greensand and earlier layers in

the east, but cross-cuts (is *unconformable on*) the tilted Jurassic and New Red Sandstone layers in the west. Note also that the Jurassic, Wealden and Upper Greensand layers are thicker in the east than in the west, providing further support for the idea that eastern areas were moving downwards more than those in the west.

The oldest bedrock visible in this region occurs in the Brendon and Quantock Hills of Somerset (northwest of Taunton), which are the eastward continuation of the Exmoor hills of north Devon (Fig. 95). The bedrock here consists of Devonian sandstones and mudstones, formed during an episode when sands, muds and thin limestones accumulated in environments that varied from fresh water (rivers and alluvial flats) to brackish and salt water (shallow sea and coastal). The area was sinking during Devonian times, allowing sediment to accumulate along a broad swathe as the coastline moved progressively inland. During the convergent movements that caused the Variscan mountain building, the Devonian sediments were moved into folds and sliced by fractures, and the mudstones were cleaved to form slates.

The next bedrock episode represented is the New Red Sandstone. This was deposited after the Variscan mountains had grown as a result of the plate convergence and compression of the crust. The New Red Sandstone was deposited on and against the eroded surface of the deformed older material, as outlined in Chapter 4, and was itself the product of erosion of the higher areas of the Variscan mountains. The New Red Sandstone consists of distinct layers of sandstone, conglomerate and mudstone, and there is an overall trend towards finer-grained material in the younger layers (for example, the very fine-grained Mercia Mudstones of Triassic age). This finer material indicates a trend towards less vigorous river transport of debris as the high ground of the Variscan mountains was being carved and lowered by erosion, leading to gentler river channel gradients. Much of the New Red Sandstone was deposited by rivers and in lakes on land, though in later times the area was sometimes submerged by the sea.

Lying on top of the New Red Sandstone, the Jurassic bedrock succession in the west outcrops most dramatically along the *Jurassic Coast*, a World Heritage Site considered in more detail in Area 4. For now, it is enough to note that the full succession represents most of the 50 million years of Jurassic time, and consists mainly of mudstones, thin limestones and some sandstones that accumulated in the seas of the Southeast England Basin. Many types of fossils have been found in these rocks, and in some localities they are extremely abundant. The Jurassic ammonites are particularly famous, and form the basis for dating this succession, while fossil vertebrates – including dinosaurs – have

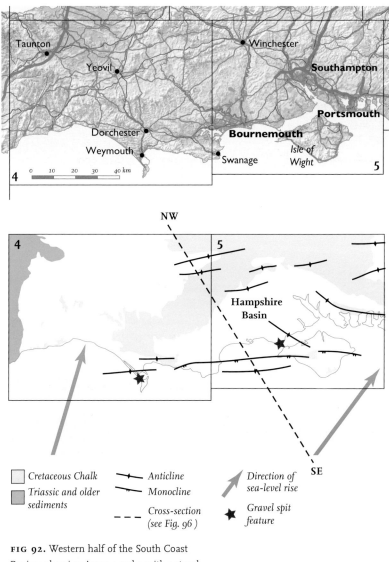

FIG 92. Western half of the South Coast Region, showing Areas 4 and 5, with natural and man-made features of the landscape (above), and bedrock and other natural features (below).

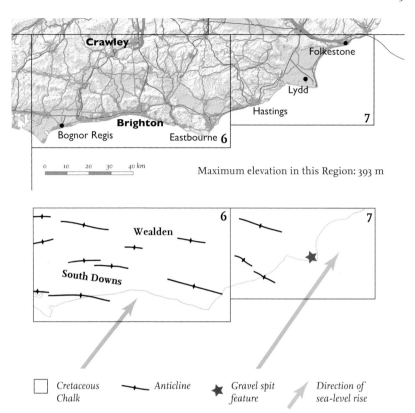

FIG 93. Eastern half of South Coast Region, showing Areas 6 and 7, with natural and man-made features of the landscape (above), and bedrock and other natural features (below).

played an important role in the early days of geological science and are still being studied today. The layers in the Jurassic that have resulted in extensive topographic features are primarily the Bridport Sand (from the Early Jurassic) and the limestones, especially the Purbeck and Portland limestones from the very latest Jurassic.

The Late Jurassic materials were formed in an arm of the sea that became increasingly shallow and coastal as time passed. By the Early Cretaceous, the local environments were changing and the Wealden deposits were formed in lakes that were clearly separated from the sea and were periodically invaded from the north by sand-carrying rivers. Eventually the sea invaded again from the south,

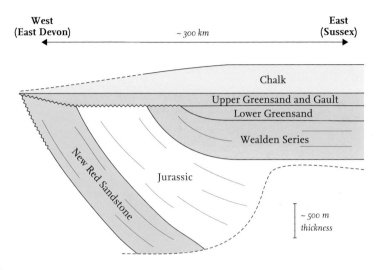

West
(East Devon)   ~ 300 km   East
                                                           (Sussex)

Chalk
Upper Greensand and Gault
Lower Greensand
Wealden Series
New Red Sandstone
Jurassic
~ 500 m
thickness

FIG 94. Sketch section showing the Western Unconformity visible in the layers across the Southeast England Basin. The zigzag lines represent the unconformities.

and in younger Early Cretaceous times sands (later forming the Greensands) and muds accumulated in shallow coastal seas. Eventually these coastal environments became the remarkably uniform seas of the Late Cretaceous in which algal calcareous muds formed, ultimately turning into the Chalk after burial and compression by further sediments.

Above the Chalk, the succession contains a distinct time gap of about 20 million years in the record of sedimentation, during which the already deposited Jurassic and Cretaceous bedrock was subjected to crustal movements, and the pattern of sediment accumulation was interrupted. When the record starts again in Early Tertiary times, the material deposited was being formed in seas that extended only over an area now represented by the Hampshire and London basins. The succession of Tertiary layers preserved in the Hampshire Basin (located on Fig. 92) is beautifully visible in some localities, for example Alum Bay at the western end of the Isle of Wight. The succession in the Hampshire Basin spans the time from about 58 million years ago to 28 million years ago (mid Paleocene to mid Oligocene). The layers vary from about 200 to 700 m in total thickness from west to east, and the proportion of sediment that was deposited in the sea rather than on land also increases eastwards, confirming the idea that the eastern part of the Southeast England Basin was the most strongly subsiding.

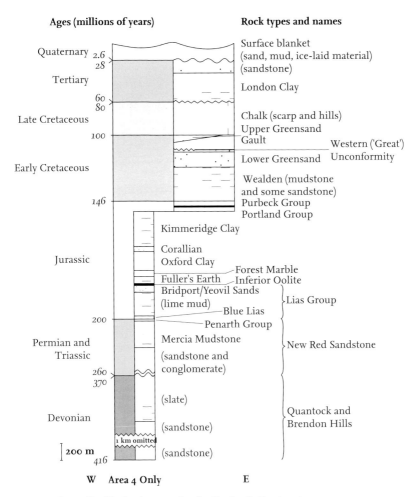

Ages (millions of years)

Quaternary 2.6
28
Tertiary
60
80
Late Cretaceous
100
Early Cretaceous
146
Jurassic
200
Permian and
Triassic
260
370
Devonian

| 200 m
416

W   Area 4 Only   E

Rock types and names

Surface blanket
(sand, mud, ice-laid material)
(sandstone)

London Clay

Chalk (scarp and hills)
Upper Greensand
Gault
Lower Greensand   Western ('Great')
Unconformity

Wealden (mudstone
and some sandstone)
Purbeck Group
Portland Group
Kimmeridge Clay

Corallian
Oxford Clay
Fuller's Earth   Forest Marble
Bridport/Yeovil Sands   Inferior Oolite
(lime mud)   Lias Group
Blue Lias
Penarth Group
Mercia Mudstone   New Red Sandstone
(sandstone and
conglomerate)

(slate)   Quantock and
Brendon Hills
(sandstone)

1 km omitted
(sandstone)

FIG 95. Generalised bedrock succession for the South Coast region.

Bedrock movement, uplift and erosion by rivers

The overall geographical arrangement of the bedrock layers is largely the result of gentle folding, which took place after the Tertiary sedimentation described above. The distinctive Late Cretaceous Chalk layer acts as a clear marker for this late episode of large-scale movement (Fig. 96). From northwest to southeast the Chalk marker curves round the broad Weald uplift (or *anticline*), is buried by Tertiary clays in the Hampshire Basin downfold (or *syncline*), and arrives at the surface again at the Isle of Wight stepfold (or *monocline*), which extends across

Areas 4 and 5. There are also other gentle fold structures in the area, and it is clear that they are the surface expression of a series of west-to-east trending faults deeper in the crust which formed after the end of Tertiary sedimentation (Figs 92 and 96). An early phase of extension or stretching, particularly in the Jurassic, appears to have generated a series of normal faults, which became inactive and were buried by continuing sediment deposition. A later phase of mid-Tertiary compression and convergence reactivated these faults but in the opposite direction, pushing the sediment layers above into gentle folds. This model of crustal deformation seems a more likely explanation of the South Coast mid-Tertiary folds than one linking them to the severe plate boundary convergence that generated the Alps and the Pyrenees many hundreds of kilometres to the south, over the same period of time.

The absence, on land, of bedrock of later Tertiary age suggests that the land surface of Southern England was uplifted at this time (beginning about 20 million years ago), allowing river and stream erosion to begin to carve the scenery. Indeed, some features of the present-day scenery are thought to date from mid-Tertiary times, and the local evidence for this is covered in detail in the Area discussions that follow.

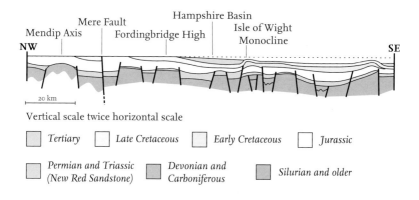

FIG 96. Dorset cross-section from the northwest to the southeast, located on Figure 92. Note the Hampshire Basin and the Isle of Wight monocline.

THE SOUTH COAST REGION · 127

Modification under Ice Age conditions

The whole of the South Coast Region lies south of the areas covered by ice sheets during the Ice Age. However, there is no doubt that surface conditions during much of the Ice Age must have been periglacial (near-glacial), similar to those of Arctic Canada and Russia at the moment. The subsoil and upper bedrock would have been permanently frozen (forming the *permafrost* layer), while the upper layer of the soil thawed during spring and summer and froze in the winter. Weathering processes such as the freeze–thaw shattering of rocks and down-slope mass movement, due to the unfrozen top layer of soil slowly sliding over the permafrost layer, began to shape the landscape.

These Ice Age conditions also help to explain the dry valleys that are such a feature of some local scenery, particularly where Chalk forms the bedrock, for example in the North and South Downs. The dry valleys were initially carved by seasonal water flow and slope movement when the ground was frozen at depth, preventing the water from seeping away into the usually permeable Chalk. When the Ice Age ended, the disappearance of the permafrost layer allowed water to percolate down through fractures in the bedrock, leaving the valley floors dry. Some Chalk streams today are *winter-borne*, only flowing when the water in the Chalk is at a high level, and then becoming dry in the summer and autumn.

Coastal shape and location

The spectacular 100 km long coastline is the defining feature of this South Coast Region. As outlined in Chapter 2, worldwide sea level was around 120 m lower than at present only 18,000 years ago, and has been at or near its current level for only 5,000 years, at the most (Fig. 20). This means that the impressive coastal features that can be examined along the South Coast today have formed within a very short space of time, though some of them almost certainly involve relicts of earlier scenic features created by previous high sea levels (for example during the Ipswichian, 130,000 years ago; Fig. 13).

The overall east–west trend of the coastline is parallel to the folding that formed during the mid Tertiary (see above). This is particularly so in the west, where these folds have locally controlled the arrangement of the resistant Jurassic limestones and the Late Cretaceous Chalk to produce spectacular, narrow headlands that dominate the scenery. In the east of the Region, the coastline of Areas 6 and 7 swings northwards and cross-cuts the mid-Tertiary folds, which themselves curve to the southeast and link up with similar folds in the bedrock of northern France. This northwards curve of the coastline was produced during low-sea-level conditions when a river flowed where the English

Channel is now, carving a wide valley through the bedrock structures. At the end of the Ice Age cold episodes, the sea flooded this valley to create the English Channel (Fig. 21).

Another feature of the present coastline that strongly influences its local shape is the presence of large accumulations of gravel in the form of active gravel spits. Examples of these are Chesil Beach, Hurst Spit (5 km south of Lymington) and Dungeness. In all these cases, the gravel accumulations appear to have been transported into this area by powerful rivers during Ice Age times, and are now being reworked and reshaped by modern-day wave action.

AREA 4: EAST DEVON, SOMERSET AND DORSET

This area (Figs 97 and 98) includes most of the Jurassic Coast, a stretch of the coastline that became a World Heritage Site in 2001. This coast holds a special place in the history of geological discovery, providing a beautifully varied and colourful range of bedrocks that cover some 250 million years of the Earth's history. It is famous for Jurassic fossil collecting and also provides a laboratory for studying coastal erosion, land-slipping and sedimentation processes, as well as for exploring the natural history of the coastal zone. Oil-producing rocks are also visible along the coast and oil is currently being extracted from parts of southeast Dorset (at Wytch Farm – see Area 5).

FIG 97. Location map for Area 4.

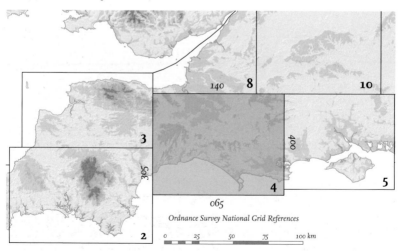

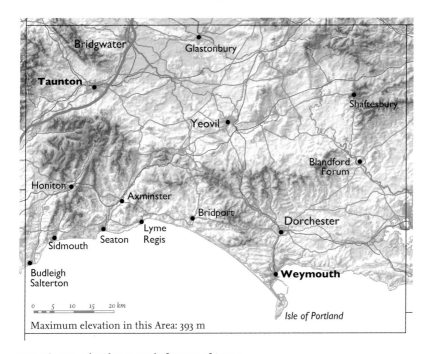

FIG 98. Natural and man-made features of Area 4.

As well as most of Dorset, Area 4 includes parts of Devon, Somerset and Wiltshire. It is a topographically complex Area with many different landscapes (Fig. 99). I have divided the area into nine Landscapes, labelled **A** to **I**, simplifying the Countryside Agency's character area scheme (Fig. 100).

Landscape A: The Brendon and Quantock Hills, Vale of Taunton and East Devon Redlands

The Vale of Taunton and Quantock Fringes consist generally of low-lying, flat farmland that extends to the north coast of Somerset in Area 8, and separates the upland areas of the Brendon and Quantock Hills. The Brendon hills (**a1**) are a continuation of the North Devon hills, while the Quantock hills (**a2**) form a high ridge covered by well-drained heathland, giving breathtaking views across to Exmoor in the west and the Blackdown Hills to the south in Landscape C. The hills here owe their height to the resistance to weathering and river erosion offered by their Devonian bedrock, in clear contrast to the surrounding lowlands that are underlain by the easily eroded Mercia Mudstone (part of the New Red

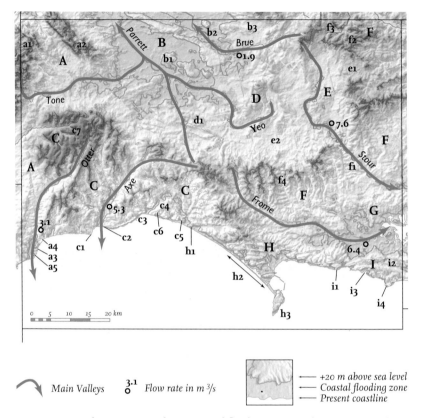

FIG 99. Area 4, showing river pathways, coastal flooding zone, Landscapes **A** to **I** and localities (**a1, a2** etc.) mentioned in the text.

Sandstone). Further west, however, the New Red Sandstone bedrock also contains sandstones, pebble beds and breccias that have resisted erosion more successfully and formed hills. The presence of these coarser-grained sediments represents the more vigorous erosion and transport that occurred in early New Red Sandstone times along the fringes of the Variscan mountains.

North of the Tone valley, the Brendon Hills are separated from the Quantock Hills by a distinct valley, occupied by the Taunton to Minehead road and the West Somerset railway line. The bedrock in this valley is again New Red Sandstone, and its detailed mapping shows that the layers have been much cut by faulting since they were first deposited. The southwestern edge of the Quantock Hills is straight, steep and often reaches 200 m in height above the valley floor

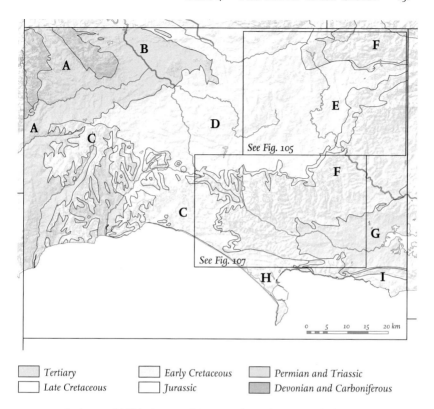

Tertiary   Early Cretaceous   Permian and Triassic
Late Cretaceous   Jurassic   Devonian and Carboniferous

FIG 100. Geology and hillshade map of Area 4, with Landscapes marked.

(Fig. 99). This edge may be an eroded fault scarp, but it could also be an ancient topographic feature, perhaps a slope dating from New Red Sandstone times that was excavated again during the Tertiary.

The New Red Sandstone extends down the western edge of Area 4 and continues into Areas 2 and 3 (Fig. 100). The most characteristic features of the East Devon Redlands are the red soils and buildings, both of which have been made from the New Red Sandstone. The bedrock is largely Mercia Mudstone, but there are earlier Triassic sandstones and coarser pebble beds in the west, because the Triassic rivers tended to deposit their coarsest material closest to their sources in the hills of the Southwest Region.

The Redlands extend down the valleys of the Exe and the Otter, which drain to the south coast. Beautiful cliffs of gently eastward-sloping red sediments of Triassic age are striking features of this part of the coastal scenery, particularly

FIG 101. Looking northeastwards across Ladram Bay (Fig. 99, a3) towards Sidmouth, showing the gently sloping layers of Triassic age in the New Red Sandstone. (Copyright Dae Sasitorn & Adrian Warren/www.lastrefuge.co.uk)

between Ladram Bay (**a3**) with its sea stacks and Peak Hill (**a4**). These Triassic sediments can be seen in Figure 101.

To the west of Budleigh Salterton (**a5**) are cliff exposures, including the Budleigh Salterton Pebble Beds, which are evidence for a Triassic episode of transport of unusually coarse-grained gravels in very vigorous floods. The material forming many of these pebbles seems to have been carried by the rivers from source areas similar to those presently exposed in Brittany in northwest France, which were also part of the Variscan mountain belt.

Landscape B: The Somerset Levels and Moors and the Mid-Somerset Hills

The Somerset Levels and Moors are low and very flat fingers of land that extend southeastwards from the coast of the Bristol Channel. Although the whole area is commonly known as the Somerset Levels, more precisely the Levels are the coastal areas underlain by clay, while the inland peat areas are called the Moors. Low ridges and isolated hills of higher ground, such as the Polden Hills (**b1**) and Glastonbury Tor (**b2**), extend into the Levels. Further north, Landscape B extends into Area 8 in the direction of the Mendip hills.

Before the concerted drainage efforts of the eighteenth and nineteenth centuries, the Levels and Moors were wetland areas frequently flooded by the rivers or the sea. Drainage and agriculture created today's characteristic Somerset Levels landscape: flat straight-sided fields of lush pasture, bounded by artificial streams (called *rhynes*), willows and occasional poplar trees. The rhynes augment the natural drainage provided by the rivers Parrett and Brue.

The bedrock of this Landscape varies considerably. The hills and ridges of higher ground are formed mainly of Triassic and Jurassic clays and limestones that have resisted erosion by the ancestors of the present-day rivers and streams. Much younger sediment has accumulated in the lower ground, particularly during the later stages of the Flandrian transgression that followed the last cold episode of the Ice Age. In the inland areas, the clay is buried under a surface blanket of peat, the youngest sediment in the region, which formed between 7,000 and 2,000 years ago.

The low but often distinctive Mid-Somerset Hills are due to the resistance to erosion offered by thin limestones in the lowermost part of the Blue Lias, which forms the oldest layer of Jurassic bedrock. The sharpness of the toes of the slopes just above the flat ground of the Levels suggests that the hills may have been eroded not only during the Flandrian sea level rise, but also during the earlier (Ipswichian) high-stand of the sea, about 130,000 years ago.

Glastonbury Tor (**b2**) and the Pennard Hills (**b3**) are very clearly defined features of the Mid-Somerset Hills, both of which have been eroded from layers

FIG 102. Glastonbury Tor (Fig. 99, **b2**) and some of the Somerset Levels. (Copyright Dae Sasitorn & Adrian Warren/www.lastrefuge.co.uk)

within the Early Jurassic Lias group. The distinctively shaped Tor of Glastonbury is capped by Bridport/Yeovil Sand and owes its well-defined form to the resistance of this material to erosion (Fig. 102). The lower slopes of Glastonbury Tor and most of the Pennard Hills are composed of earlier Jurassic silts that also appear to have resisted erosion more than the surrounding mudstones. One possible explanation for this is that mineralisation from hot water migrating up faults has strengthened the surrounding bedrock: the Pennard Hills, Glastonbury Tor and Brent Knoll (in Area 8) are all associated with northeast–southwest trending faults.

Landscape C: The Blackdown Hills and Sidmouth to Lyme Bay

This Landscape consists of flat-topped hills dissected by numerous valleys, extending from the Blackdown Hills (**c7**) on the Devon–Somerset border to Sidmouth and Lyme Regis (**c6**) on the Jurassic Coast.

The extensive flat caps of these hills are made of a resistant sheet of Early Cretaceous Gault (marine silts and clays) and Upper Greensand (marine sands and silica-rich, flint-like cherts), and the geological map shows that every ridge is underlain by a finger of this bedrock. In the general introduction to this chapter I described the Western Unconformity that forms the western edge of the Southeast England Basin (Fig. 94). The resistant cover of Early Cretaceous sediments forms the upper cap of this unconformity.

FIG 103. Looking northeastwards over Lyme Regis, with Golden Cap in the right background (Fig. 99, **c6**). (Copyright Dae Sasitorn & Adrian Warren/www.lastrefuge.co.uk)

Locally, the Early Cretaceous layer is covered by patches of Late Cretaceous Chalk, and there is also often a widespread soil cover known as *Clay-with-flints*. This is interpreted as an ancient (possibly early Tertiary) weathering product, involving solution of the underlying Chalk bedrock to yield a concentrate of less soluble flint and chert materials.

The surface of the Western Unconformity is visible in this Landscape over an area approximately 30 km by 30 km, and it slopes very gently to the southeast, from an elevation of 230 m inland to just 70 m around Lyme Regis (Fig. 103). As the unconformity was originally formed by erosion at sea level about 100 million years ago, it provides an indication of land movements since that time, relative to present-day sea level. The net uplift of ~250 m inland and ~100 m around present-day Lyme Regis may have included several downward movements, but it is unlikely that any significant horizontal movement has taken place.

The coastline of this Landscape is famous for its spectacular cliffs and abundant fossils. From Sidmouth to Beer Head (**c1**), red Triassic sandstones are capped by Cretaceous Upper Greensand that slopes gently eastwards, occupying more and more of the coastal cliff face. About 1.5 km west of Beer Head the base of the Cretaceous bedrock passes below sea level and the New Red Sandstone disappears from view, until it is brought back to the surface by a north-trending fault at Seaton Bay. The Late Cretaceous Chalk is also present in the upper parts of the cliffs in this area, forming spectacular near-horizontal layers picked out by flints. The flints have been used as building materials in Beer along with a distinctive form of Chalk known as 'Beer Stone', which was quarried in a remarkable system of caves and tunnels.

From Seaton (**c2**) to Charmouth (**c3**), the coastal hill plateau consists largely of Cretaceous bedrock, showing up as a yellow cap in the distance on the right of Figure 104 and resting upon gently sloping layers of New Red Sandstone and Jurassic materials. Because much of this older material is made of mudstone, which tends to slip when wet, there are numerous examples of land-slipping in this area. The Bindon landslide of 1839 attracted widespread contemporary interest, and movements at Goat Island and Black Ven in 1995 have greatly changed the look of the coastline.

Whereas the New Red Sandstone formed in river and lake environments and generally lacks fossils, the Lias of the Early Jurassic is marine and contains

FIG 104. Black Ven landslip with Charmouth (Fig. 99, **c3**) in the foreground, and Lyme Regis (**c6**) beyond. (Copyright Landform Slides – Ken Gardner)

abundant fossils that can be seen in the museums and fossil shops of Lyme Regis and Charmouth. Ammonites are among the commonest of these fossils, but marine reptiles such as plesiosaurs and ichthyosaurs are probably the most famous.

The Marshwood (**c4**) and Powerstock (**c5**) vales are drained southwards by the Char and Brit rivers and are surrounded by typical flat-topped hills and ridges capped by Cretaceous Upper Greensand, as in the Blackdowns. Gentle folding in this area has elevated the rocks into a dome structure (called a *pericline*), bringing soft Jurassic mudstones to the surface in the centre of the dome and leaving younger, less easily eroded Cretaceous sediments around the edges. Erosion has had the greatest impact on the mudstones, so flat and low-lying topography has formed within the vales, which are surrounded by ridges and hills made of the tougher Cretaceous sediments.

Golden Cap, 6 km east of Lyme Regis, is the highest cliff on the South Coast and owes its name to the yellow colour of the Upper Greensand that forms its crest. The permeable Greensand sits on top of impermeable Gault and Lias clays, and landslides are therefore common along this stretch of coastline. Rainwater percolates readily through the Greensand but cannot penetrate the clays so easily, resulting in a build-up of fluid pressure at the interface between the two layers. This pressure works to destabilise the cliff face and, combined with erosion of the cliff base by waves, can result in large and dangerous landslides as the Greensand slides over the underlying Jurassic clays.

Landscape D: The Yeovil Scarplands
The northward-draining Yeovil Scarplands are underlain entirely by bedrock of Jurassic age, so the pattern of hills and valleys is not easily explained by the simplified geological map in Figure 100. Moreover, the Jurassic bedrock here is extremely variable, not only between its layers but also within a single layer, from one place to the next. Discrete layers of resistant sandstones and limestones, picked out by erosion in one area, often die out laterally to be replaced by more recessive mudstones and clays. The diversity of the Jurassic rocks is due to highly variable local environments in Jurassic times, when the sediments were accumulating. For example, the Ham Hill Stone is a famous calcareous building stone much used in Dorset, but it is only found at a small number of locations, such as at Ham Hill (**d1**). This is because the stone originally formed in a ~5 km wide Jurassic tidal channel, bounded on either side by islands of less calcareous Bridport/Yeovil sand.

Another reason why the pattern of hills and valleys in this Landscape is unclear is that the bedrock has been cut by large numbers of faults that were active after the Jurassic sediments had been deposited. It is difficult to see any simple pattern in the fault directions: groups of faults trend roughly north–south, but east–west faults are also important. The faults influence the scenery because they sometimes juxtapose very different bedrock materials at the surface, and these differences are quickly picked out by erosion to form a complex landscape.

Despite the complexity of much of this Landscape, some of the most spectacular scenery is easily understood. For example, the local topography of north Dorset is due to the presence of particular layers in the bedrock that have resisted erosion, such as the Blue Lias limestones, the Bridport/Yeovil Sands and the Inferior Oolite. In contrast to the Cotswold Hills to the north, many of the other Middle Jurassic layers that produce striking topography are much less important or absent in this Landscape.

Landscape E: Blackmoor Vale and the Vale of Wardour

This Landscape also does not define itself easily in terms of its pattern of hills and valleys. It occupies the area of hills and vales between the main northward-draining catchment of the Parrett and Brue (Landscapes **B** and **D**) and the Chalk Downs (Landscape **F**) to the south (Fig. 99). The Landscape drains largely southeastwards via the River Stour, breaking through the main Chalk rim near Blandford Forum (**f1**). The Vale of Wardour (**e1**) lies between the Wiltshire Downs and Cranborne Chase, while Blackmoor Vale (**e2**) is largely defined by the catchment of the River Stour before it enters the Dorset Chalk. The landscape is of typical 'wooded clay vale' with rich pastureland underlain by soft Jurassic clays, similar to Marshwood Vale (**c4**), described on page 137.

Although the topography of the area is complex (Fig. 105), the map pattern of the bedrock geology and its effects on the local scenery are easier to understand. In the Vale of Wardour (**e1**), detailed mapping of the bedrock has revealed that the margins of the Vale are bounded by high ground underlain by Upper Greensand and Chalk, forming the Wiltshire Downs to the north and Cranborne Chase to the south (Fig. 106). The low ground of the Vale of Wardour is underlain by Jurassic clays, and this has made it the natural route for railways and roads: the main southerly railway loop between London and Exeter and the main A30 Salisbury–Yeovil road both run through the Vale.

More detailed examination of the Vale of Wardour bedrock allows the reconstruction of a scenically important sequence of events. Firstly, a variety of bedrock layers was deposited during the Middle and Late Jurassic, including the Portlandian limestones, which are resistant enough to produce slopes today in the east of the Area. The deposition of these layers was followed by a general

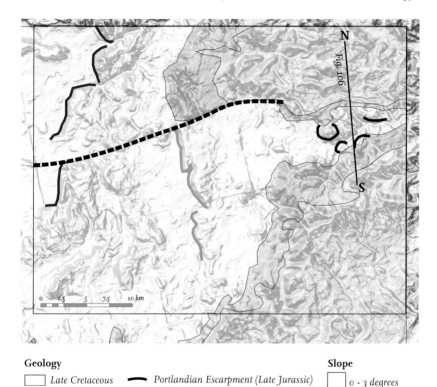

Geology

▢ Late Cretaceous
▢ Early Cretaceous
▢ Jurassic

▬ Portlandian Escarpment (Late Jurassic)
▬ Corallian Escarpment (Middle Jurassic)
▬ Middle Lias Escarpment (Early Jurassic)
▬▬▬ Mere Fault

Slope

▢ 0 - 3 degrees
▢ Above 3 degrees

FIG 105. Vale of Wardour slope (greater than 3 degrees) and hillshade map. Located on Figure 100.

FIG 106. Cross-section through the Wiltshire Downs, Vale of Wardour and Dorset Downs, showing both normal and reverse faulting. Located on Figure 105.

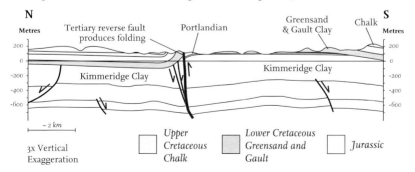

stretching of the crust across the whole South Coast Region, resulting in normal faulting and mild folding of the bedrock layers. The rocks were then subject to erosion as the sea flooded the Region, followed by the deposition in the Cretaceous of the Gault clays, the Greensand and the Chalk. In mid-Tertiary times the crust of the area was deformed under horizontal compression to produce reverse faulting and some localised folding in the fault zones. The uplift associated with this compression exposed the surface rocks to erosion, removing the Early Tertiary deposits from everywhere except the Hampshire Basin. The northern edge of the Vale of Wardour also formed at this time.

Erosion of the land surface has continued since, and more resistant levels in the bedrock have been picked out while valley slopes have formed as sediment is transported down the streams and rivers. One of the layers that has been picked out during this ongoing erosion process is the Chilmark Stone, a well-known building material used in the construction of Salisbury Cathedral. It was quarried from the Chilmark Oolite, a unit of the Portland Limestone Formation brought to the surface by compression and subsequent erosion in the Vale of Wardour.

To the west of the Vale of Wardour is the area round Sherborne and Blackmoor Vale. Here the scenery of hills and valleys reflects the presence of various resistant layers of the Middle and Late Jurassic, particularly the limestones of the Corallian, Forest Marble, Inferior Oolite and Fuller's Earth Rock, and the sandstones of the Yeovil Formation. The pattern is complicated, partly by the lack of continuity of some of these resistant layers (reflecting lateral changes in Jurassic environments of deposition), but also due to local faulting (Figs 105 and 106).

Landscape F: The Wiltshire and Dorset Downs and Cranborne Chase

In the north of Area 4, this Chalk landscape includes part of the Wiltshire Downs (**f2**), forming the northern margin of the Vale of Wardour. Compared with the large area of Chalk Downs that makes up Salisbury Plain further to the northeast (see Area 10), these Chalk hills are high and deeply dissected, particularly along the indented western margin of the Chalk, where Brimsdown Hill (**f3**) reaches 284 m in elevation. Large valleys here generally tend to have a valley floor consisting of mass-flow deposits, called head, and river deposits, called *alluvium*, which usually consist of mass-flow deposits that have been eroded, locally transported and deposited by streams.

More centrally within Area 4, the Dorset Downs (**f4**) are the westernmost chalk uplands in England. They form the northern and western edges of the Hampshire Basin, which extends towards the east across Areas 5 and 6. The Chalk layer slopes gently southeastwards from the escarpments around the

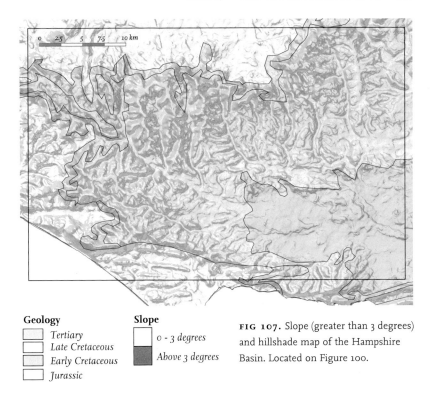

Geology
☐ Tertiary
☐ Late Cretaceous
☐ Early Cretaceous
☐ Jurassic

Slope
☐ 0 - 3 degrees
■ Above 3 degrees

FIG 107. Slope (greater than 3 degrees) and hillshade map of the Hampshire Basin. Located on Figure 100.

northern and western edges of the basin towards its centre, which is filled by sediments of early Tertiary age (see Landscape **G**). Although Chalk slopes also bound the southern edge of the basin, they are much narrower because the Chalk layer here dips much more steeply. In fact, it is almost vertical in some localities, for example the narrow Chalk ridge of the Purbeck Hills (see Landscape **I**). This difference between the northern and southern structures is due to the mid-Tertiary compressional movements discussed above.

The Dorset Downs are a classic area for studying features of Chalk scenery. The typical rolling, grass-covered tops and the steep-sided valleys, sometimes with flat bottoms, show up beautifully on the slope map in Figure 107. Many small valleys and hollows in the faces of the Chalk hills are dry, having been formed by slope failure and stream flow during the Ice Age when the subsurface was frozen (see the general introduction to this chapter for more detail).

The present drainage of this Landscape takes place to the east and south, towards the centre of the Hampshire Basin. Major rivers are the Frome, through Dorchester, and the Stour, which cuts through the Downs at Blandford Forum (**fi**).

Landscape G: The Dorset Heaths

This Landscape, lying between the Dorset Downs and the Purbeck Chalk ridge, is underlain by flat-lying bedrock of Early Tertiary age. This bedrock occurs in a shallow basin centred on Poole Harbour that also contains the large conurbation of Poole and Bournemouth (see Area 5).

Although there are layers in the Early Tertiary succession that are assigned to the London Clay, other layers below and above this are more prominent and much richer in sand. This gives rise to the widespread acid-soil heathland with a vegetation cover of heather, bracken and gorse, though much of this habitat has now been converted to farmland or conifer woodland. The hills and slopes of the area are low and poorly defined, sometimes marking sandy layers in the Early Tertiary bedrock. There are also patches of gravel and alluvial terraces forming a surface blanket, representing episodes in the much younger Quaternary development of the landscape.

Landscape H: The Weymouth Lowlands and the Isle of Portland

The Weymouth Lowlands stretch along the coast from Burton Bradstock (**h1**) to Weymouth, bounded to the north by the Chalk ridge that forms the edge of the Dorset Downs. The bedrock of the area is Jurassic in age and consists of east–west trending limestone ridges interspersed with clay vales.

The Weymouth Lowlands have been eroded downwards to reveal a very broad upward fold in the bedrock – the Weymouth Anticline – which has an east–west trending axis and gentle slopes, steepest in the north where the slope reaches 10 degrees. The oldest layers, exposed by erosion in the central part of the anticline, are of Middle Jurassic age, but a full succession of younger Jurassic strata is also visible. Many faults have been discovered in these strata by drilling and seismic work aimed at the detailed exploration of possible oil-bearing reservoirs. Most of the faults are normal faults, suggesting that they formed during a period of extension or stretching of the crust, though the gentle folding of the Weymouth Anticline implies a later period of crustal compression. Some 5 km east of Weymouth, a tighter upfold (the Poxwell Anticline) runs east to west, parallel to but inland from the coast, and contains Early and Late Cretaceous layers to both north and south. Inclinations of up to 65 degrees have been measured on the very steep north slope of this fold, contrasting with the gentle southern slope, which confirms that the overturning movement during this late compressional phase was in the same northward direction as occurred in other late movements in this area.

The Isle of Portland (**h3**) is a limestone plateau which slopes southwards, from high northern cliffs to barely 10 m above the sea. This slope and the layers visible in the northern cliffs of Portland are part of the southern limb of the

FIG 108. Looking southeastwards along Chesil Beach (Fig. 99, **h2**) to the Isle of Portland (**h3**). (Copyright Dae Sasitorn & Adrian Warren/www.lastrefuge.co.uk)

Weymouth Anticline. The Isle is famous for its bedrock, the Portland Stone, a shelly, often oolitic, limestone that has been widely used as an ornamental stone in important British building projects such as St Paul's Cathedral in London. The Portland Stone has been quarried since Roman times and the Isle is extensively scarred by old quarries and spoil heaps.

The Isle of Portland is connected to the mainland by Chesil Beach (**h2**), a remarkable coastal feature (Fig. 108). It is a coast-parallel gravel barrier some 28 km long, and for most of its length it is separated from the mainland by the tidal lagoon known as the Fleet. The pebbles are roughly pea-sized at the northwestern end of the beach at West Bay, and potato-sized at the Portland end. The larger pebbles are thought to be transported the longest distances along the beach because of the impact of the prevailing storm waves on their larger surface area. Local folklore has it that smugglers could tell exactly where along the beach they had landed just by looking at the size of the pebbles.

Chesil Beach is one of several large gravel landforms that occur along the South Coast. During the last (Ipswichian) interglacial, about 125,000 years ago, sea level was slightly higher than now, and the coastal slope was eroded by storms and landslips just as today. During the subsequent cold phases of the Ice Age, the former coastal debris would have been spread widely by river action over the areas now covered by the sea, and was then transported inland again by the rising sea during the most recent (Flandrian) sea-level rise. Chesil Beach was formed about 10,000 years ago, but is constantly being reshaped by the waves. It seems that the beach is currently moving inland over the tidal muds of the Fleet, as its outer face often reveals peats that appear to have formed in the Fleet and then been over-run by the gravel ridge migrating landwards.

Landscape I: South Purbeck

This Landscape consists of a narrow strip of coastline, never more than 7 km wide, running along the coast from Lulworth (i1) to Swanage on the Isle of Purbeck. The area is defined topographically by the dramatic, west-to-east trending stepfold (or *monocline*) in the bedrock. To the north, the stepfold is expressed at the surface by steeply dipping Chalk and older layers immediately south of the Dorset Heaths (see Landscape G). Typically, the Chalk has resisted erosion to form a narrow ridge known as the Purbeck Hills (i2), running inland from just north of Swanage and crossing the Isle of Purbeck before reaching the coast again at Lulworth. East of Lulworth (i1) and south of the Chalk, the layers at the surface span the full local succession from Early Cretaceous to Late Jurassic, though they are flat-lying by the time the south coast is reached.

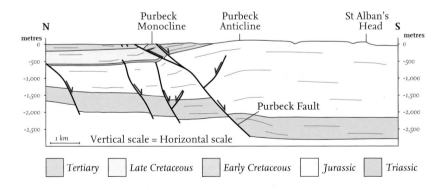

FIG 109. Cross-section running north–south through St Alban's Head (Fig. 99, i4), South Purbeck.

The Purbeck Ridge is breached by the northward-draining Corfe River, which flows into Poole Harbour. Corfe Castle and its small town have grown in this breach, which acts as the gateway to the low-lying Corfe Vale, underlain by Early Cretaceous Wealden sandstones and mudstones. To the south of this is a plateau, carved at an elevation of 120–140 m above sea level, and underlain by Late Jurassic Kimmeridge Clay and limestones and mudstones of the Portland and Purbeck groups. The Portland Stone Formation is particularly resistant to weathering, and its historic importance as a building stone is shown by the remarkable number of abandoned quarries on this plateau.

FIG 110. Looking westwards along the coast towards the Isle of Portland. Lulworth Cove (Fig. 99, i1) is in the foreground. (Copyright Dae Sasitorn & Adrian Warren/ www.lastrefuge.co.uk)

FIG 111. Durdle Door, 2 km west of Lulworth Cove (Fig. 99, **i1**). (Copyright Dae Sasitorn & Adrian Warren/www.lastrefuge.co.uk)

The structure of the Isle of Purbeck area is well illustrated by a cross-section through St Alban's Head (**i4**), as shown in Figure 109. Further west, Lulworth Cove (**i1**) is one of the most famous features of this stretch of coast, demonstrating the control of the coastal geometry by the folding of the bedrock (Fig. 110). The outer coastal wall of the Cove is formed by steeply layered, erosion-resistant Portland limestone, which has been breached by wave action during storms. The breach probably first occurred at the mouth of a former stream

FIG 112. Cliffs at Kimmeridge Bay (Fig. 99, i3) showing the typical bedrock layering, often cut by faults. (Copyright Dae Sasitorn & Adrian Warren/www.lastrefuge.co.uk)

flowing into the sea where the entrance to the Cove is now, allowing waves to erode the softer sediments behind the limestone barrier. The Cove was then excavated in relatively weak Wealden mudstone, and has now cut back far enough to expose the tougher Late Cretaceous Chalk as a steep-sided cliff at the back of the bay. The remarkably regular, circular form of the Cove seems to be a response to the diffraction (or bending) of the crests of storm waves as they enter the mouth of the Cove, fanning out and causing longshore transport of the available debris.

Just west of Lulworth Cove, Stair Hole displays a beautiful example of a small fold called the Lulworth Crumple.

About 2 km west of Lulworth Cove is Durdle Door, another famous feature of the Jurassic Coast. In this case, a steeply sloping limb of the Purbeck Stepfold (or *monocline* – Fig. 109) is exposed in the Portland Stone, where it has been eroded into a spectacular doorframe-like arch.

Just east of Lulworth Cove is a famous locality where a 'fossil forest' may be seen. It is on the coastal footpath just within the boundary of a large military firing range, so access is not permitted at certain times. Tree trunks of large conifers and ferns that flourished in the Late Jurassic were preserved here when the Jurassic sea level rose and the trunks became surrounded by mats of primitive plant material, preventing their decay.

The steep bedrock layers of Chalk and limestone that cause the spectacular scenery of Durdle Door and Lulworth Cove continue eastwards along the coast, before striking inland to form the Purbeck hills. Along the coast, they are replaced by increasingly flat-lying layers of clay and limestone. Land-slipping is common in this area, where the cliffs have permeable, resistant tops overlying soft, easily eroded Kimmeridge Clay.

Kimmeridge Bay (**i3**; Fig. 112) is much visited by scientists. This is partly because its name has been adopted for one of the worldwide subdivisions of Jurassic time, but it is also of interest because it is the original locality that gave its name to the Kimmeridge Clay, a layer that provides a high proportion of the oil wealth of the North Sea. The grey mudstones exposed in Kimmeridge Bay are rich in fine-grained organic material generally referred to as *kerogen*. If this material has been buried deeply enough, and subjected to high temperatures, for long enough, the kerogen becomes altered, releasing oil that can migrate along and through any permeable layers in the bedrock. The oil can either seep out at the surface or become trapped by folds, faults or loss of permeability to form a natural reservoir, which may then be exploited as an oil field. The contribution of the Late Jurassic Kimmeridge Clay to the economy of Britain has been enormous.

AREA 5: HAMPSHIRE AND THE ISLE OF WIGHT

This area includes the striking coastal scenery of the Isle of Wight, as well as the seaside cities of Bournemouth and Portsmouth. Southampton sits in the centre of the area within the low-lying Hampshire Basin, while to the north Salisbury and Winchester lie within Chalk hills (Figs 113 and 114).

The bedrock succession of this Area records a variety of episodes starting in the Late Jurassic, through the Cretaceous and into the early Tertiary, representing 150 million years of Earth history. Although the total thickness of the bedrock layers shown in Figure 115 is around 2 km, this figure is misleading because it does not represent subsidence of the Earth's surface by this amount at any one place. In fact, some of the layers (e.g. the Early Cretaceous Wealden and the Tertiary) accumulated in certain parts of the Area while crustal movements uplifted other parts, causing them to be eroded and to supply – rather than receive – sediment. A general review of the changing environments of sedimentation for the whole Region is included in the general introduction to this chapter.

FIG 113. Location map for Area 5.

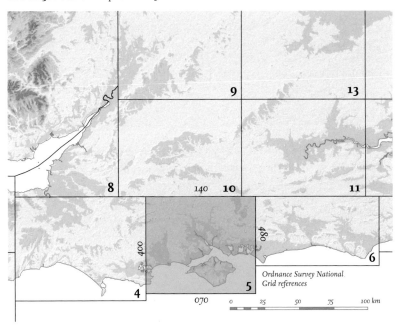

Ordnance Survey National
Grid references

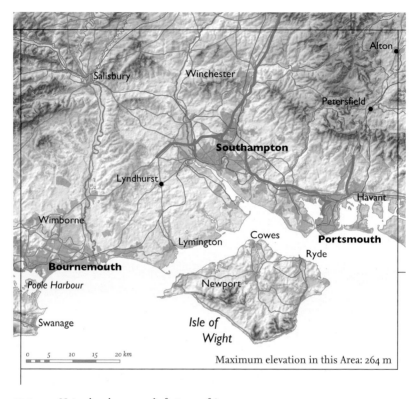

Maximum elevation in this Area: 264 m

FIG 114. Natural and man-made features of Area 5.

The pattern of the Late Cretaceous Chalk on the geological map (Fig. 116) provides a useful marker in this Area, as it does for most of Southern England. It records well the broad movement pattern that developed after the main bedrock succession had formed, and explains the distribution of hills and downs on the one hand, and basins on the other. The large northern areas of Chalk that form Salisbury Plain, the Hampshire Downs and the South Downs are replaced southwards by the Early Tertiary sediments that fill the Hampshire Basin. South of these sediments, the Chalk reappears at the surface in the Portsdown Ridge, and in the northward-facing stepfold (monocline) that extends across the Isle of Wight and South Purbeck (Figs 116 and 117).

As Figure 116 shows, I have divided this Area into seven Landscapes (**A** to **G**), which are treated separately below.

Ages (millions of years)   **Rock types and names**

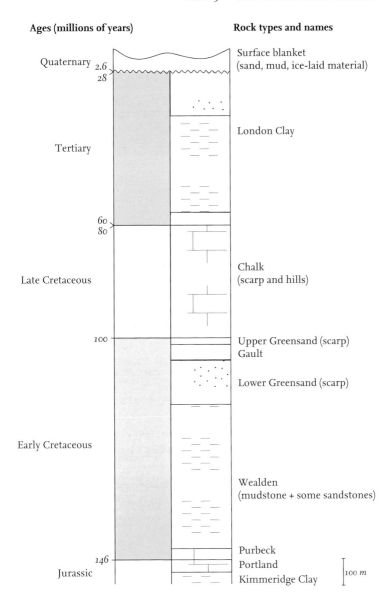

Quaternary 2.6
28

Surface blanket
(sand, mud, ice-laid material)

Tertiary

London Clay

60
80

Late Cretaceous

Chalk
(scarp and hills)

100

Upper Greensand (scarp)
Gault

Lower Greensand (scarp)

Early Cretaceous

Wealden
(mudstone + some sandstones)

146

Purbeck
Portland
Kimmeridge Clay

Jurassic

100 m

FIG 115. Generalised bedrock succession for Area 5.

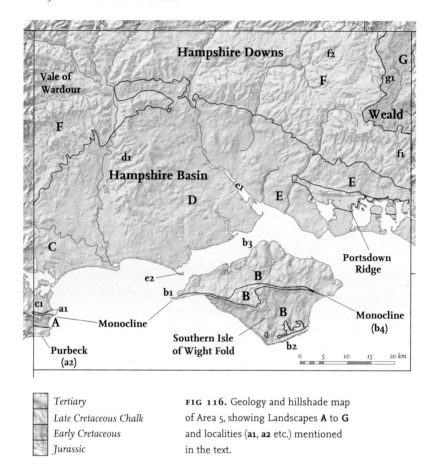

Tertiary
Late Cretaceous Chalk
Early Cretaceous
Jurassic

FIG 116. Geology and hillshade map of Area 5, showing Landscapes **A** to **G** and localities (**a1**, **a2** etc.) mentioned in the text.

Landscape A: The Isle of Purbeck

A description of the westward continuation of this Landscape is given in Area 4. Here it is enough to note that, as in Area 4, the Isle of Purbeck is defined by two distinctive ridges. The northernmost of these is the Chalk ridge north of Swanage, which has been formed by the erosion of the stepfold that also runs through the Isle of Wight (Fig. 117). Figure 118 shows the cliffs around Old Harry (**a1**), where the near-horizontal Chalk has been eroded by storm waves to create numerous small bays. The remarkable feature of this erosion is the way that the waves swing round to attack both sides of the main headland, resulting in well-defined, almost parallel-sided 'bites' in the cliff line. The southernmost distinctive ridge is formed by the Late Jurassic/Early Cretaceous Portland and

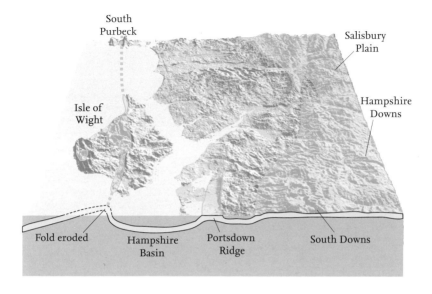

Late Cretaceous Chalk

FIG 117. Oblique block view of the crustal geology, starting 10 km west of the eastern edge of Area 5 and looking westwards.

Purbeck limestones, which form a high plateau (a2) south of Swanage. Jurassic Kimmeridge Clay forms the base of the cliffs along the south coast of Purbeck, and its preferential erosion by storms has undermined the cliffs in many places, causing frequent land-slipping (Fig. 119). Swanage itself lies in the low ground of the Corfe Valley, on soft Wealden mudrock.

The cross-section in Area 4 (Fig. 109), a few kilometres west of the boundary with Area 5, is relevant to this area, since the same bedrock pattern continues eastwards through this Landscape. The Triassic, Jurassic and Early Cretaceous layers in this section have been cut by a number of normal faults, indicating stretching movement of the crust in a north–south direction, linked to subsidence and increasing amounts of sediment accumulation to the south. This contrasts with the folding and faulting that is visible in the Purbeck Stepfold or Monocline, with reverse faulting that indicates convergence of the crust and increased sedimentation to the north in mid-Tertiary times. The same patterns, involving two distinct phases of movement, are also visible where the stepfold crosses the Isle of Wight.

FIG 118. Looking southwestwards across the eastern Isle of Purbeck. Note the embayments and sea stacks cut into the Chalk, including Old Harry and Old Harry's wife (Fig. 116, **a1**). (Copyright reserved Cambridge University Collection of Air Photographs)

FIG 119. Looking eastwards over Dancing Ledge, South Purbeck. (Copyright Dae Sasitorn & Adrian Warren/ www.lastrefuge.co.uk)

Landscape B: The Isle of Wight

The variety of landscapes and relative ease of access have added greatly to the popularity of the Isle of Wight. The mild climate and long hours of summer sunshine have brought large numbers of tourists to the island since Victorian times.

The landscapes here range from the lush pastures and creeks of the north, particularly in the area west of Cowes (**b3**), across the windswept downs and cliffs of the central belt, to the open fields and wooded 'chines' (narrow, deep ravines) of the south. All these features have formed during the long history of erosion of the underlying bedrock geology. The most dramatic geological structure is the spectacular, northward-facing stepfold in the Chalk known as the Isle of Wight Monocline, running east–west through the centre of the island (Fig. 117). The steep layers of the Chalk form the Needles (**b1**) at the western end of the island and extend eastwards across the island as a high ridge, although the steeply-dipping layers temporarily flatten out near Newport, where another fold crosses the stepfold. Culver Cliff (**b4**) marks the eastern end of the Chalk ridge.

FIG 120. The Needles (Fig. 116, **b1**) and Alum Bay, western Isle of Wight. (Copyright reserved Cambridge University Collection of Air Photographs)

North of the central belt and its stepfold, the Isle of Wight is underlain by soft-weathering early Tertiary materials that have been dissected by local stream and river erosion. The multicoloured cliffs of Alum Bay (Fig. 120) are formed of steeply tilted (locally vertical) early Tertiary sediments that have been folded along with the Chalk. The colours of the sandstones and mudstones in the cliffs are exceptionally bright and varied, and collections of multicoloured sand samples in transparent tubes are carried home from Alum Bay by holidaying families every year. White sands are made of pure quartz, whose grains lack the thin coating of iron oxide that colours the Bay's red to yellow sands. Green sands have been coloured by the iron-bearing mineral *glauconite*, preserved when reducing conditions are generated by organic material in the sediment. Dark layers of *lignite* (a coal-like material) were formed by the burial of ancient vegetation. These striking bands of colour were formed during deposition, when the layers were in their original near-horizontal orientation, before they were tilted to near-vertical by folding and faulting as the stepfold was created.

South of the Isle of Wight central belt, the bedrock consists of Early Cretaceous Wealden strata, which form the core of the southern Isle of Wight Anticline or upfold. The elevated area near the south coast is a remnant of Chalk grassland lying above the Wealden. The southern face of the coast (**b2**), between St Catherine's Point and Dunnose, has cliffs that tower above terraces stepping down to the shore. This coastal strip is one of the largest areas of land-slipping in western Europe, because overlying materials have slipped down the coastal slopes created by storm erosion, lubricated by underlying muddy layers after prolonged periods of rain.

Landscape C: The Dorset Heaths

This Landscape passes westwards into Landscape **G** of Area 4. In Area 5, it is covered largely by Poole Harbour and the City of Bournemouth, so its typical heath landscape is only developed over rather small areas, where the Early Tertiary sandstones produce acid-soil vegetation. Although the landscape here is very subdued, there are small hilly features created by erosion of the varying materials in the bedrock, or by unsteady erosion of the rivers Stour, Avon and their tributaries. In fact, the southern part of this Landscape is covered with many levels of unconsolidated surface materials, consisting mainly of gravels brought down by ancestral versions of the rivers draining the Chalk terrain to the north.

Just on the western edge of Area 5, below this young spread of Early Tertiary and Quaternary sediment, is the Wytch Farm oil field (**c1**), the largest oil field in Europe that has been drilled from land. The field was developed by BP and taps porous New Red Sandstones of Triassic age which have been tilted and faulted into a valuable reservoir pattern. The oil itself appears to have come from Jurassic source sediments.

Landscape D: The New Forest

The New Forest became the newest National Park in Britain when an official Park Authority was designated in April 2005. It occupies the distinctive part of the Hampshire Basin between the Hampshire Avon to the west and Southampton Water and the River Test to the east.

The New Forest has had special status for over 1,000 years, initially as a royal hunting ground. The grazing and hunting of deer were particularly favoured by the balance of open and mixed woodland cover, resulting from the generally acid soils that have formed on the Tertiary bedrock and the younger cover of Quaternary sediments, particularly gravels. To maintain the mix of open ground and woodland cover, grazing by ponies, donkeys, cattle and pigs has been actively encouraged for centuries by laws defining the rights of local Commoners. At the same time, large-scale settlement has been discouraged.

Detailed mapping of the Early Tertiary bedrock and the surface blanket of the area has shown that the bedrock here has only loosely controlled the gently hilly topography. One of the most obvious patterns is visible in the area east of Fordingbridge (**d1**), where distinct ridges and valleys have been carved into the Early Tertiary strata, draining southwestwards into the Hampshire River Avon. The ridges are capped by what were, at one stage, defined as the 'Plateau Gravels', though these are now regarded simply as the earliest of a very large number of river terraces that are preserved across much of the New Forest. The gravels are very largely composed of flints, originally derived by erosion of the Chalk, although material derived from *Sarsen Stones* (hard sandstones of Tertiary age) is also present. In the absence of fossil evidence it is very difficult to be sure whether these gravels represent stages in the history of the rivers draining this area, or evidence for episodes of deposition from high-stands of sea level.

Landscape E: The South Hampshire Lowlands and the western South Coast Plain

The South Hampshire Lowlands form the ground between the South Downs to the north and Southampton Water and the Gosport–Portsmouth coast to the south. The bedrock is predominantly Tertiary mudrock and sandstone, except just north of Portsmouth where the Portsdown Ridge has formed by erosion of the Tertiary material, revealing an east–west trending upfold of Late Cretaceous Chalk (Fig. 116). This ridge rises some 130 m above sea level and is clearly visible

FIG 121. Looking northwards across Portsmouth Harbour, with Gosport to the left and the Hampshire Downs in the distance. (Copyright Dae Sasitorn & Adrian Warren/ www.lastrefuge.co.uk)

north of the M27 motorway, just north of Portsmouth. Since Napoleonic times, the Portsdown Ridge has repeatedly been used as a site for fortifications (for example, Palmerston's Follies) to oversee the important harbour and settlement centres of Portsmouth to the south.

The coastal stretch south of the Portsdown Ridge marks the western end of the South Coast Plain. The bedrock consists entirely of gently folded Early Tertiary mudrocks and sandstones, but there is a widespread cover blanket of younger river-terrace sediment, including much fine-grained material often referred to as *brickearth*. The highly indented coastline around Portsmouth Harbour (Fig. 121) was formed at the end of the last cold phase of the Ice Age,

FIG 122. Hurst Castle Spit (Fig. 116, **e2**). (Copyright Dae Sasitorn & Adrian Warren/www.lastrefuge.co.uk)

as the rising water flooded the low-lying land and created broad expanses of sheltered water, edged by a mix of mudflats, marshes, wetland scrub, low-lying fields and the occasional creek.

The sea-level rise also created drowned valleys such as Southampton Water (**e1**). Today this body of sea water receives water from the rivers Test, Itchen and Hamble, but during the last cold spell of the Ice Age, Southampton Water was the trunk river valley into which the present rivers flowed as tributaries. When it filled with the rising sea water it became the estuary on which Southampton grew to become one of Britain's premier ports for international shipping.

The gravel beds of southward-draining rivers provided much of the material that now forms the large number of gravel spits, bars and ridges that are such a feature of this area (e.g. Calshot Spit, Hurst Castle Spit (**e2**) and Poole Harbour (**c1**)). These coastal features have been shaped by storm waves and the strong tidal flows that are active in these coastal waters.

Hurst Castle Spit (Fig. 122) extends into the western Solent towards the Isle of Wight, leaving a channel less than 1.5 km wide. This gives the spit great strategic importance, and a castle was first built on it by Henry VIII in 1544. The spit was last manned for defence during the World War II.

Landscape F: The southern Salisbury Plain, Hampshire Downs and western South Downs

In the northern half of Area 5, the Hampshire Downs form part of the broad belt of Chalk linking Salisbury Plain in the west with the South Downs in the east. To the south, the Chalk dips gently under the Early Tertiary sandstones and mudstones of the Hampshire Basin.

The scenery of the Hampshire Downs has the open and exposed character typical of most regions with Chalk bedrock, with rolling downland scarps, hill tops and valley walls. Chalk grassland covers steep scarps and is a particular feature of the South Downs. Most of the smaller valleys are dry, except in winter, and have a distinctive branching pattern.

The uniformity of much of the Chalk bedrock is one of its most distinctive features, although the presence of a ~5 m thick hard band (the Stockbridge Rock Member) about two-thirds of the way up the Chalk succession has influenced the local shape of many of the ridges and slopes in this area.

In the area around Salisbury, the Chalk bedrock is strongly dissected by the upper valley of the Avon and its various tributaries. The scenery of wide valley floors, with floodplains and river terraces between steep valley-side slopes, is very typical of the area and provides a fine setting for Salisbury Cathedral. This section of the Chalk is quite well populated, in contrast to the high plains further north in Area 10.

About 10 km west of Salisbury, erosion of the fault and fold structure of the Vale of Wardour has brought Early Cretaceous Gault and Upper Greensand bedrock to the surface (see Area 4 for more detail). Unlike Area 4, where it is more fully developed, the Vale of Wardour is not well defined in Area 5.

The Test and Itchen river valleys (Fig. 123) have cut particularly clearly across this typical downland scenery, providing the trunk drainage of the area southwards towards Southampton Water. Some 3 km south of Winchester, the large and controversial excavation made for the M3 motorway through Twyford Down demonstrates very clearly the way the erosion of the Itchen valley has cut into the Chalk. Water meadows are a traditional feature of many of the larger valley floors, being flooded early in the season to keep off frosts and provide fresh vegetation for stock. The Watercress Line, a steam railway running from Alresford to Alton, takes its name from the crop grown in these water meadows.

The northeastern edge of the Hampshire Downs is an undulating plateau covered by Clay-with-flints, a surface blanket of material that appears to have formed by weathering of the Chalk under very variable climates, leaving a residue of flints and clay. This surface blanket has formed on different layers within the upper part of the Late Cretaceous Chalk, but has distinct margins with slopes facing eastwards over the Weald uplift in Landscape **G** (**g1**) and westwards over the upstream branches of the River Itchen (**f2**). These Clay-with-flints deposits often support small patches of woodland, unlike the thin, dry Chalk soils elsewhere that are covered by grassland and pastureland.

The high ridge of the South Downs (**f1**) rises out of the Hampshire Downs south of Winchester, gaining definition as it runs east towards Sussex. In Area 5, the South Downs occupy only a thin sliver of country about 10 km wide, extending from the Itchen valley near Winchester in the west to a few kilometres east of the A3 trunk-road between Havant and Petersfield. Along the whole of this stretch, a remarkable plan-view pattern of arrowhead-like Vs can be seen on the south side of the ridge pointing northwards (see Fig. 123, for example). Both this pattern and the narrowness of the Chalk belt are the direct result of the regional tilting of the Chalk layers, which steadily slope southwards at between 2 and 6 degrees.

Landscape G: The western outcrop area of the Wealden Greensand

In the northeastern corner of Area 5, the Chalk is replaced by older (Early Cretaceous) bedrock that has been brought to the surface by erosion of numerous gentle, open folds. Together they produce the Weald uplift, a regional-scale structure that dominates the bedrock geology of southeastern England south of the Thames, described more fully in Area 6.

The youngest of the Early Cretaceous layers is the Upper Greensand. This 5 m thick sandstone and siltstone, often richly cemented with iron, forms a clear series of ridges round the western end of the Weald uplift, particularly near Selborne (**g1**). The Upper Greensand ridges change sharply in direction around the town of Petersfield, from a broadly southwesterly direction to an easterly direction, running approximately parallel to the escarpment of the South Downs.

Below the Upper Greensand is the mudstone-rich Gault and, below that, the alternating sandstones and mudstones that make up the thick Lower Greensand. In Area 5, the Gault lies east of the Upper Greensand, and has generally been eroded into low-lying, featureless country, whereas the Lower Greensand sandstones further east have resisted erosion. To the northeast of Petersfield the topography reflects the way that river erosion has picked out fault displacements of these Lower Greensand layers.

Review of the landscape history

Most of the inland slopes and valleys have been created during the evolution of the river and stream systems that occupy the valley bottoms. These systems have not only drained the landscapes, but they have also generated sediment as they have eroded and carried it away, causing an overall lowering of the ground surface.

FIG 123. Main river pathways and coastal flooding zone for Area 5.

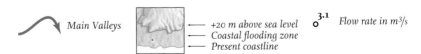

The present-day drainage provides a template for this key aspect of the landscape evolution, though the exact locations of the rivers will have changed considerably over time. We can simplify the pattern by selecting the main valleys and labelling them as the 'main river pathways', as in Figure 123. This general pattern is likely to be over 20 million years old.

The coastline of this area has taken up its familiar form and position only in the last few thousand years. During the previous 12,000 years, the coastline has advanced inland great distances because of a rise in sea level of about 120 m, due to the melting of the ice sheets formed during the last cold episode of the Ice Age.

At the time of the Devensian Glacial, about 20,000 years ago, a continuous belt of hilly ground underlain by Chalk extended across most of the southern part of Area 5 (now largely covered by the sea), from an area south and east of the present Isle of Wight to the present Isle of Purbeck. The headland of Culver Cliff at the eastern end of the present-day Isle of Wight marks the stump of this Chalk belt left by wave erosion today. West of the present Isle, the wave erosion eventually broke through what must have been a continuous line of Chalk hills (Fig. 124), exposing the softer Tertiary rocks to the north to intense wave erosion and creating the broad concave coastline around Bournemouth. All that remains of the Chalk ridge today are the headlands of Ballard Point with Old Harry on the Isle of Purbeck, and the Chalk Downs stretching from the Needles to Culver Cliff on the Isle of Wight.

We can visualise further the effect of this 120 m sea-level change by considering the present Isle of Wight and its surroundings. At the time of low sea level 20,000 years ago, the area now occupied by the Isle of Wight was simply an area of higher ground surrounded on all sides by lower land. To the north, a large Solent River flowed eastwards along a valley where the Solent seaway is today (Fig. 124). The river transported water and sediment from much of Dorset and all the main rivers of Hampshire, as well as from the south, where the higher ground of the present Isle of Wight was continuous with Chalk hills now covered by the waters of the English Channel, as described above. The rivers of Southern England and northern France drained into this plain, eventually flowing into the Atlantic west of Cornwall (Fig. 21). This involved a change in direction from eastwards to westwards for the waters of the Solent river as it negotiated the topography and bedrock contrasts generated by the fold and fault movements of the Purbeck–Isle of Wight stepfold.

Some 20,000 years ago the view shown in Figure 125 would have looked across the open valley of the Solent river, with no sea visible. The Flandrian sea-level rise has flooded a large valley, creating the present Solent and making the

FIG 124. The ancient Solent River drainage before the Flandrian sea-level rise.

distant Chalk hills into the Isle of Wight. In the foreground, the rising sea has also flooded the mouth of the Lymington tributary of the former Solent river, and storms and tides have mobilised sediment to produce the pattern of river-mouth islands.

Flint tools and ancient trees dating from before the Flandrian rise in sea level have been found towards the middle of the Solent, providing evidence to support the ideas described above. However, worldwide sea level largely stopped rising about 6,000 years ago, yet much younger artefacts have also been found submerged below the present sea. For example, Saxon sheep pens, perhaps 1,000 years old, have been found offshore between the Isle of Wight and the English mainland. The main Flandrian global sea-level rise due to ice-sheet melting cannot account for this, because most of it was over long before Saxon times. This implies that some younger downward movement of the bedrock,

FIG 125. Lymington river, looking southeastwards towards the Isle of Wight.
(Copyright Dae Sasitorn & Adrian Warren/www.lastrefuge.co.uk)

due to changes within the Earth, must have taken place very recently in some
local areas.

Some scientists now believe that during the last few thousand years sea level
was briefly higher than it is today, though this is far from certain, and estimates
of sea level during earlier interglacials are even less clear. Figure 123 attempts to
show the effects of a 20 m rise in sea level, ignoring any of the effects of local
bedrock rising or sinking that may have taken place. This is relevant to today's
worries over rising sea level, although the extent of the contribution made by our
own species to the undoubted present warming is not clear.

AREA 6: SUSSEX

A north–south traverse through the centre of this Area runs from Crawley through Haywards Heath to the coast at Brighton. The western edge of the Area adjoins Area 5, and runs from Haslemere via Midhurst to Chichester and Selsey Bill on the coast. The eastern edge adjoins Area 7, and runs from Royal Tunbridge Wells via Hailsham to Beachy Head and Eastbourne on the coast (Figs 126 and 127).

Area 6 extends across the central and southern part of the Weald of southeastern England, an area neatly defined by the presence of the Early Cretaceous bedrock known as the Wealden (Fig. 128). The name *Weald* derives from Old English, and refers to the woodland cover that is still an obvious feature of this area, particularly when looking across from the escarpments of younger Chalk or Greensand that form its border to the north, west and south. This rim acts as the frame of the broad and gentle *Weald uplift* in the bedrock, formed by a phase of compression and upward movement in the crust about 30 million years ago. The neat map pattern of concentric layers of bedrock

FIG 126. Location map for Area 6.

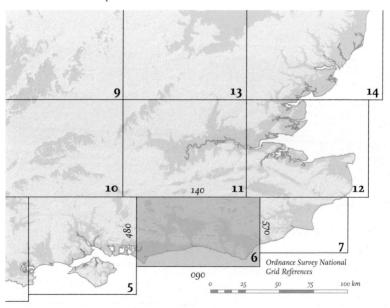

(Fig. 129) and scenery is the direct result of the way the Wealden structure has been bevelled downwards as river and stream erosion has lowered the ground surface over those last few tens of millions of years. Figure 129 also shows that some of the mapped boundaries between the main layers are locally quite jagged; a result of the presence of much smaller local faults and folds, often trending, very approximately, east–west. These small features have probably formed as a result of the movement of larger faults at greater depth.

Six distinctive Landscapes can be identified in Area 6, labelled **A** to **F** in Figure 129. These are discussed in turn below.

Landscape A: The High Weald

This Landscape forms the northeastern corner of the Area. It is framed to the south, west and north by Landscape **B**, the Low Weald. The scenery of the High Weald is typically one of small wooded hills and valleys distributed in a weakly radial pattern, so that some of the High Weald drainage is to the west and the north, draining via the Medway into the Thames estuary. The rest of the drainage is southerly, via the headwaters of the Adur, Ouse and Cuckmere to the south coast, along valleys carved through the South Downs (Fig. 136).

The hills of the High Weald range in elevation between about 50 m and 250 m, whereas the Low Weald is generally much lower and flatter. Erosion in the High Weald to the west of Mountfield has exposed bedrock of latest Jurassic age

FIG 127. Natural and man-made features of Area 6.

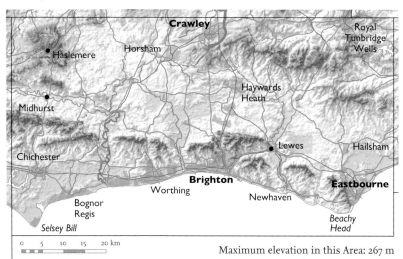

Maximum elevation in this Area: 267 m

Ages (millions of years)   **Rock types & names**

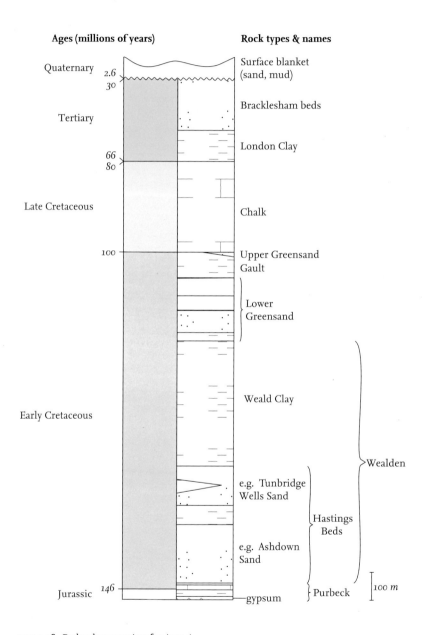

FIG 128. Bedrock succession for Area 6.

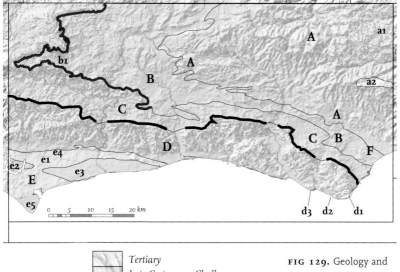

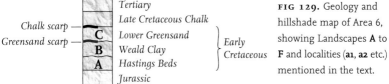

Chalk scarp —	Tertiary
Greensand scarp —	Late Cretaceous Chalk
	Lower Greensand
	Weald Clay
	Hastings Beds
	Jurassic

Early Cretaceous

FIG 129. Geology and hillshade map of Area 6, showing Landscapes **A** to **F** and localities (**a1**, **a2** etc.) mentioned in the text.

identified as the lower part of the Purbeck beds (**a2**). In addition to mudstones and thin limestones, these Purbeck deposits contain gypsum (calcium sulphate) which has been mined commercially for plasterboard. All the rest of the bedrock at the surface of the High Weald is Early Cretaceous in age and assigned to the Hastings Beds that make up the greatest thickness and lower part of the Wealden Series (Fig. 128).

In Early Cretaceous times the material that now forms the Wealden Series was deposited in a low-lying, subsiding basin that extended southwards from a flat upland area where London is now. This Wealden Basin was occupied by lakes and extensive mud flats that were invaded from the north by rivers flowing and shifting across plains with channels and sandbars. The sediments deposited in these mud- and sand-flats became mudstones and sandstones as they were buried by more sediment as the area continued to subside. The sandstone sheets have now been eroded to form slopes, and locally even form distinctive areas of cliffs that provide challenges for rock climbers, particularly in the Tunbridge Wells area.

In mid-Tertiary times, the surface of the Wealden area began to move upwards, and erosion by rivers and streams began to cut downwards into the Wealden bedrock, eventually creating the topography of hills and valleys that we see today (Fig. 130). The crude radial pattern of this drainage (described above) reflects the erosion of the rising, dome-like Weald uplift. In addition, local geological mapping has shown that many of the sandstone sheets have been cut by faults that often trend approximately east–west, particularly in the lower parts of the Hastings Beds. These faults have often provided bedrock contrasts that have influenced the local directions of the young valley systems.

The High Weald was the focus of a remarkable iron industry from the fifteenth to the seventeenth centuries. The source of the iron was siderite, an iron carbonate mineral that grew as a precipitate in the wet muds of the Wealden lakes. The small valley networks of the High Weald were ideal for the construction of dams and ponds (known as 'hammerponds'), and these in turn

FIG 130. Typical High Weald landscape, looking eastwards over Bewl Lake (Fig. 129, **a1**). Copyright Dae Sasitorn & Adrian Warren/www.lastrefuge.co.uk)

powered bellows for the smelting of the iron and forge hammers for working it. The forges were fuelled using charcoal from valley and slope woodlands, and the industry eventually died because the northern British coalfields became recognised as a more efficient source of heat and power.

Landscape B: The Low Weald
In Area 6, the Low Weald extends in a belt to the south and west of the High Weald, from Haslemere in the west, past Horsham and Haywards Heath, and on towards the sea between Eastbourne and Hailsham, where it passes into the Pevensey Levels (Landscape F).

This rather flat and featureless Landscape owes its lack of topography to the uniformity of its bedrock, which is the upper division of the Wealden beds known as the Weald Clay (Fig. 128). There is an obvious contrast in elevation and the presence of slopes between this Weald Clay landscape and the higher and more hilly topography seen in Landscapes A and C. In a few locations, the Weald Clay does contain thin sandstones and freshwater limestones which create some topography, but they are much less common here than in the Greensand below and the Hastings Beds above.

The Vale of Fernhurst (b1) at the western edge of Area 6 has a floor of Weald Clay sandwiched between scarps cut in the Lower Greensand. In some places, these scarps are due to the presence of an important, erosion-resistant sandstone (the Hythe Beds) in the lower part of the Lower Greensand. In other places, distinct slopes seem to have been carved in the Wealden below the actual Lower Greensand boundary.

Landscape C: The Wealden Greensand
Much of the sediment that accumulated in Area 6 during the later part of the Early Cretaceous has been assigned to the Lower Greensand. This unit consists of alternations of mudstones and sandstones, ranging up to a maximum total thickness of about 400 m. The sediments seem to have formed in a shallow sea, and shelly fossils found in them have allowed a fairly precise age for the rocks to be worked out. The deposits vary from place to place, depending on their position in the succession, and this reflects the changing patterns of the Early Cretaceous shallow marine environment and the variable way that sandy material was being supplied to the sea floor by rivers.

In the western third of this Landscape, the lowest thick sandstone layer of the Lower Greensand (the Hythe Beds) has resisted stream and river erosion to produce an escarpment that is particularly clear between Midhurst and Haslemere. Here the Vale of Fernhurst (b1) has been eroded down into the Low

Weald by what is now a small stream flowing along the line of a gentle west-to-east trending upfold. The small stream runs parallel to the much larger River Rother, which flows about 10 km further to the south, under the shadow of the South Downs Chalk escarpment (Figs 129 and 136). Valley-slope processes in the Vale of Fernhurst have resulted in escarpments to the north and south that are steep enough to have collapsed by land-slipping.

Further east in this Landscape, the bedrock has not produced any clear slope features in the Wealden Greensand belt.

Landscape D: The South Downs

The South Downs provide a classic example of a linear range of hills that have been formed by the erosion of a bedrock succession containing a sloping, more resistant, layer, in this case the Chalk. In Area 6, the slope is typically southwards at only a few degrees, although gentle and open folds with higher slopes are present locally.

The most famous scenery of this Landscape occurs where the sea has cut the spectacular coastal cliffs between Eastbourne, Beachy Head (**d1**), the Seven Sisters (**d2**) and Seaford Head (**d3**). The Beachy Head photograph (Fig. 131) shows how a recent rock fall produced a lobe of debris extending outwards towards the lighthouse. Further to the west, the Seven Sisters provide a beautiful example of the way that receding coastal cliffs can reveal a perfect cross-section through a pre-existing landscape of parallel ridges and valleys (Fig. 132). Beyond is the valley of the Cuckmere, where an artificial channel has been used to bypass the highly meandering lower stretch of the river (Fig. 133). The object of this was to improve drainage to make the floodplain less liable to flooding.

The special properties of the Chalk give its scenery the classic features seen in most other Chalk bedrock areas in Southern England. Chalk is a remarkably homogeneous and fine-grained sediment, generally giving rise to hills that are smoothly rounded and separated by distinct valleys. However, the lack of clear bedding or layering also means that it has responded to the inevitable stresses within the Earth's crust by fracturing, where many other rock types would have responded by slipping along layers. This fracturing makes much of the Chalk permeable to rainwater, so most Chalk valleys now are dry for much – if not all – of the year. Chalk valleys, therefore, were probably excavated mainly during the cold episodes of the Ice Age, when frozen ground conditions sealed the bedrock and made it impermeable, and surface erosion could remove material in the short summers.

The northward-facing escarpment is the most striking feature of the scenery of the South Downs, and corresponds directly to the position of the base of the Chalk layer. The escarpment shows up very clearly, for example, in Figure 127,

FIG 131. Beachy Head (Fig. 129, **d1**) seen from the west. (Copyright Sheila Smart)

FIG 132. The Seven Sisters (Fig. 129, **d2**) from above, showing the parallel valleys intercepted by the cliff line. (Copyright Dae Sasitorn & Adrian Warren/ www.lastrefuge.co.uk)

FIG 133. Looking northwestwards over the western Seven Sisters and the Cuckmere valley. (Copyright Aerofilms)

reflecting the contrast in erosional resistance of the Chalk compared with that of the underlying Early Cretaceous Gault or Upper Greensand. Looking at the form of the line marking the base of the Chalk in Figure 129, a number of deflections mark distinct departures from a simple straight line. These are due to local folds that have deformed the Chalk layer. Another feature of the escarpment is that it consists of large numbers of *coombes* or hollows, usually less than 1 km across, which appear to have formed by local slope collapse of the Chalk under Ice Age conditions of thawing and freezing. Other evidence of the effects of this slope collapse is the jumbled deposits of Chalk mud and fragments (known as *head*) resulting from flows of debris into the floors of many of the valleys.

Many scientists have considered the way that the river and stream drainage pattern of the Weald may have developed. A focus of this interest has been the way that a rather regular series of large valleys cuts right through the South Downs, carrying water southwards from Landscapes **A**, **B** and **C** (Fig. 136). From west to east, the Arun, Adur, Ouse and Cuckmere pass through clear valleys sometimes called water gaps, and it has been concluded that they are the descendants of rivers that originated early in the history of the Weald uplift as the bedrock layers became tilted. On the high ridge of the South Downs, between these cross-cutting *water gaps*, a similar number of *wind gaps* or low points have been identified. It has been suggested that they may represent early valleys that were abandoned by their rivers as the drainage pattern evolved and tributaries cut back to deflect or capture other streams.

Landscape E: The South Coastal Plain

This remarkable coastal-plain Landscape stretches all the way from Southampton Water and Portsmouth in the west (see Area 5) eastwards, via Selsey Bill (Fig. 134), as far as Brighton (Fig. 135). It provides clear evidence of the way that coastal processes, coupled with sea-level changes, have created a zone where bedrock structures have been planed down by storm-wave action and covered by a thin veneer of gravel and wind-blown *brickearth* (a fine-grained sand).

The bedrock structure here involves the folding of the Chalk and Early Tertiary sediments (the London Clay and Bracklesham Beds; Fig. 128) into the distinctive *Chichester downfold* (**e1**), the *Portsdown upfold* (**e2**) and the *Littlehampton upfold* (**e3**).

Boxgrove (**e4**), about 4 km northeast of central Chichester, has attracted a lot of interest because of the remarkable information it has provided on the conditions at the northern edge of the coastal plain here during the middle Pleistocene. A number of gravel pits have revealed an ancient cliff line cut into the Chalk forming the toe of the South Downs. Marine sediments rest on a

FIG 134. Selsey Bill (Fig. 129, e5), looking northwestward. (Copyright Dae Sasitorn & Adrian Warren/www.lastrefuge.co.uk)

wave-cut platform in the Chalk bedrock and are covered by layers formed by periodic slumping of Chalk debris that alternate with lagoonal sediments, soils and freshwater deposits. The special interest of this situation is that fossil bones of early humans have been found here, along with stone artefacts and the remains of rhinoceros, horse and red deer that appear to have been butchered by the humans. These people appear to have been an archaic form of *Homo sapiens*, referred to by some as Heidelberg man, rather than Neanderthal. The deposits probably date from episodes before the Anglian cold episode, perhaps 500,000 years ago.

FIG 135. Hove and Brighton, looking eastwards. (Copyright Dae Sasitorn & Adrian Warren/www.lastrefuge.co.uk)

Landscape F: The Pevensey Levels

The Pevensey Levels, between Eastbourne and Hailsham, are a distinctive low-lying Landscape formed by recent coastal processes of erosion and deposition. The Levels consist largely of gravels deposited by storms on beaches fringing an embayment that has existed periodically just north of the South Downs (Landscape **D**) during times of high sea level. Salt-marsh and river deposits have also been added to this gravel material in some areas.

Review of the landscape history

The present-day scenery of this Area started to develop about 30 million years ago, when the Weald uplift began to form in response to stresses generated within the Earth's crust. Although in country-wide terms this is a large structure (approximately 150 km by 80 km), it is simply one part of a much larger pattern of gently tilted layers that resulted from continental movements during mid-Tertiary times. More locally, 1 km scale folds and faults formed as part of the same movement episode, and are clearly apparent in the pattern of mapped geological boundaries. Many of these local effects were due to the presence of earlier faults in the bedrock that moved again during the later episode, often in the opposite direction.

As soon as the Weald uplift produced high ground, patterns of local river and stream drainage started to develop, particularly by cutting valleys back from the coastlines into the areas of newly formed high ground to produce a generally radial drainage pattern. The variable resistance of the bedrock to erosion has strongly influenced the landscape, creating some of the most spectacular scenic features. The other variable in this valley erosion was the climate, which influenced the amount of rainfall and the occurrence of the floods that do much of the work in eroding and removing material from the landscape. Valley slopes are also critically affected by climate changes, which determine vegetational cover and, during cold episodes of the Ice Age, the permeability and stability of the bedrock. It seems likely that the dry valleys visible today on the South Downs formed during cold phases when the ground was frozen.

Sea-level change, particularly in response to vigorous changes of climate during the Ice Age, is the other major factor that has influenced the scenery. It is now understood that, about 20,000 years ago, sea level was some 120 m lower than at present. Since then it has invaded the land, rising to within 10 m of its present level approximately 6,000 years ago, although minor fluctuations more recently have been important in local coastal development, both natural and man-made. Over the previous 2.6 million years of Pleistocene time, sea-level changes between about 100 m below and 10 m above present sea level have occurred many times, at approximately regular intervals (see discussion of this under Area 7).

Figure 136 shows the present coastline of Area 6, and the present land up to an elevation of 20 m above sea level as the 'coastal flooding zone'. Sea level may not have reached as high as this 20 m level, but river and stream systems of the past would certainly have been influenced by invading seas, causing ponding-up of their flow to about this level at some earlier times. The whole of the South Coastal Plain (Landscape **E**) and the Pevensey Levels (Landscape **F**) are clearly within this coastal flood zone, and it is also interesting to note how the 'water gaps' of the rivers Arun, Adur, Ouse and Cuckmere allow the flooding zone to extend inland, to invade Landscapes **B** and **C** and even parts of Landscape **A**. One conclusion is that anywhere within this zone will have been influenced by coastal advance and retreat processes over the past few million years of the Ice Age. Another conclusion is that anywhere within this zone is liable to be influenced by future rise of sea level.

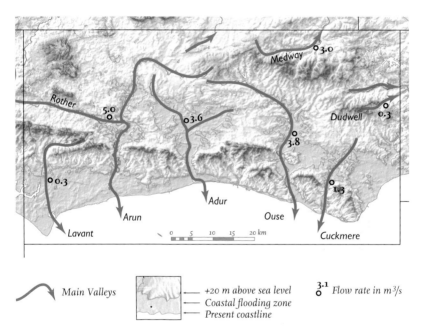

Main Valleys

+20 m above sea level
Coastal flooding zone
Present coastline

3.1 Flow rate in m³/s

FIG 136. Main river pathways and coastal flooding zone of Area 6.

AREA 7: EAST SUSSEX AND SOUTHEAST KENT

More than half of this Area rectangle is occupied by the sea (Figs 137 and 138). The coastline extends from Bexhill in the west, where the sea is eroding cliffs in the Early Cretaceous High Weald bedrock, to Folkestone in the northeast, where the cliffs have been formed by erosion of the Early Cretaceous Lower Greensand and Gault and the Late Cretaceous Chalk. Between these two sections of coastal cliffs is a large area of young surface blanket forming Dungeness and Romney Marsh.

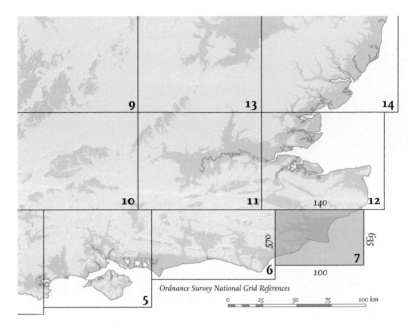

FIG 137. Location map for Area 7.

FIG 138. Natural and man-made features of Area 7.

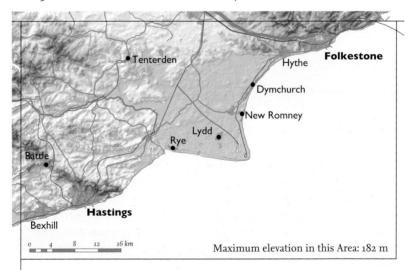

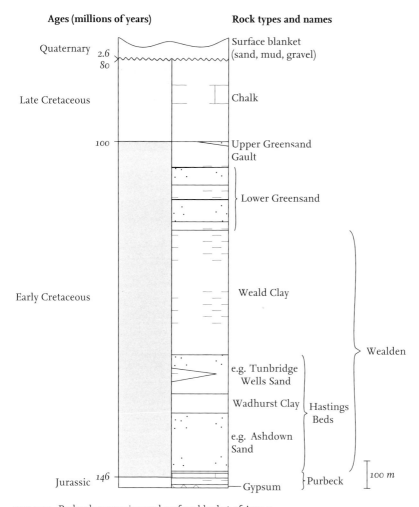

Ages (millions of years)	Rock types and names

FIG 139. Bedrock succession and surface blanket of Area 7.

Almost all of the land of Area 7 is underlain by bedrock of Cretaceous age. The only exception to this is a small area of bedrock in the High Weald, just north of Battle, which is of Late Jurassic (Purbeck) age (Fig. 139).

Five distinctive Landscapes can be identified in Area 7, labelled **A** to **E** in Figure 140. The first four of these are defined by their successively younger bedrock, while the last one is defined by its surface blanket of young material.

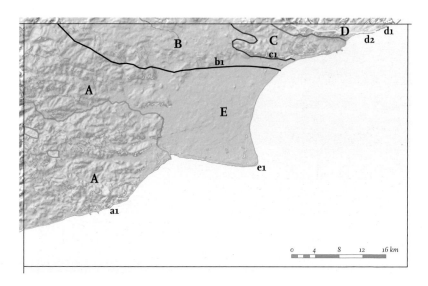

Main Bedrock Boundaries

 Base of Chalk
Top of Lower Greensand
Top of Weald Clay
Top of Hastings Beds

Top of Purbeck Limestone

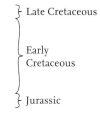 } Late Cretaceous

} Early Cretaceous

} Jurassic

FIG 140. Geology and hillshade map of Area 7, showing the boundaries of important bedrock layers, Landscapes A to E and localities (a1, b1 etc.) mentioned in the text.

Landscape A: The High Weald

Most of the land of Area 7 is underlain by the Early Cretaceous Hastings Beds, though in the centre of the Area this is covered by the surface blanket of younger sediment that forms the Dungeness and Romney Marshes. The hilly ground to the west of the Area is therefore a continuation of the High Weald Landscape of Area 6, and many aspects of its history are discussed more fully under that Area.

Only rarely do the hills of this part of the High Weald exceed 100 m in elevation, but the topography consists generally of many small valleys and ridges, so there are very few substantial areas of flat ground. The small size of the topographic features made this Landscape ideal for damming streams to provide local sources of power, and so, as in Area 6, an iron-smelting industry flourished here between the fifteenth and seventeenth centuries.

FIG 141. Hastings Castle, foreshore and cliff (Fig. 140, **a1**).
(Copyright Sylvia Cordaiy Photo Library Ltd)

The layering of the Hastings Beds in this Landscape is generally near to
horizontal, and consists of alternations of sandstones and mudstones on many
scales. The sandstones were mainly deposited in Early Cretaceous river channels
and at river mouths, while the mudstones were formed in lakes or on river
floodplains. Two groups of sandstone layers are particularly important: an early,
lower group called the Ashdown Sand and a later, upper group called the
Tunbridge Wells Sand. They are separated by a mud-rich interval known as the
Wadhurst Clay (Fig. 139). These changes of rock type have locally influenced the
slopes that have formed during the erosion of much of the topography. At
Hastings (**a1**), the castle was constructed on a prominent sandstone layer within
the Wadhurst interval, which has been eroded by coastal storms to produce a
distinctive cliff feature (Fig. 141).

The bedrock was cut by faults that became active during the movement
of the crust in mid-Tertiary times, when the Weald uplift was forming.
Displacements along these faults have disrupted the regular layer pattern of
the bedrock, which has, in turn, caused variation in local slope erosion.
The commonest fault direction is WNW–ESE, and some of the main valleys, such
as those of the Rother and Brede, locally trend parallel to particular faults
(Fig. 149, page 192).

Landscape B: The Low Weald

The Low Weald is defined by the presence of the Early Cretaceous Weald Clay just below any surface blanket that happens to be present locally. It forms a wide and rather featureless belt of scenery along the northern margin of Area 7.

To the east of this Landscape, the Weald Clay bedrock forms an irregular but generally linear slope feature that was eroded in the Bilsington area (**b1**) before the coastal-zone deposition of Dungeness and Romney Marsh began. The irregularities of this slope may reflect the way the weak mud material of the Weald Clay has tended to collapse and flow down-slope.

As the coastal town of Hythe is approached, the Weald Clay bedrock becomes covered up by the surface blanket of Romney Marsh. The area underlain by the Weald Clay generally becomes much narrower in Area 7, at least partly because the total thickness of the Clay in the bedrock succession decreases here to just over 100 m, compared with some 500 m near Guildford in Area 11. Changes of thickness of this sort usually reflect variations in the downward movements of the Earth's crust during the accumulation of the sediment, but may also reflect variations in the amount of sediment supplied to the environment in which the Weald Clay accumulated.

Landscape C: The Wealden Greensand

Coastal erosion in the Hythe and Folkestone area has produced vegetated cliffs cut into Early Cretaceous Lower Greensand and Gault bedrocks (Fig. 142). These units have a combined thickness of about 150 m in the Folkestone area and consist largely of mudstones, except for a lower sandstone layer (the Hythe Beds) and an upper sandstone layer (the Folkestone Beds). The sandstones have preferentially resisted erosion to produce slopes in the local scenery, particularly in the case of the Hythe Beds, which contain thin, hard limestone layers inter-bedded with sandstones containing grains of the dark green, iron-bearing mineral glauconite. These alternations of hard and soft bands were known as 'rag and hassock' by local quarrymen in earlier times, and 'Kentish Rag' is still a source of road stone and concrete aggregate.

The Hythe beds have been eroded into a distinct scarp for some 10 km along the northern margin (**c1**) of Romney Marsh, west of Hythe. In more recent times, the margin of this scarp has been made less distinct by land-slipping and surface modification, as the Hythe Bed sandstones have collapsed downwards over the underlying softer mudstones.

FIG 142. Looking northeastwards past Hythe (in the foreground) to Folkestone (with the pier) and the White Cliffs of Dover (in the distance). (Copyright Dae Sasitorn & Adrian Warren/www.lastrefuge.co.uk)

Landscape D: The North Downs

Area 7 contains a very small area of Late Cretaceous Chalk bedrock along its northeastern margin, which can be identified as Landscape **D**. The Chalk continues northwards into Area 11, where it forms the North Downs, extending from Dover northwestwards via Chatham, and on westwards south of London. All three subdivisions of the Chalk are present in the Folkestone area, the Lower and Middle each about 70 m thick, and the Upper about 200 m thick.

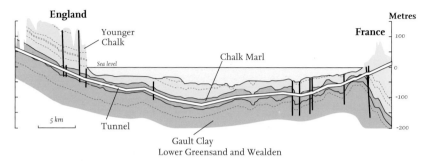

FIG 143. Diagram showing the way the Channel Tunnel was excavated within the Chalk Marl, the lowest layer in the Late Cretaceous Chalk. (Redrawn from drawing by Nigel Woodcock)

The design of the Channel Tunnel (completed in 1994) involves three tunnels, one for each of the two traffic directions, and a smaller one for emergency and maintenance work. The tunnels are excavated as far as possible within the lowest unit of the lower Chalk, known as the Chalk Marl (Fig. 143). This material consists of a mixture of clay minerals and fine-grained calcium carbonate, making it largely impermeable to water flow, yet plastic enough to suit the tunnelling machinery. It is also not so brittle that it contains cracks and fractures that would cause collapse and flooding by groundwater.

Excavation took place simultaneously from both France and England and took about three years. Spoil from the tunnels on the English side was used to construct a 1 km by 300 m extension to the coastline just west of Shakespeare Cliff (**d1**), most of which is now used as the Samphire Way Country Park.

The decision was also taken to locate the tunnel mouths very well inland, some 2.5 km north of the coast in central Folkestone (Fig. 144). The route of the tunnels crosses the coastline below Shakespeare Cliff (**d1**), some 2 km from the Western Docks of Dover and almost 10 km from the tunnel mouths north of Folkestone. This 10 km of tunnelling below land was felt to be preferable to locating the tunnels closer to the coastal cliffs, which had proved to be extremely unstable in the past, particularly along the 3 km coastal stretch just northeast of Folkestone known as the Warren (**d2**). Cliff erosion of the soft Early Cretaceous Gault overlain by the Late Cretaceous Chalk in this area has caused continuous land-slipping here. The decision to construct the first railway line to Dover across the Warren required frequent movement and re-cutting of the line, culminating in a major landslip in 1915 which carried away a complete train (Fig. 145).

FIG 144. Aerial view eastwards, looking at the mouth of the Channel Tunnel. To the right is Folkestone and to the left is the edge of the Late Cretaceous Chalk. (Copyright Dae Sasitorn & Adrian Warren/www.lastrefuge.co.uk)

FIG 145. The Folkestone Warren landslip, 1915. Note the train in the foreground. (Photo from British Railways, Southern Region)

The dry valleys and steep slopes that are developed so clearly in many areas of Chalk downland in Southern England are very clear in the Downs to the north and northwest of Folkestone and Dover. A detailed investigation of the landscape history has been carried out in Holywell Coombe, north of Folkestone and just south of the A20 tunnel mouth a few hundred metres from the Channel Tunnel portal. This showed that the Chalk slopes were actively retreating because of freeze–thaw collapse during the Dimlington and Loch Lomond cold periods (see Chapter 2, Fig. 19), providing clear evidence that this Chalk landscape was actively evolving in very recent geological terms.

Landscape E: The Dungeness and Romney Marshes

Dungeness is one of the largest beach-gravel promontories of the whole coastline of Britain. It adds a highly distinctive shape to the coast of the Strait of Dover, the narrowest section of the English Channel.

FIG 146. Photograph looking northwestwards over Dungeness and the nuclear power stations (Fig. 140, **e1**). The lines or ridges on the surface of the promontory mark the positions of former coastlines. (Copyright Dae Sasitorn & Adrian Warren/www.lastrefuge.co.uk)

The surface of the main Dungeness promontory is only lightly vegetated, and very clearly shows large numbers of distinct lines or ridges, locally called 'fulls' and visible in Figure 146. Groups of these ridges trend in different directions, and excavations made during the construction of the power station show that they mark the tops of sedimentary layers, sloping downwards towards the sea at about 9 degrees. These layers were formed during storms when gravel was deposited on the sloping surfaces of old beaches. This means that the pattern of lines provides a record of the positions of active beaches over time, making it possible to plot the way the promontory has grown and changed in the past (Fig. 147). Where the lines have been truncated by the present coast, an earlier episode of deposition by storms must have been followed by a later episode of net removal, causing the movement of the coast landward.

As Figure 147 shows, analysis of these lines provides evidence for an early episode of build-out of the coastline in the southwest of this Landscape, near Rye. The building of the large promontory of present-day Dungeness, further to the east, has occurred more recently, and has been accompanied by large amounts of erosion south of Rye (Fig. 148), as well as some lesser erosion to the northeast, about 5 km southwest of Hythe, where a wall has been constructed to protect the coastline.

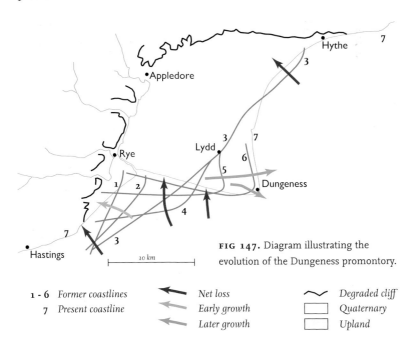

FIG 147. Diagram illustrating the evolution of the Dungeness promontory.

1 - 6 *Former coastlines*	*Net loss*	*Degraded cliff*
7 *Present coastline*	*Early growth*	*Quaternary*
	Later growth	*Upland*

FIG 148. Looking southeastwards down the River Rother, with Rye in the foreground. The gravel beaches of the present coastline of Rye Bay extend further to the left into Dungeness. (Copyright Dae Sasitorn & Adrian Warren/www.lastrefuge.co.uk)

Inland from the shingle-covered areas are large areas of flat-lying, open, agricultural land with distinctive dykes and marshes. Although there are many local names, these flat-lying areas are often grouped under the general name of the Romney Marshes.

Muds and sands are widespread just below the surface of the Marshes, and peats are common a few metres down. It is possible to date these peats using radiocarbon methods, and it is also possible to use related fossils to determine whether the peats formed in wetlands that were freshwater or becoming salty because of flooding due to sea-level rise. This work has confirmed that all the Marsh deposits have been formed during the last period of the Flandrian transgression (rise) of the sea. Some 6,000–7,000 years ago, sea level was about 10 m lower than at present and it rose progressively to reach its present level within the last few hundreds of years. However, it is also clear that horizontal movement of features such as tidal channels, beach barriers, wetlands and salt marshes can be responsible for local vertical changes, without requiring any change of overall sea level.

There is no question that the global rise of sea level since the last (Devensian) cold spell has been the major factor controlling the arrival and deposition of all the sediment in the Dungeness and the Romney Marshes. However, on a more local scale, it seems that small-scale variations in the climate have also been important, controlling both the supply of sediment to the marshes and the power and frequency of storms.

One regional feature that needs to be stressed is the special location and geometry of Dungeness in relation to the geography of land and sea. The Dungeness promontory is situated in an exposed position, at the mercy of prevailing Atlantic storms driven from the southwest up the English Channel, and also from winter storms caused by depressions passing over the northern North Sea. Both of these processes act to transport sediment into and around the Dungeness promontory. At the same time, the proximity of the promontory to the coast of France means that winds from the southeast, which are unusual anyway, do not have sufficient reach to cause erosion that would counteract the tendency for Dungeness to grow.

Another striking feature of this Landscape is the *degraded cliff* that marks the boundary between the areas of bedrock control, to the north and west, and the flat-lying area of the Marshes covered with surface blanket, to the south and east (Fig. 147). This cliff feature runs on the landward side of the Royal Military Canal, which was constructed for communication and defence purposes under threat of a Napoleonic invasion. As the 'degraded cliff' name implies, this distinctive slope feature is regarded as a cliff line eroded by the sea before deposition of the young Marsh. Although it is generally assumed that it formed just before the Marsh sediments themselves, within the last 7,000 years or so, it is also possible that it is much older. For example, in some areas along the coast of East Anglia, cliff-forming erosion took place during the last (Ipswichian) interglacial, about 125,000 years ago, when sea level was a few metres higher than it is at present. It is possible that the Romney Marsh cliffs formed by similar processes, and that their degradation took place over the 125,000 years that followed.

Review of the landscape history

The oldest features of the scenery of Area 7 must be the major river valleys of the Rother, Tillingham and Brede, which started to erode downwards into the rising land surface when the Weald uplift began some 30 million years ago. These rivers have excavated the intricate valley patterns of the High Weald, the low and subtle drainage patterns of the Low Weald, and the more marked scarps and valleys of the Wealden Greensands and Chalk.

The second group of landscape features are those that reflect changes in sea level. There is no clear dating evidence for high-stands of the sea earlier within the Tertiary, but the evidence for Holocene flooding by postglacial sea-level rise is abundant and has been discussed above. So also has the possibility that the Romney Marshes degraded cliff line may date from the high sea level associated with the Ipswichian interglacial, some 125,000 years ago. The evidence for this is based not on direct dating, but on the configuration of the land as represented by the 'coastal flood zone' shown in Figure 149. This figure highlights the inland valley patterns, and also identifies the large proportion of the Area sensitive to fairly small changes in sea level.

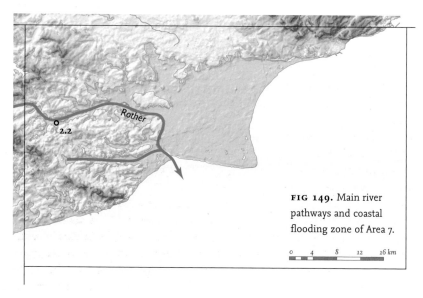

FIG 149. Main river pathways and coastal flooding zone of Area 7.

0   4   8   12   16 km

Main Valleys

+20 m above sea level
Coastal flooding zone
Present coastline

$o^{3.1}$ Flow rate in m³/s

CHAPTER 6

The Severn Valley Region

GENERAL INTRODUCTION

I HAVE LINKED AREAS 8 AND 9 together to form the Severn Valley Region (Fig. 150). This is because the Bristol Channel and the Severn and Avon valleys form one of the most important landscape features of this part of Southern England. Another dominant feature of this Region is the Cotswold Hills, extending from Bath northeastwards through Banbury.

The generalised bedrock succession for this Region (Fig. 151) contains a major unconformity or time gap. At this gap, the scale used to represent the thickness of the rock successions shown in Figure 151 has been changed, because the Carboniferous and older bedrock generally involves much greater thicknesses than the younger bedrock. This provides evidence for a slowing in the rate of sediment accumulation in this Region towards the end of the Carboniferous, which suggests that Earth movements were more active in earlier times, when the raising and lowering of the Earth's surface resulted in vigorous production of sediment and its trapping in subsiding basins.

The time gap in the succession can be mapped across the Region and is known as the *Variscan Unconformity*. Figure 151 shows this gap spanning the time between 305 and 299 million years ago, but this is misleading because 305 million years is the youngest age found in the underlying layers, while 299 million years is the oldest age found in the overlying layers. In most localities in the Region the time gap is much longer in duration.

The Variscan Unconformity is spectacularly exposed along the coastline at Woodhill Bay, Portishead, some 10 km west of central Bristol (Fig. 152).

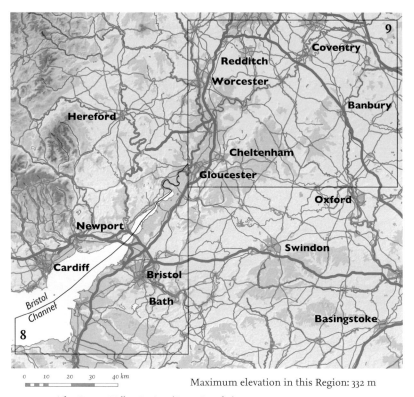

0   10   20   30   40 km

Maximum elevation in this Region: 332 m

FIG 150. The Severn Valley Region (Areas 8 and 9).

The lower part of the unconformity here consists of Devonian rocks of the Lower Old Red Sandstone, deposited as more-or-less flat beds about 400 million years ago. These beds were tilted and then eroded to form a flat surface during the Variscan mountain building, before being covered by layers of Triassic dolomitic conglomerate about 270 million years ago. These rocks provide a vivid record of the Variscan mountain building in this Region: the Devonian strata were tilted by folding, moved upwards and then eroded, before being covered by sediment derived, at least partly, from Variscan mountains that still existed nearby.

The Severn Valley Region contains an unusual diversity of scenery and bedrock because it straddles an important boundary represented by the Variscan Unconformity, dividing the older and newer bedrock successions of England and Wales (Fig. 153). Carboniferous and older bedrock geology underlies most of the Southwest, Wales, northwestern England and some parts of the English West Midlands. New Red Sandstone and younger bedrock dominates most of the rest

Ages (millions of years)   **Rock types and names**

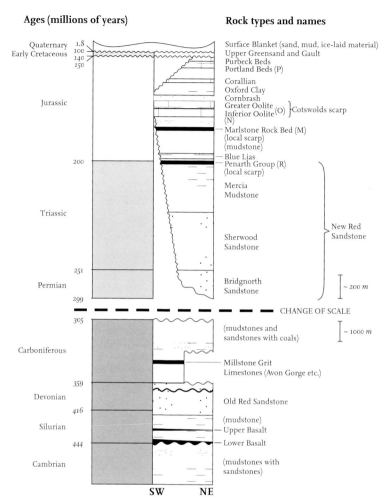

SW   NE

FIG 151. Generalised bedrock succession for the Severn Valley Region.

of Southern England and the eastern part of northern England. The map in Figure 153 shows the trend of Variscan folds generated during the plate convergence that caused the Variscan mountain building. South of the line marked 'Variscan Front' the main fold trends run east–west, representing convergence in a roughly north–south direction. North of the Variscan Front, in Areas 8, 9 and 10, folds of similar age trend generally north–south and result from a different pattern of movement.

FIG 152. The Variscan Unconformity spectacularly exposed at Woodhill Bay, Portishead. The upper rocks are dolomitic conglomerates of Triassic age, resting upon the tilted Lower Old Red Sandstones of the Devonian. (Copyright British Geological Survey)

The other landscape feature of Regional interest here is the valley system of the River Severn and Bristol Channel. Figure 153 shows the extent of the Bristol Channel Basin, outlined by the pre-New Red Sandstone unconformity and filled mainly with New Red Sandstone sediment. This basin formed as an area of persistent downward movement during the latest stages of the Variscan mountain building. The soft sediment fill of the basin made it more susceptible to erosion than the surrounding older, harder rocks, allowing the Bristol Channel to form as it is now.

East of the Basin, the Bristol Channel narrows and becomes an estuary, until it ceases to be tidal near Gloucester. This northeasterly reach, largely in Area 8, is characterised by the change in fold and fault trends referred to above, from east–west in the south, to northeast–southwest, and then north–south in the north. It seems likely that the change in direction of the estuary and the river has resulted from erosional topography controlled by the presence of these structures.

Further north, the eastern edge of the Severn–Avon catchment is formed by the watershed of the Cotswold Hills. We shall see in Area 9 how the drainage divide here is controlled by various resistant layers in the Jurassic bedrock, which slope regionally and very gently to the southeast. In this Region, the gentle tilting movements appear to have been influenced partly by uplift of the Atlantic margin in the west and partly by the lowering of the North Sea to the east. Area 9 also contains evidence of possible late-stage uplift of the Cotswolds in response to erosional unloading of the Severn Valley. The River Severn itself flows generally southerly through Area 9, much of it near parallel to the north–south trending Malvern Line to the west. In contrast, in its upper reaches, it flows generally easterly and southeasterly, from headwaters that are less than 20 km from the sea at Cardigan Bay. In our consideration of Area 9, we shall review evidence that this highest section of the Severn began as the headwaters of an ancestor of the River Thames and flowed eastwards all the way across Southern England to the ancestral North Sea.

FIG 153. Map of western England and Wales showing the main Variscan fold trends and the Variscan Front. The surface cover of younger rocks (from Permian New Red Sandstone to Early Cretaceous age) is also shown, along with the catchment area of the Severn–Avon river system.

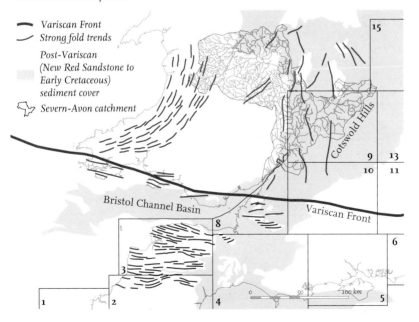

AREA 8: BRISTOL

The boundary of this area runs along the coast of the Bristol Channel, up the Severn Estuary and along the banks of the River Severn (Figs 154 and 155). Bristol and Bath are the most important cities. We shall consider the origins of the complex pattern of hill areas and the landscapes of gorges (Avon) and caves (Cheddar, Wookey Hole etc.). In contrast, we shall also examine the origins of the low and very flat Somerset Levels.

The following detailed discussion of the scenery of Area 8 is organised into six Landscapes, labelled **A** to **F** in Figure 156. The main river pathways and coastal flooding zone are shown in Figure 157.

Landscape A: The Quantock Hills and Fringes

The patch of higher land in the southwest corner of Area 8 is the northern tip of the Quantock Hills, which rise to an elevation of 310 m at Beacon Hill (**a1**), some 3 km from the coast of the Bristol Channel. The bedrock underlying the

FIG 154. Location map for Area 8.

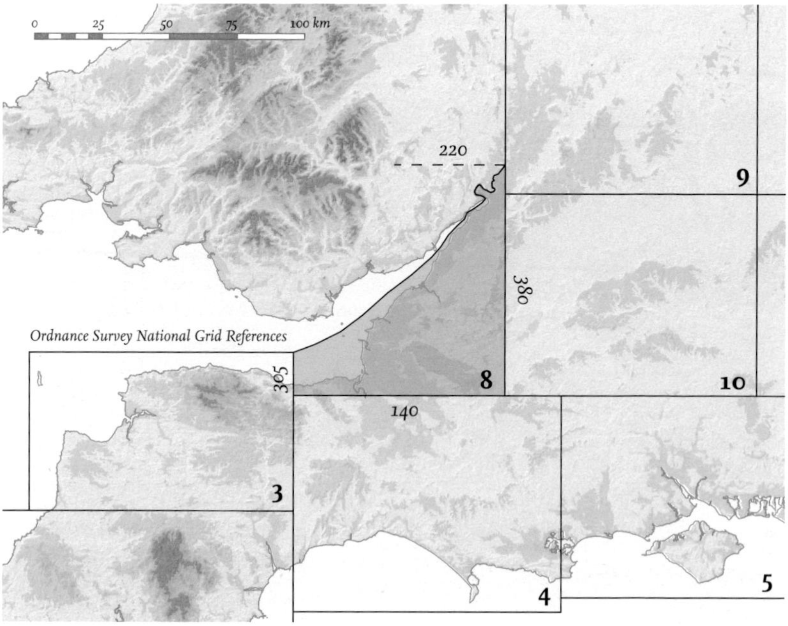

Quantocks is hard-wearing Devonian sandstone and slate, similar to the bedrock of Exmoor in the west. The resistance of this bedrock to landscape weathering and erosion is the reason for the high ground in both cases.

As in the rest of Area 8, the Variscan Unconformity marks the important end-of-Variscan episode when the Triassic and Jurassic layers surrounding the Quantocks were deposited on folded Devonian bedrock (Fig. 152). Much of the younger, overlying material is mudstone, which has been eroded preferentially over the last few million years to form small hills and valleys at a lower level than the Quantocks themselves (the Quantock Fringes landscape). Geological mapping of the unconformity reveals the ancient landscape of the Variscan mountains, carved into the Devonian and older bedrock between 300 and 200 million years ago, and subsequently buried by Triassic and Jurassic sediments.

FIG 155. Natural and man-made features of Area 8.

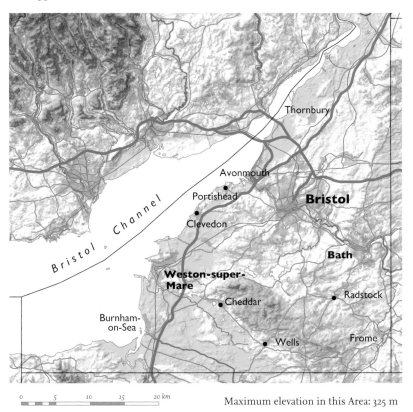

Maximum elevation in this Area: 325 m

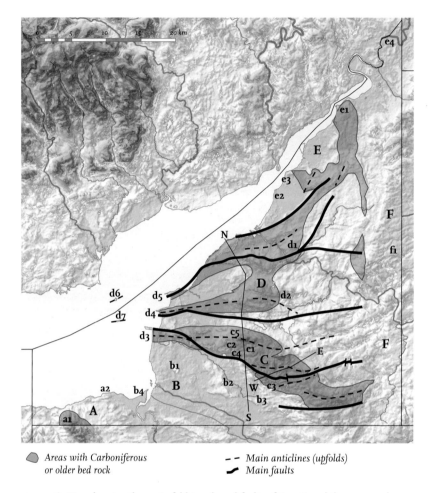

Areas with Carboniferous
or older bed rock

– – Main anticlines (upfolds)
↗ Main faults

FIG 156. Map showing the main fold trends and faults of Area 8, and the areas underlain by bedrock of Carboniferous age or older. Landscapes **A** to **F** are also marked, along
with localities (**a1, a2** etc.) mentioned in the text.

This Landscape's Bristol Channel coastline runs approximately from west to
east and is a continuation of the Exmoor coast (see Area 3). Both run parallel to –
and have been controlled by – the main Variscan folds. Hinkley Point (**a2**) is
notable as the site of two nuclear power stations, one of which is in the process
of being decommissioned. The intertidal zone of this stretch of coastline
consists largely of a wave-cut bedrock platform, exposed to view at low water on

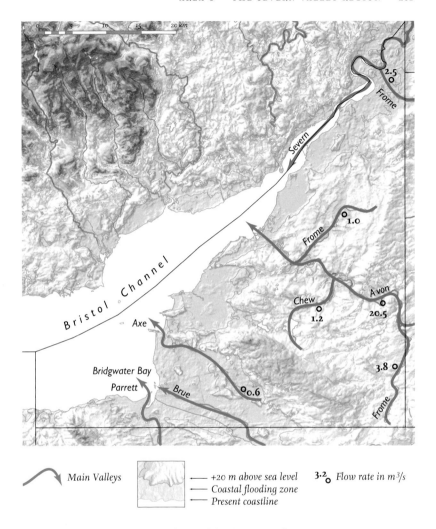

Main Valleys

—— +20 m above sea level
—— Coastal flooding zone
—— Present coastline

3·2 o Flow rate in m³/s

FIG 157. Main river pathways and coastal flooding zone of Area 8.

medium tides. Most of the bedrock is Early Jurassic in age and consists of grey mudstone with a clear, regular layering of thin limestones. Examination of the layering shows that this bedrock has been folded locally and fractured by numerous faults that trend east–west. Because these movements have deformed the Jurassic bedrock, they must have occurred distinctly later than the mountain-building episode represented by the Variscan Unconformity, and may have formed during the creation of the Bristol Channel Basin (Fig. 153).

A narrow beach of sand and mud is present along much of this coastline at the upper limit reached by normal high tides. Inland from this, there is generally a small cliff line that is only reached by storms during high tides. It seems likely that this cliff line was created by storm action relatively recently, after the sea rose to within about 10 m of its present level some 6,000 years ago. However, as along many other stretches of the coast of Southern England, initial erosion may have taken place some 130,000 years ago during the Ipswichian, when the sea was last as high as it is today.

Landscape B: The Somerset Levels and Moors and the Mid-Somerset Hills
The flatness of this Landscape is one of its most remarkable features. In Southern England, the only other flat area of comparable size is the Fens of East Anglia (Area 15). Both the Fens and the Somerset Levels owe their flatness to the presence of easily eroded mudstone bedrock in areas that have experienced repeated invasions and retreats of the sea during the last 2 million years. These repeated invasions have resulted in large flat surfaces of eroded bedrock covered by young, surface-blanket sediments, deposited by low-lying rivers along the coasts or washed inland by the sea. In the Somerset Levels, the flat areas are underlain by the soft mudstones of the lower Lias (Early Jurassic), which are often covered by a surface blanket of Quaternary muds, formed during the late stages of the Flandrian sea-level rise. Some areas, locally called moors, are peat-rich and were formed in wetland landscapes.

The hills, although low, often present abrupt slopes overlooking the flat lands. Brent Knoll (**b1**) is a striking conical hill rising over 100 m above the surrounding Levels, and best visible to people travelling southwards along the M5 motorway. It consists of flat layers of Early Jurassic mudstones capped by a small patch of Middle Jurassic limestone and a prehistoric fort. Brent Knoll owes its existence to its cap of limestone, which is a more resistant bedrock layer than the mudstones underneath it. Erosion of the slopes of the Knoll was active both during times of warm climate and high sea level, and during cold episodes, when freeze–thaw action led to slumping of bedrock material and soil down-slope to produce the conical form we see today.

To the east, the Wedmore to Wookey ridge (**b2** and **b3**) is another distinctive feature of the northern part of the Somerset Levels. The zigzag plan shape of the ridge follows the pattern of a number of faults that cut limestones of Late Triassic and Early Jurassic age. This is another example of deformation (in this case faulting) that has taken place since the Early Jurassic, changing the pattern of resistant bedrock and resulting in a distinctive present-day geometry in the scenery.

The stretch of coastline bordering Landscape **B** has a low-lying hinterland because it marks the area in which the main Severn Valley is joined by the River Parrett (**b4**; Fig. 158). The Parrett is one of the main tributaries of the Severn, bringing water and sediment from much of Somerset. At the maximum of the last cold episode of the Ice Age, some 20,000 years ago, the entire Bristol Channel was dry land at least as far as Land's End and westernmost Wales. Since then the sea has advanced to its present position by flooding this landscape of rivers, valleys and hills. The River Parrett flows into Bridgwater Bay (Fig. 157) where an array of channels and bars is covered and modified twice a day by the exceptionally large tides of the Severn Estuary. These tides have the greatest range of anywhere on the British coast: up to 15 m between low and high tide. This remarkable range is a result of the unique interaction between the orientation, shape and location of the Bristol Channel, and the patterns of tides that move around this part of the eastern Atlantic margin.

FIG 158. Meandering lower reaches of the River Parrett (Fig. 156, **b4**), near Burnham-on-Sea. (Copyright Dae Sasitorn & Adrian Warren/www.lastrefuge.co.uk)

Away from the channels and bars of the river mouth, the intertidal zone is unusually extensive, with 2–4 km of land exposed at low tide. Much of the exposed material is mud, although it tends to be sandy and locally gravel-rich near the high water mark, where stronger wave action (especially under storm conditions) has sorted and moved the sediment. Although there is obviously a large amount of sediment movement offshore along this coast (as shown by the muddy waters), it is not known whether the sediment predominantly comes from the land via rivers, or from the floor of the recently flooded Bristol Channel.

Above the high water mark there is commonly a belt of wind-deposited dunes, up to 1 km wide. The dune belt was built largely under storm conditions after the sea stabilised at its present position. Low islands of bedrock appear locally from beneath this spread of young sediment and, as at the mouth of the Parrett, they have sometimes become incorporated into the coastal bars and spits of the present-day coastline.

Landscape C: The Mendip Hills
The Mendip Hills extend across the Somerset–Gloucestershire border, from Weston-super-Mare in the west to Frome, some 40 km to the east. They rise to over 300 m above sea level, and their landscape of limestone cliffs, plateaus and gorges provides a striking contrast with the surrounding lowlands.

The Mendips are defined by a number of anticlines (upfolds) that have brought Devonian Old Red Sandstone and Carboniferous Limestone to the surface. These older rocks have resisted erosion to form uplands distinctly higher than the surrounding softer and younger bedrocks. The pattern of anticlines and small faults was created during the Variscan mountain-building episode some 300 million years ago.

A cross-section through the North Hill upfold (Fig. 159), just north of Wells, illustrates some of the features found in many of the Mendip anticlines: a core of Devonian sandstone is flanked by layers of Carboniferous Limestone that are steeply tilted (to about 40 degrees) and cut by small faults. The Devonian and Carboniferous bedrocks have resisted erosion and form rolling upland plateaus, possibly relics of some earlier erosion event. Perhaps they are wave-cut platforms, recording a time in the past when sea level was very high and/or the land was lower, similar to the wave-cut platforms identified in the Southwest granites. The highest elevation of the cross-section is in the Devonian bedrock, at 305 m.

Another cross-section (Fig. 160) reconstructs the wider Variscan fold and fault pattern in a north-to-south direction across much of Area 8. We can picture a geometry of this sort forming by using an analogy: imagine a weak paper tablecloth violently pushed over the table-top. The paper will fold and tear as it is

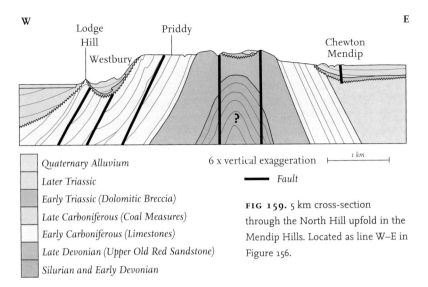

W   E

Lodge Hill   Priddy   Chewton Mendip

Westbury

☐ Quaternary Alluvium

☐ Later Triassic

☐ Early Triassic (Dolomitic Breccia)

☐ Late Carboniferous (Coal Measures)

☐ Early Carboniferous (Limestones)

☐ Late Devonian (Upper Old Red Sandstone)

☐ Silurian and Early Devonian

6 x vertical exaggeration   ├── 1 km ──┤

━━ Fault

FIG 159. 5 km cross-section through the North Hill upfold in the Mendip Hills. Located as line W–E in Figure 156.

bunched up. Similarly, the upper layers of bedrock have folded and faulted as they slid northwards over a flat-lying surface (the table-top) and over each other. The flat-lying surface must have formed by fracturing along some weak layer deep in the ancient (Silurian or older) bedrock.

During the Variscan deformation, the rock now forming the Mendips was part of a massive convergent mountain belt. The intense heat and pressure created by the convergence led to metal ores being deposited in the rocks by hot-water (hydrothermal) circulation, similar to the circulation which deposited tin and lead in the granites of Cornwall. As in Cornwall, the Mendips have been

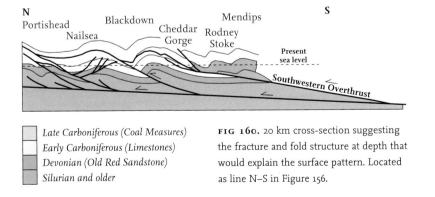

N   S

Portishead   Blackdown   Mendips

Nailsea   Cheddar Gorge   Rodney Stoke

Present sea level

Southwestern Overthrust

☐ Late Carboniferous (Coal Measures)

☐ Early Carboniferous (Limestones)

☐ Devonian (Old Red Sandstone)

☐ Silurian and older

FIG 160. 20 km cross-section suggesting the fracture and fold structure at depth that would explain the surface pattern. Located as line N–S in Figure 156.

mined for their metal ores, particularly those containing lead and zinc. The Romans were the first to exploit these ores, and the industry reached its peak in activity during the seventeenth century, but continued until much more recently. Mining activity has left considerable evidence of surface working in local landscapes, particularly in the areas around Charterhouse (c1) and Shipham (c2).

The Mendips are also known for their cave complexes, resulting from moving water dissolving and enlarging crack systems in the limestone bedrock. A famous example is Wookey Hole (c3), just north of Wells. In some areas, most famously Cheddar Gorge (c4; Fig. 161) and Burrington Coombe (c5), roof collapse of large cave systems has generated spectacular landscapes that attract large numbers of visitors. Large limestone quarries are a man-made feature of the Mendip scenery, often of similar size to the famous natural collapses.

One particularly interesting feature of Area 8 is the relationship between the folded and faulted Variscan bedrock, as exemplified in the Mendips by the bedrocks of Devonian and Carboniferous age, and the overlying New Red Sandstone of Triassic age. Careful examination of the contact between these rocks reveals episodes when hilly scenery was being 'drowned' in Triassic times by angular conglomerates (*breccias*), sandstones and mudstones. These, of course,

FIG 161. Cheddar Gorge seen from the Heights of Abraham (Fig. 156, **c4**). (Copyright Landform Slides – Ken Gardner)

are further examples of the Variscan Unconformity (Fig. 152). In some localities, kilometre-scale valleys have been eroded into Carboniferous bedrock and then plugged up by sediment. It seems clear that much of this sediment must have been transported from source areas some distance away from the valleys themselves. Figure 159 presents an example of this situation, where, at the western end of the cross-section, around Westbury, the Carboniferous Limestone has been tilted and fractured, and then eroded to produce a distinct valley almost 1 km across. This valley was then plugged by Triassic sediments consisting of angular coarse blocks (breccias) derived from the nearby valley walls and sandstones derived from nearer the valley centre. Local hollows in the hills are preserved in the same section on the Mendip upland east of Priddy, and on the northern Mendip flank near Chewton Mendip.

Landscape D: The Bristol and Avon Valleys and Ridges
This Landscape lies north of the Mendips and west of the Cotswolds, and includes the city of Bristol and the coastline from Weston-super-Mare to Avonmouth. North of Avonmouth the landscape merges into that of the Severn Vale. The region is hilly but does not reach the heights of the Mendips. The main river is the Avon, which runs northwest towards the Severn, passing through Bath and Bristol on the way.

Like the Mendip Hills to the south, the discrete hill features of this scenery are the result of Variscan fold structures in the bedrock. However, the folds are less regular and continuous in their arrangement than in the Mendips, because the Bristol Landscape appears to have developed across the transitional zone of the Variscan Front. Here the east–west trends of the main Variscan mountain belt give way northwards to a more open arrangement with a general north–south trend.

In spite of this important difference in the regularity and trend of the folds, the basic bedrock components are very similar to those of the Mendips. Carboniferous Limestone is the most distinctive feature of the folds, and one of its most famous features is the Avon Gorge (**d1**; Figs 162 and 163) at Bristol. The cliffs of the gorge are up to 100 m high, and have been formed partly by rainwater dissolving the rock and partly by gravitational collapse of the highly fractured limestone.

Away from the hills, the surrounding landscape is often underlain by a sequence of Late Carboniferous sediments broadly grouped as the Coal Measures. The Coal Measures are predominantly mudstone, but also contain coals and sandstones. Being mostly mudstone, the coalfields have tended to be preferentially eroded by younger rivers and streams, resulting in rather lower landscapes. This was also the case during Triassic times, because the distribution

FIG 162. The Avon Gorge, looking downstream from the Clifton Suspension Bridge (Fig. 156, **d1**). (Copyright Landform Slides – Ken Gardner)

FIG 163. Looking eastwards over Bristol with the Avon Gorge and Clifton Suspension Bridge in the foreground (Fig. 156, **d1**). (Copyright Dae Sasitorn & Adrian Warren/ www.lastrefuge.co.uk)

of Triassic sediment in many of the coalfield areas provides evidence that these areas were low-lying when sediment was accumulating. The large volume of Triassic sediment present indicates that much of it was not simply being derived from local sources, but was being transported over longer distances, probably from the central peaks of the Variscan mountain range to the south.

A number of small areas of Jurassic sediment occur in the western part of Area 8. The most prominent of these forms Dundry Hill (**d2**) on the southern edge of Bristol. Dundry, rising to 233 m above sea level, is a flat upland made of limestones of the Middle Jurassic Inferior Oolite. It is ringed by a broad zone where the limestones have landslipped downwards on slopes of Early Jurassic (Lias) mudstones. In the eastern part of Area 8, the surface is underlain by Early Jurassic mudstones occupying relatively low ground, rising eastwards towards a scarp of the Middle Jurassic limestones that define Landscape **F**, the Cotswolds.

FIG 164. Looking northeastwards across Weston-super-Mare, with the headlands of Weston Woods (Fig. 156, **d4**) and Sand Point (**d5**) behind. (Copyright Dae Sasitorn & Adrian Warren/www.lastrefuge.co.uk)

The striking features of the stretch of coastline around Weston-super-Mare are the isolated sections of Carboniferous bedrock that form the strongly projecting headlands of Brean Down (**d3**), Weston Woods (**d4**) and Sand Point (**d5**). The combination of hilly headlands with wide bays provides attractive views (Fig. 164), though the strong tides and abundant availability of muddy sediment make many of the beaches too muddy to attract many visitors. The headlands, along with the offshore islands of Flat Holm (**d6**) and Steep Holm (**d7**), are the tops of ridges that are the relics of faulted folds made largely of Carboniferous Limestone, deformed during the Variscan mountain building and then eroded and draped with Triassic sediments. More recent river erosion has subsequently modified the hill form of the Carboniferous features. Finally, Flandrian sea-level rise has deposited yet another layer of sediment on the low-lying land (now beaches) between these old hill features.

Between Clevedon and Portishead the coast displays another example of a Variscan faulted fold, although in this case it runs northeasterly, forming a ridge parallel to the coast. Inland from the ridge is the Gordano Valley, with the M5 motorway running along its southeasterly slope. The low ground of the Gordano Valley was probably carved out by an episode of erosion when the main River Severn occupied this part of its valley slope. Mapping of the bedrock in this area shows that the present-day coastal ridge was also a ridge in Triassic times, a relict of the early Variscan landscape similar to the Weston-super-Mare headlands and Westbury Valley in the Mendips.

Landscape E: The Severn Vale

This Landscape consists of the flat areas lying between the hills of folded Devonian and Carboniferous bedrock of Landscape **D** and the coast of the Severn Estuary, north of Avonmouth. Locally, these flat areas are interrupted by hills underlain by folded ancient bedrock typical of the Bristol area. The largest of these is near Berkeley (**e1**), where a major bedrock structure of tilted and faulted Carboniferous, Devonian, Silurian and Cambrian bedrock runs northward across the estuary. As in the Bristol Landscape (**D**), the older bedrock was folded by the Variscan episode, then covered by more-or-less flat-lying Triassic New Red Sandstone, which was then covered by Jurassic bedrock. These flat-lying strata can be seen below both of the Severn Road Bridges, at Severn Beach (**e2**) and Aust (**e3**).

As explained in greater detail in Area 9, it seems clear that an important episode in the erosion of the Severn Valley has taken place during the last 500,000 years. The removal of soft Triassic and Early Jurassic mudstones from the valley floor unearthed discrete hills made of the folded Carboniferous and earlier bedrock and left patches of relict Triassic and Early Jurassic rock. During this time, the river channel of the Severn has moved laterally across its floodplain, widening the floor of the valley and resulting in the deposition of a surface blanket of even younger river and estuarine sediments.

This Region is bounded to the northwest by the estuary of the River Severn. The river is notable for its tidal *bore*, a surge involving several waves up to 3 m in height that moves upstream in the uppermost tidal reaches of the Severn at high tide. People now compete to surf the longest upstream distance on the best bores. The largest bores occur when a particularly high tide is combined with critical values of freshwater inflow from the River Severn, atmospheric pressure and wind direction. Predictions and information on locations from which to observe the bore (such as at Minsterworth, **e4**) are posted on numerous Severn Bore websites. This is the only location in Britain where this phenomenon occurs so clearly and so often, and indicates the special nature of the tidal regime and the shape of the Severn Estuary and Bristol Channel.

Landscape F: The Cotswolds

The Cotswold Hills form the eastern margin of Area 8 and consist of erosion-resistant oolitic limestone of Middle Jurassic age. These hills were extensively

FIG 165. The Cotswold Edge near Wooton-under-Edge, looking northwestwards towards Wortley. (Copyright Landform Slides – Ken Gardner)

explored and understood by William Smith (often referred to as 'the Father of English Geology') between 1794 and 1799. Working as a canal and coal-mine engineer, he was able to demonstrate clearly for the first time, by careful examination of the landscape, that individual layers of characteristic appearance and fossil content can be followed from one place to another. He was also a pioneer in demonstrating how these layer arrangements can be presented in diagrammatic form, preparing and publishing the first systematic geological map of England and Wales in 1815.

The hill ridges stand up above the nearest valleys because of the way that their limestones have resisted erosion better than the surrounding softer rocks (Fig. 165). A remarkable point is that this erosion may have contributed to further upward movement of the landscape: parts of the Cotswolds crust may have been uplifted (or rebounded) by about 30–40 m when the Severn Valley was eroded, removing the weight of 100 m of sediment and producing a compensating flow in the deep crust. This process is discussed further under Area 9.

The Cotswold Hills are generally capped by limestone layers of Middle Jurassic age, but it is remarkable how many of the valley slopes below these caps are also underlain by blocks of limestone – many tens of metres or more across – that have moved down the slopes over the underlying mudstones as the valleys have been carved. This is particularly clear north of Bath, where, apart from isolated ridges capped by limestones that are still in place, local geological mapping has shown that the intervening valley slopes and floors are underlain largely by detached limestone blocks, producing areas of *foundered strata*.

In the area between Frome and Bath the bedrock pattern changes. Near Frome the Early Jurassic succession is very thin, apparently because it was a shallow-water shoal in the Jurassic sea. Sediment tended to be moved by wave action off the shoal and into surrounding areas, where greater thicknesses accumulated in deeper water. In this same area, the Middle Jurassic Inferior Oolite is also thin and unusually sandy, while the equivalent of the Great Oolite is a largely mudstone layer known as the Forest Marble. Much of this bedrock succession is interrupted by southwest–northeast running faults that locally run parallel to the directions of the sloping layers in the Carboniferous strata of the Mendip Hills. In the Bath area itself, the topography is dominated by the meandering and incised valley of the Avon. Ten kilometres north of Bath, the main layer capping the Cotswold Hills is the Great Oolite, which is more resistant than its southerly equivalent, the Forest Marble. The narrow valleys carved with an ESE–WNW trend into this Cotswold Landscape give it a particularly distinct form in the area around Marshfield (**fi**).

AREA 9: THE COTSWOLDS AND THE MIDDLE SEVERN

The landscapes of Area 9 (Figs 166 and 167) are dominated by the Cotswold Hills, stretching from the southwest near Gloucester to the northeast near Rugby. They separate the drainage that flows down the Avon and Severn valleys into the Bristol Channel from the drainage of the smaller rivers that flow eastwards and southwards, eventually to the North Sea. Area 9 therefore occupies a central position in the landscape of England and Wales, and the fact that it sends stream and river drainage in such different directions reflects this position.

We shall be considering why the Cotswold Hills exist, why they are located and oriented the way they are, and why they have such a clearly defined edge south of Evesham. We shall also consider why the River Severn flows southwards down the western edge of the Area, and why the large cities of Birmingham and Coventry have developed along the northern edge of the Area. On their eastern and southern flanks, the Cotswold Hills generally lack a well-defined margin, although important cross-cutting valleys there have provided routes for the roads, railways and canals that run between London and the Welsh Borders.

FIG 166. Location map for Area 9.

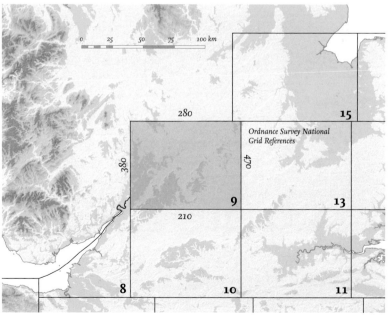

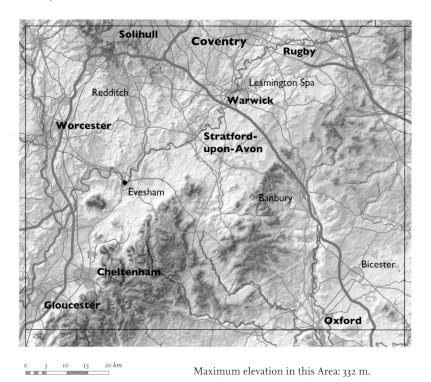

0   5   10   15   20 km

Maximum elevation in this Area: 332 m.

FIG 167. Natural and man-made features of Area 9.

The general introduction to this chapter provides an overview of the bedrock geology of the Severn Valley Region as a whole. It also includes a generalised succession for the bedrock layers below the surface blanket (Fig. 151). Although, like the rest of Southern England, this Area has much bedrock of Jurassic and Cretaceous age, it also includes older layers more typically seen further north and west. In terms of the bedrock near the surface, this Area is on the border between the newer and older bedrock regions of Britain.

For the more detailed discussion of the influence of the bedrock on the scenery the Area can be divided into four Landscapes, labelled **A** to **D** on Figure 168. I have simplified the bedrock succession, representing it as a succession of layers of rock ranging in thickness between a few metres to over a kilometre. Each of the layers was formed over a period of time in the distant past when totally different landscape patterns prevailed in the Area. Each consists of sedimentary rock (most commonly mudstone) that was deposited in the sea or by rivers over a period of millions of years. The layers are distinguished from the

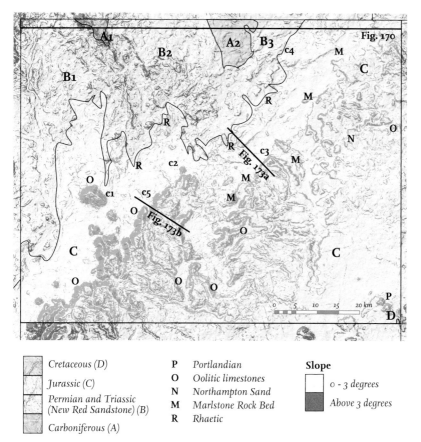

Cretaceous (D)

Jurassic (C)

Permian and Triassic
(New Red Sandstone) (B)

Carboniferous (A)

P   Portlandian
O   Oolitic limestones
N   Northampton Sand
M   Marlstone Rock Bed
R   Rhaetic

Slope

0 - 3 degrees

Above 3 degrees

FIG 168. Slope map showing the main divisions of the bedrock by age. Landscapes **A** to **D** and localities (**c1**, **c2** etc.) mentioned in the text are also marked.

older and younger layers below and above them by the types of rocks present, their arrangement and, in most cases, by characteristic fossils.

During and after the formation of this succession of layers there were distinct episodes of local movement of the Earth, now recorded in the rocks by gentle differences in the slope or tilt of the layers. The last of the episodes left even the youngest of the bedrock layers with a gentle southeasterly tilt. This episode appears to be linked to a general rising of western Britain due to the emplacement of hot, molten rock at depth, linked to the opening of the Atlantic Ocean. The North Sea was also sinking at this time, causing a lowering of eastern Britain and adding to the southeasterly tilt. For Area 9, the important point is that the tilting of the bedrock means that the oldest and lowest material is exposed in the northwest of the Area (the Carboniferous rocks of Landscape **A**), while the youngest and highest material is exposed in a very small patch in the far southeast (the Cretaceous rocks of Landscape **D**).

Landscape A: Carboniferous and earlier bedrock

The northern edge of Area 9 contains the southern ends of two areas distinguished by bedrock of Carboniferous and earlier age. The presence of Carboniferous material near the surface here has strongly influenced the ways in which settlement has occurred in these areas: the presence of coal at depth resulted in the development of the South Staffordshire and Warwickshire coalfields, which in turn brought widespread industrial activity to the Birmingham and Coventry areas (Fig. 169).

FIG 169. Old and new cathedral buildings in the city centre of Coventry mark its bombing during World War II, reflecting the industrial importance of the city. (Copyright Dae Sasitorn & Adrian Warren/www.lastrefuge.co.uk)

The two examples of the Carboniferous Landscape represented in Area 9 have rather different geology. In the case of the westernmost, South Staffordshire area (**A1**), the structure is dominated by an upfold. The core of this upfold is a fault-bounded strip of Ordovician Lickey Quartzite that has been eroded into the distinctive narrow ridge of the Lickey Hills (Fig. 170). This quartzite consists of quartz sand grains, themselves strongly cemented together by later growths of quartz, which make it very resistant to the processes of weathering. The quartzite is the result of an Ordovician episode (roughly 480 million years ago) when the sea flooded across central England, which had, at that time, been weathered and eroded into a very flat landscape. Repeated storm wave activity during this flooding resulted in sand that was unusually rich in pure quartz grains. These grains later became a tough, erosion-resistant quartzite upon burial by further sediment and cementation.

FIG 170. Diagrammatic cross-section across the top edge of Area 9 (located on Fig. 168).

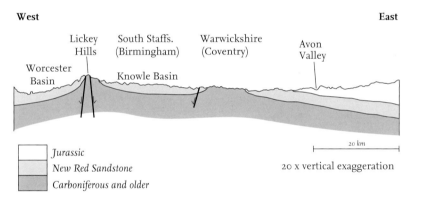

The easternmost (Warwickshire) part of this Landscape (**A2**) has not created distinctive present-day scenery, probably because rather weak Carboniferous mudstones dominate the near-surface materials. Unlike Landscape **A1**, this area corresponds to a gentle downfold in the Carboniferous layers, although its subsequent movement history has tended to raise the central area of Carboniferous bedrock while lowering its margins, giving something of an upfolded appearance in Figure 170. This movement pattern has included the formation of a southeastern boundary where the earlier bedrock has been eroded and then covered by gently tilted Triassic and Jurassic bedrock. In contrast, the western boundary consists of the steep Warwick Fault (shown in Fig. 170).

Landscape B: New Red Sandstone bedrock

The two areas of Landscape **A** described above are surrounded by areas of New Red Sandstone, which constitute Landscape **B**. It is convenient to divide this Landscape geographically into **B1**, the Worcester Basin; **B2**, the Knowle Basin, and **B3**, the Avon Valley Basin.

The New Red Sandstone provides the red (iron oxide) pigment that colours many of the soils and cliffs of the West Midlands. Detailed mapping shows that it consists of a lower (earlier) division called the Sherwood Sandstone Group, made largely of sandstones but also containing coarser-grained conglomerates and breccias (with rounded and angular pebbles, respectively). This is overlain by an upper (later) division called the Mercia Mudstone Group, made up largely of mudstones. In older maps and reports these two divisions are often labelled as *Bunter* and *Keuper*, using the terminology first invented for the excellent outcrops of the New Red Sandstone in Germany.

The red (oxidised) colour of the New Red Sandstone, together with the absence of fossils that are typical of seawater deposits, suggests that it was originally deposited from fresh water, particularly in rivers on land. The lower Sandstone Group appears to be largely Triassic in age but may contain some Permian material. The coarse grain size of these deposits suggests they were deposited by relatively fast-flowing, vigorous rivers. The upper Mudstone Group is entirely Triassic in age, and its relatively fine grain size suggests that it formed on the floodplains of more gentle rivers, although distinct sandstone horizons (often referred to as Arden Sandstone) may mark episodes of more vigorous flow. The minerals gypsum and rock salt occur in distinct layers in the Mudstone Group and have been extracted commercially in some localities. These sulphate and chloride minerals formed by precipitation from the waters of saline lakes or coastal lagoons and reflect arid climatic conditions, rather like those of the present-day Dead Sea.

From the present landscape point of view, the coarser deposits of the Sherwood Sandstone Group have locally resulted in hills and slopes. In contrast, the Mercia Mudstone Group tends to have been eroded to form lower ground, except where more resistant sandstone layers (the Arden Sandstone) have produced small scarps.

The New Red Sandstone sediments of the Worcester Basin (**B1**) have been gently moved into a downfold, with the younger Mudstone Group bedrock preserved in its centre below Worcester and Droitwich. The older Sandstone Group forms the flanks of this downfold, closer to the older bedrock of Carboniferous age (**A1**). The scenery locally reflects this change in bedrock type:

in the east a number of northwest–southeast ridges reflect landscape erosion of distinct sandstone layers, sometimes further picked out by the presence of northwest–southeast trending faults. In the centre, slopes cut into the mudstone are small, largely reflecting episodes in valley erosion by relatively small tributaries of the River Severn. In the Kidderminster area, valley slopes have been cut by the River Severn and its major east-bank tributary, the Stour. These have cut into the sandstones, and local variations in sandstone erosional behaviour and in-valley down-cutting histories have resulted in distinct sandstone ridges.

In the Knowle Basin (**B2**), the upper (younger) Mercia Mudstone is the bedrock nearest to the surface, so the only slope features tend to be small and due either to Arden Sandstone layers or to features of the surface blanket.

The Avon Valley Basin (**B3**) extends from Warwick via Leamington Spa towards Rugby. There is a layer (up to 50 m thick) of Sherwood Sandstone along its northwestern edge, resting on the Carboniferous area of **A2**. Apart from that, the local bedrock is the Mercia Mudstone Group and the scenery is dominated by a surface blanket of ice-laid and river deposits that are discussed below.

Landscape C: Jurassic bedrock
Younger than the New Red Sandstone bedrock – and above it in the succession – are distinctive layers of Jurassic age found extensively in the southeastern parts of this Area and beyond. This reflects a widespread change of environment, from the deposition of New Red Sandstone in lakes and rivers during the Triassic to deposition in shallow seas during the Jurassic. In the seas, subtle changes in environment may produce widespread and distinctive changes in the resulting bedrock. Because of this, the Jurassic succession contains many distinct marker layers, and can be divided up and traced like a layer-cake much more readily than the New Red Sandstone. There are five marker layers that have been resistant enough to produce distinct erosional topography in Area 9 (see Fig. 151 for their place in the bedrock succession).

(1) The Rhaetic (labelled R on Figs 151 and 168)
Although most of the Early Jurassic rocks (historically known as the Lias) consist of soft mudstones that have not generally produced features in the scenery, they are underlain by a group of distinctive beds that, together, have produced steep slopes where the landscape has been carved out by erosion. We use the label *Rhaetic*, borrowed from central European geological usage, to refer to this layer (also called the Penarth Group). This group of beds is now regarded as partly latest Triassic and partly earliest Jurassic in age. It contains at least one surface representing a relatively short time gap in the deposition and includes

mudstones, limestones and fossil beds, up to and including material called the Blue Lias. These beds represent the arrival of coastal and lagoonal conditions after a long period of New Red Sandstone river and lake sedimentation. There are numerous small scarps, particularly in the lowlands of the Avon valley around Evesham and Leamington Spa, which mark the resistance to erosion of this Rhaetic material.

(2) The Marlstone Rock Bed (labelled M on Figs 151 and 168)
In the middle part of the Early Jurassic succession, the Marlstone Rock Bed tends to form distinct slopes because it contains limestones and iron-rich materials, making it a valuable resource that has been extensively quarried. At Edge Hill (**c3**; see also Fig. 173) the Rock Bed caps a 100 m escarpment, straddling the A422 between Stratford-upon-Avon and Banbury, some 5 km southwest of the

FIG 171. Radway Village and the gently undulating flatlands of the battlefield below the Edge Hill scarp (covered with trees at the right of the photograph) (Fig. 168, **c3**). (Copyright Dae Sasitorn & Adrian Warren/www.lastrefuge.co.uk)

M40 motorway. This escarpment results from the resistance to local river erosion of the Marlstone Rock Bed, but is more famous as the setting for the Battle of Edge Hill (Fig. 171). The area below the scarp of Edge Hill is still often called the Vale of the Red Horse, although the carvings that once gave it this name are no longer visible. The Vale gained fame because the colour of its rocks was so spectacular, due to the red iron oxide of the Marlstone Rock Bed.

We allow ourselves to be diverted here to outline the way the Battle of Edge Hill was influenced by this feature of the landscape. The battle, the first large engagement of the English Civil Wars, took place on 23 October 1642. King Charles I was the commander of the Royalist army and the Parliamentarians were commanded by Robert Devereux, Earl of Essex. The troops and the field commanders on both sides were generally inexperienced and unsure, and there was no clear winner in the battle. The king decided that the strategic advantage offered by the Edge Hill scarp was such that he chose to position his army of some 15,000 infantry and cavalry there. Because of the steepness of the upper slopes, the Royalists moved some of their cavalry to the toe of the escarpment before making their charge down onto the similar-sized Parliamentarian army, which had been drawn up on the ground below (now occupied by a large Ministry of Defence munitions depot!). In spite of this move, the charge by the Royalist cavalry was so vigorous that it not only scattered the Parliamentarian cavalry, but overran the infantry lines in its pursuit and became disorganised. Some 3,000 men, including some influential figures of the time, were killed or wounded in the chaos that followed, but the armies then disengaged and regrouped. Over the next days and weeks, the Royalists established themselves in Oxford, while the Parliamentarians consolidated their hold on the London area.

(3) The Northampton Sand (labelled N on Figs 151 and 168)
In the northeast of Area 9, the Northampton Sand at the base of the Middle Jurassic is important not only as a hard material that resisted erosion during the creation of the present landscape, but also because it has been quarried widely as an economically important source of iron.

(4) The Middle Jurassic oolitic limestones (labelled O on Figs 151 and 168)
The Middle Jurassic of this Area was one of the earliest successions anywhere in the world to be analysed in detail and traced from place to place. This pioneering work was carried out by William Smith, as described in the treatment of Area 8. He divided this limestone-dominated, fossil-rich part of the Jurassic succession into two major subdivisions, the Inferior Oolite (lower and older) and the Great Oolite (higher and younger), and was able to trace and map them over many tens

FIG 172. The Lygon Arms Hotel in the village of Broadway (Fig. 168, **c5**), 8 km southeast of Evesham. The hotel is typical of many traditional Cotswolds buildings and is made using Middle Jurassic oolitic limestones. (Copyright Peter Oliver, Herefordshire and Worcestershire Heritage Trust)

of kilometres, although the two divisions together are normally no more than 100 m thick. Although these Middle Jurassic sediments also include mudstones, sandstones and ironstones, a wide variety of limestones is present which dominate the local landscapes, forming the Cotswold Hills, one of the main scenic features of Southern England. Most of these layers of sediment were deposited in the shallow tropical seas that covered Southern England during the Middle Jurassic. The variation in the sediment layers reflects changes in the environments of sedimentation, including periodic invasions of muddy material brought in by rivers. Much of the limestone is honey-coloured, and its wide use as a building stone is one of the most attractive features of the villages and towns of the Cotswolds (Fig. 172).

Ebrington Hill (c2), 5 km northeast of Chipping Camden, is the northernmost point on the well-defined section of the Cotswold Edge, where the scarp is capped by Middle Jurassic oolites. This hill reaches an elevation of 259 m and looks out over the floor of the Avon Valley some 200 m below. The lower slopes are formed in the Marlstone Rock Bed (marked **M** in Fig. 168), while the top is made of the resistant limestones of the Oolite layer.

Bredon Hill (c1) dominates the low ground where the Rivers Severn and Avon meet. It has a similar structure of resistant layers to Ebrington Hill, though many of the steeper slopes have been covered by blocks of limestone that have collapsed from the edge of the outcrop and slipped down the slopes. The isolation of Bredon Hill from the main Cotswold Edge is due to vigorous back-cutting by the headwaters of eroding streams. These streams must have increasingly encircled and detached this prominent – but previously attached – point on the Edge.

The position and direction of trend of the Cotswold Hills, particularly the well-defined Cotswold Front, is a direct result of the level to which the landscape of the Area has been eroded at the moment. As erosion continues to lower the landscape the Front will move to the southeast, because that is the direction in which the layers slope.

The slope pattern of the Cotswold Hills (Fig. 168) reflects directly the distribution of these Jurassic marker layers. The well-defined Cotswold Edge that extends southwesterly from Ebrington Hill (c2) corresponds to the thickest development of the oolitic limestones, due to environmental conditions or gentle tilting by Earth movements in Jurassic times. Similarly, the replacement of the prominent Oolite scarp further to the northeast by a more widespread array of lesser scarps (due to the Marlstone Rock Bed, Northampton Sand and a thinner Oolite scarp) is an erosional response to changes in the layer pattern that reflect variations in Jurassic environments and movements (Fig. 173).

a) Edge Hill Profile

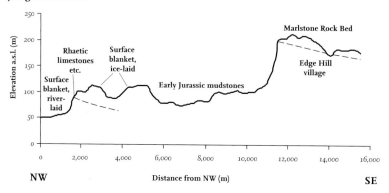

b) Fish Hill Profile

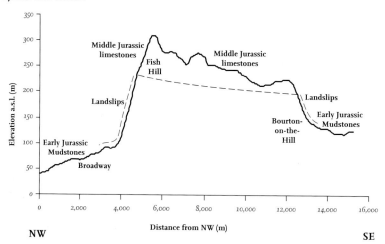

FIG 173. Comparison of topographic profiles across the northwestern edge of the Cotswold Hills, contrasting the northeastern, multi-scarp sector at Edge Hill (a) with the higher, single-scarp sector at Fish Hill (b). The sections are located on Figure 168.

(5) The Portlandian (labelled P on Figs 151 and 168)

The layers above the Oolites are of Late Jurassic age and generally consist of mudstones. Most of this younger Jurassic bedrock has not produced distinct topography on erosion, except in the southeast of the Area, east of Oxford, where limestones of latest Jurassic age ('Portlandian') cap some well-formed hills.

Landscape D: Early Cretaceous bedrock

The tops of some of the distinct hills in the southeast corner of Area 9 contain small areas with thin layers of Early Cretaceous material. This situation is discussed more fully in the treatment of Areas 10, 11 and 13; in Area 9 these are very small features of the landscape.

Younger drainage and erosion patterns

The discussion of this Area concludes with a review of the present drainage systems (Fig. 174) and their Tertiary and Quaternary evolution, because it is largely the rivers that have been responsible for the shape of the present landscape.

FIG 174. Main river pathways and coastal flooding zone of Area 9.

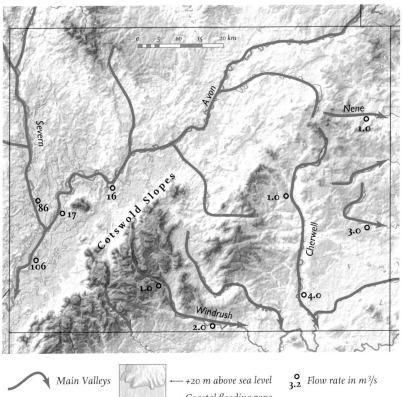

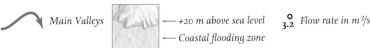

Main Valleys   ⟵ *+20 m above sea level* $\overset{\text{o}}{3.2}$ *Flow rate in m³/s*

⟵ *Coastal flooding zone*

The National River Flow Archive gives us insights into the present drainage pattern by providing estimates of mean flow rates (in m³/s) for the main rivers, together with figures for the upstream areas (in km²) being drained by the rivers in question. Here I have selected some of these flow data to demonstrate the present-day important role of the River Severn and its major tributary, the Avon. The very largest mean river flow rate is 106 m³/s at the downstream end of the Severn–Avon system. This station has a catchment area of 9,900 km², which reflects its drainage of large parts of central Wales and the Midlands. For comparison, the Thames at Kingston has a mean river flow rate of 66 m³/s from a catchment of very similar size (9,948 km²), reflecting lower general rainfall and different groundwater conditions. The gauging stations on the south and east side of the Cotswold drainage divide are the sources and upper reaches of the Nene, Great Ouse, Cherwell and Windrush, with catchment areas in Area 9 of no more than a few hundred square kilometres, and mean river flows of no more than 4 m³/s.

Drainage to the Severn Estuary
As described above, the Severn and Avon river systems have by far the largest catchments and river flows in Area 9. Where the River Severn flows into Area 9, it has generally incised a few tens of metres into a landscape underlain by New Red Sandstone. A distinct floodplain, typically half a kilometre in width, has been built by river sedimentation during the Holocene (postglacial) rise of sea level, but there are often small patches of river terraces at higher levels representing earlier floodplains. Along the rest of its downstream course across Area 9, the Severn continues to display similar features (Fig. 175). However, increases in the width of the young floodplain, the extent of ancient river terraces, and the size of meander bends all correspond to the steady increase in mean flow downstream as the catchment area and number of tributaries increase.

The River Avon is the largest tributary of the Severn, joining it near Tewkesbury after flowing parallel to the Cotswold drainage divide. The tributaries of the Avon that join it from the southeast have been the main agent in eroding the northwestern slopes of the Cotswolds (Fig. 174).
The River Avon itself is incised into landscapes made largely of impermeable mudstones of Triassic and Early Jurassic age (Fig. 176). Its young floodplain is locally more than 2 km across, and it has particularly well-developed large meanders (several kilometres in wavelength) in the reach just above and below Evesham. The meanders become smaller – though they are still well developed – in the reach upstream towards Stratford-on-Avon, as the mean flow becomes less. In the area between Coventry and Rugby, large areas of the valley slopes are occupied by surface-blanket deposits, particularly ice-laid materials and water-

FIG 175. The River Severn flows towards us past the cathedral in Worcester. The wide floodplain contains the cricket ground (to the left of the river) and the racecourse (to the right of the river), both flooded when the photograph was taken. (Copyright Dae Sasitorn & Adrian Warren/www.lastrefuge.co.uk)

FIG 176. Looking westwards over Warwick Castle and the River Avon, which flows to the left on its way to join the Severn near Tewkesbury. (Copyright Dae Sasitorn & Adrian Warren/ www.lastrefuge.co.uk)

laid muds, sands and gravels. The most important of these, from a landscape point of view, are the Dunsmore Gravels, which form a distinct plateau southeast of the Avon, between Stratford-upon-Avon and Leamington Spa. Here they provide a clear scarp to the river Leam, a southern tributary of the Avon. The age of these gravels is not clear, but they represent a major episode of river deposition that was probably linked to one of the Ice Age cold phases. Whether this was the Anglian cold episode, about 450,000 years ago (oxygen isotope stage 12), or one of the later cold episodes is still uncertain.

The important development of surface-blanket sediment in this Area provides an excellent example of how difficult it can be to separate and distinguish events in the history of the Ice Age. Wolston Quarry (c4), between Coventry and Rugby, has given its name to the *Wolstonian*, which was claimed to be a distinct episode of ice advance and retreat later than the Anglian but before the Devensian (see Chapter 2, Fig. 13). Recent detailed interpretation of the Wolstonian surface-blanket succession recognises an early phase of near-ice-sheet river sediments, followed by ice-laid deposits and then the deposits of a lake that was probably ice-dammed and extensive enough to be given a local name: Lake Harrison. These deposits are followed by further ice-laid sediments,

FIG 177. Former rivers of Area 9.

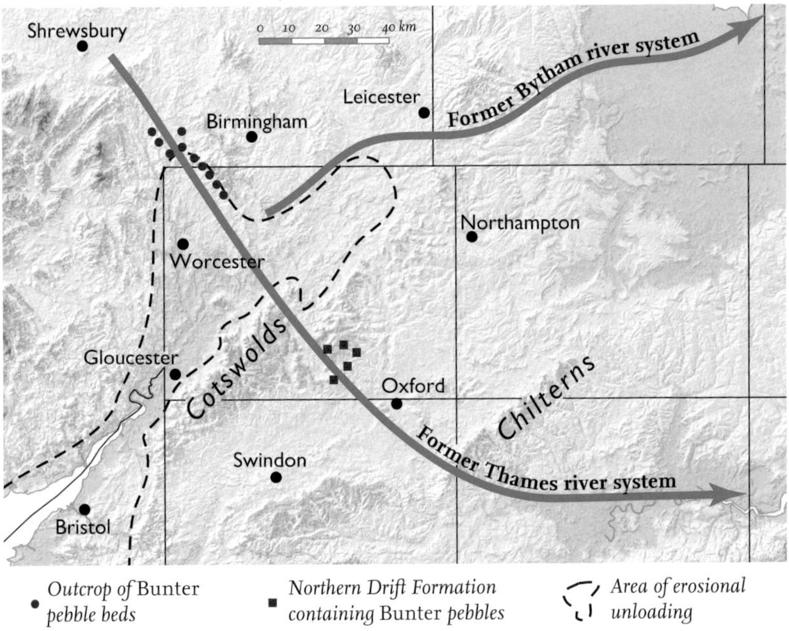

Outcrop of Bunter pebble beds

Northern Drift Formation containing Bunter pebbles

Area of erosional unloading

and finally by the river-laid deposits referred to above as the Dunsmore Gravels. Although a vivid story of environmental change has emerged from this locality, it is still not clear which of the Ice Age cold episodes is represented.

Some of the early surface-blanket, water-laid deposits of the Avon valley have been interpreted as the deposits of a now extinct river that has been called the Bytham (Castle Bytham is 10 km north of Stamford in Area 15). In Area 9, this river has been reconstructed as flowing northeastwards, roughly parallel to the present Avon, before turning eastwards near Leicester (Fig. 177). It is then supposed to have continued to flow eastwards across the present Fens before turning southwards. Along with the ancestral Thames, the River Bytham is thought to have been drastically re-routed by the arrival of the major ice sheet of the Anglian cold episode, about 450,000 years ago.

Other recent work on the landscape history of this catchment is based partly on the recognition that pebbles in old surface-blanket gravels near Oxford have been derived from New Red Sandstone outcrops to the northwest of the River Severn, and could not have been carried by rivers over the present Cotswold Hills drainage divide. Indeed, the gravels lack pebbles of material that would prove that the Cotswolds were available for erosion at that time. The suggestion is that very active erosion of the weak mudstones of the younger New Red Sandstone and Early Jurassic caused the lower River Severn to cut backwards and northwards up the Bristol Channel. This erosion was focused along the valley of the Bristol Channel, decreasing the load on the local crust and causing deep movements in the 'solid' Earth that produced regional-scale uplift (Fig. 178).

This remarkable effect has already been commented on in Chapter 3. It is now realised that loading (for example, by the arrival of an ice sheet) or unloading (for example, by erosion) of the Earth's surface can cause Earth movements that result in the surface moving upwards or downwards, like the response of a wooden boat floating in a bath. The 'floating' in this geological situation is of the upper, relatively light layers of the crust floating on deeper, denser material in the Earth. This sort of raising or lowering of the Earth's crust can happen over timescales that mean northwest England and western Scotland are still rising today, some 20,000 years after the thickest ice sheets there started to melt.

Theoretical models suggest that the margins of the Severn–Avon valley (the Welsh Borders to the northwest and the Cotswolds to the southeast) might be expected to have risen approximately 50 m due to the erosional unloading of the Severn–Avon river system. This raising of the Cotswolds could have caused the diversion of the upper former Thames to become the Welsh headwaters of the Severn, leaving the middle section of the former Thames to become the new headwaters, draining only the southeasterly flanks of the Cotswolds.

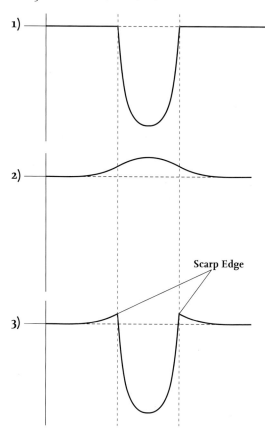

FIG 178. After valley erosion (1), the unloading of the crust resulted in deep movements within the 'solid' Earth that generated a bulge of movement near the surface of the crust (2). The two effects combined (3) produced scarp edges that may have contributed to the height of the Cotswold and Welsh Border hills.

Drainage towards the Wash on the east coast

In the northeast of Area 9, some 20 km of the headwaters of the River Nene flow eastwards from a drainage divide near Watford Gap towards Northampton in Area 13. In this westernmost part of the catchment, the Nene and its small tributaries are very gently incised – at most a few tens of metres – and the most clearly defined hills are capped by Northampton Sandstone. The area of the drainage divide is marked by flat hill tops covered with ice-laid deposits, often associated with river sediments thought to have been deposited by rivers flowing from the ice sheets. These ancient river deposits are very much concentrated along the Nene Valley, where a buried channel has been identified, demonstrating the early existence of an ancestral Nene. As in the case of the Avon Valley discussed above, the ice sheet involved may have been the Anglian, but there is some uncertainty about this. Whichever cold episode was responsible, most of the present gentle landscape topography has been created by river erosion since the ice melted.

The headwaters of the Great Ouse flow eastwards from near Brackley to Buckingham, on the edge of Area 9, and then further on towards the northern edge of Milton Keynes. This part of the catchment lacks important scarps and slopes, though it has cut gently into the Middle Jurassic Oolite. There is a surface layer of ice-laid material over much of the higher ground here, and this may have discouraged more widespread down-cutting. The River Tove, a tributary from the west and north, has cut into the Early Jurassic mudstones, but steep slopes are again not a feature. Upstream from Buckingham, well-marked meanders are a striking feature of the river scenery, though with a small wavelength to match the low average flow rates. As with the Nene, it is still uncertain which cold episode of the Ice Age resulted in the deposition of the ice-laid material, but it appears likely that the valley and hill pattern has been eroded since the ice sheet melted. River terrace deposits in the immediate Buckingham area and in the Tove tributary suggest considerable variability in the river evolution histories.

Drainage towards the Thames and the southeast coast
These tributaries drain generally southwards down the slope of the tilted bedrock layers. The headwaters of the western tributaries have cut downwards into the Early Jurassic mudstones and then, in the downstream direction, cut across the more resistant Middle Jurassic Oolite layer before flowing over the Late Jurassic mudstones. These produce distinctive valley wall slopes in the Windrush (Oxford–Cheltenham road), Evenlode (Oxford–Worcester railway) and Cherwell valleys, where the Great Oolite layer particularly tends to cap the valley wall slopes. These rivers all have low mean flow figures and minor floodplains with young alluvium, but no significant areas of ancient river terraces. Ice-laid material is present in small patches left on some of the high ground during later landscape erosion.

East of the Cherwell, the low ground drained by the River Ray is mainly underlain by Late Jurassic mudstones (quarried for brick-making east of Bicester) and is generally very flat, particularly south of Bicester and the M40 motorway. Here, Ot Moor is a remarkable local area of Fen-like appearance where faulting has brought a strip of Middle Jurassic Oolite material to the surface, and the topography and drainage reflect this. Southeast of Bicester, river erosion has picked out a number of discrete hills with caps of Portlandian (latest Jurassic) limestones and Early Cretaceous material. Between these hills and Bicester itself are two dome-like hills which have been much quarried, but lack resistant caps. These may be relics of features formed when the resistant Portlandian extended as far to the northwest as this.

CHAPTER 7

London and the
Thames Valley Region

GENERAL INTRODUCTION

THE LONDON AND THAMES VALLEY REGION includes the western
watershed between the Severn and Thames valleys in Gloucestershire
and Wiltshire, one of the main drainage divides in Southern
England. It also extends eastwards, through Oxfordshire, Berkshire and
Buckinghamshire to London, Essex, Kent and the sea. Travelling from west to
east, I have divided it into Areas 10, 11 and 12 (Figs 179 and 180).

I shall start by examining the bedrock geology, and how it relates to the
general river-valley and hill pattern of the Region (Fig. 181).

The central feature of this Region is the London Basin, bounded to the north
and south by hills of Late Cretaceous Chalk. The folding of the Chalk has formed
the London Basin downfold to the north and the Weald uplift to the south (Fig.
182). This is a classic example of how gentle folding of the bedrock can influence
landscapes and topography on a Regional scale.

Earlier chapters, particularly Chapters 5 and 6, have shown how important
the Variscan mountain building has been in the landscape evolution of Southern
England. This mountain-building episode culminated about 300 million years
ago and was followed by New Red Sandstone sedimentation during the Permian
and Triassic. Southern England then entered a period of relative stability,
although gentle regional tilting did occur, along with important variations in
sediment accumulation and minor faulting of the crust.

One important effect of the faulting has been to produce differences in the
bedrock successions to the north and south of the London Basin in layers of

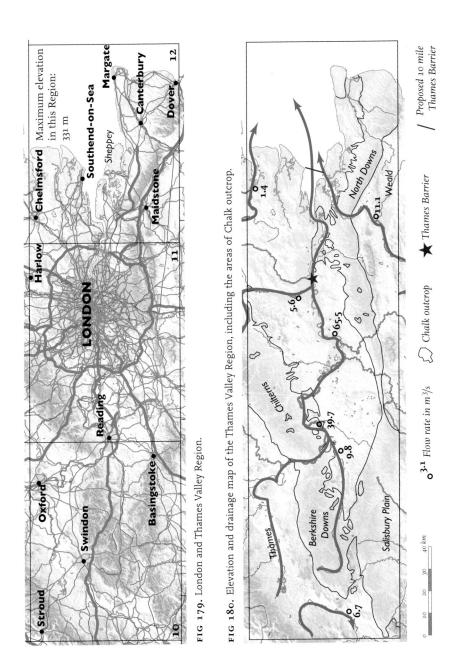

Maximum elevation in this Region: 331 m

FIG 179. London and Thames Valley Region.

FIG 180. Elevation and drainage map of the Thames Valley Region, including the areas of Chalk outcrop.

○ 3·1 Flow rate in m³/s

⟋⟍ Chalk outcrop

★ Thames Barrier

╱ Proposed 10 mile Thames Barrier

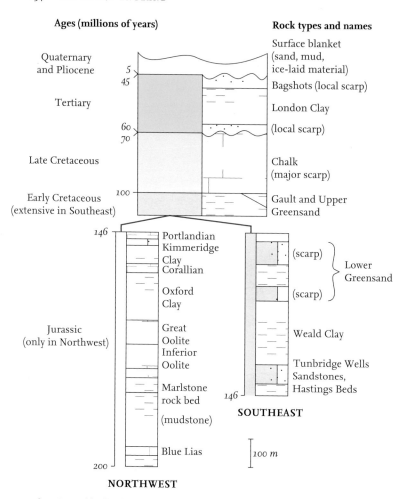

Ages (millions of years)

Quaternary
and Pliocene

Tertiary

Late Cretaceous

Early Cretaceous
(extensive in Southeast)

Jurassic
(only in Northwest)

Rock types and names

Surface blanket
(sand, mud,
ice-laid material)

Bagshots (local scarp)

London Clay

(local scarp)

Chalk
(major scarp)

Gault and Upper
Greensand

Portlandian
Kimmeridge
Clay
Corallian

Oxford
Clay

Great
Oolite
Inferior
Oolite

Marlstone
rock bed

(mudstone)

Blue Lias

(scarp)

(scarp)

Lower
Greensand

Weald Clay

Tunbridge Wells
Sandstones,
Hastings Beds

SOUTHEAST

NORTHWEST

FIG 181. General bedrock succession for the Thames Valley Region.

sediment of Early Cretaceous age or older. Most of this faulting was normal (see Chapter 3, Fig. 33), caused by stretching of the crust that fractured it into discrete blocks, some rising and some subsiding. The stretching was a local response to larger movements of western Europe, linked to the opening of the Atlantic Ocean to the west and the sinking of the North Sea area to the east. In the Thames Valley area, the result of this new pattern was that a relatively stable London crustal block (often called a *platform*) became separated by fracturing

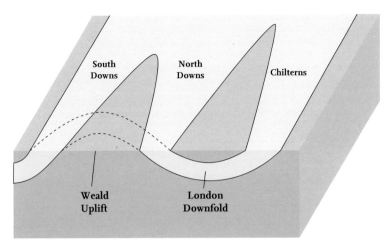

FIG 182. Block diagram, looking westwards, to show how the Chalk outcrop pattern at the surface results from erosion of the fold pattern in the bedrock.

from a subsiding Wessex Basin to the south (Figs 183 and 184). The Wessex Basin is now represented near the surface by the thick succession of Early Cretaceous bedrock in the Weald area to the south of the North Downs.

Later, in the Early Cretaceous, sea level rose substantially, flooding the previously river-dominated Wessex Basin and depositing the shallow marine sands of the Lower Greensand, which are often seen to infill ancient river valleys cut earlier into the Wealden bedrock. Later still, by the mid Cretaceous, the deeper marine Gault Clay and Upper Greensand were deposited (Fig. 181). By the Late Cretaceous, rising sea levels progressively inundated most of northwest Europe. The Thames Valley Region was submerged beneath a sea several hundred metres deep, and pure white chalk was deposited over much of Southern England.

During Early Tertiary times, the whole of Southern England was subjected to crustal convergence, causing further movements along faults and local folding of the bedrock. This occurred at roughly the same time as the major convergence that caused the tectonic-plate-related mountain building of the Alps and Pyrenees to the south. Some old faults relating to the lowering of the Wessex Basin relative to the London area were reactivated, but this time in the opposite direction: the Wessex Basin was uplifted and the London Platform subsided. The uplifted Wessex Basin was further compressed to form the Weald uplift or anticline, while in the London region a broad, eastward-opening downfold

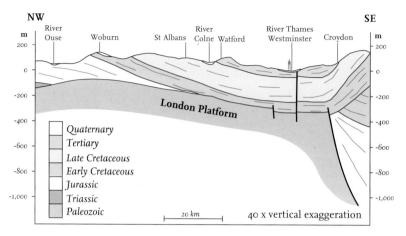

FIG 183. Bedrock cross-section through the London area, showing the bedrock structure.

(syncline) developed, creating the impressive arcuate bedrock pattern that is clearly picked out by the Chalk today (Figs 180 and 182).

As the formation of the London Basin progressed, its northern and southern edges became elevated, while its central portion was depressed, creating a shallow hollow some 80 km wide and about 500 m deep. River networks developed and began to erode the higher ground, transporting sediments inwards towards the centre of the basin. This erosion quickly picked out the strong layer of Chalk in the bedrock succession and produced the distinctive Chalk hills that mark the edges of the London Basin today.

Later in the Tertiary, sea level was rising once more, flooding the newly formed basin as far as Newbury and depositing a thick sequence of marine muds (particularly the London Clay) over a wide area. The London Clay is one of the best-known and most extensive Tertiary deposits in England, forming the bedrock beneath most of Greater London. The properties of the London Clay make it an excellent rock for excavation and tunnelling, and in 1863 the world's first underground railway was opened. Today the London Clay beneath London is riddled with tunnels, and the Underground has become a huge enterprise, used by some 3 million passengers, on average, each day.

Overlying the London Clay are the pale yellow sands of the Bagshot Formation, deposited in a shallow marine or estuarine environment as the sea retreated from the Region once again. The main outcrops are found on Bagshot Heath, an area of elevated ground around Camberley.

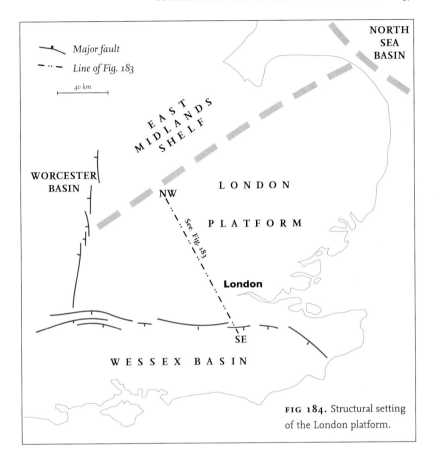

FIG 184. Structural setting of the London platform.

The most recent deposits in this Region are the extensive Quaternary terrace deposits of the modern-day Thames, predominantly sands and gravels that have been extensively quarried. In the north of the Region there are also deposits (*till*) left behind by the Anglian ice sheet 450,000 years ago.

The evolution of the London Basin downfold and the Weald uplift (see also Chapter 2, Fig. 10) can be summarised as follows:

A. Prior to about 60 million years ago, the Thames Valley Region was covered by the sea, allowing Chalk and Earliest Tertiary sediments to accumulate in approximately horizontal layers. By about 60 million years ago, sea level had dropped and/or the Region had been uplifted to expose dry land.

B. Between 60 and 45 million years ago, crustal compression began to move the bedrock units to create the London Basin downfold and the Weald uplift.

The London Basin subsided along an approximately east–west trending axis and the rocks to the north and south of this axis were tilted gently inwards by about 1 degree. The sea flooded the newly created basin from the east and sediments began to accumulate.

C. Continuing compression between 45 and 40 million years ago gradually increased the tilts of the rocks forming the fold limbs. Erosion of the uplifted ground to the north and south of the London Basin exposed the Chalk that now forms the Chilterns and North Downs respectively. Between about 40 million years ago and the present day, river networks became established on the high ground and the sea repeatedly advanced into and retreated from the London Basin. Erosion continued and intensified, lowering the landscape generally and causing the Chalk scarps to retreat inwards towards the centre of the basin.

D. Today, the landscape has been eroded to expose Early Cretaceous sediments in the core of the Weald uplift, bounded to the north and south by the Chalk scarps of the North and South Downs. Tertiary sediments are preserved within the London Basin, while to the north, at its northern margin, another Chalk scarp marks the Chiltern Hills.

Modification under Ice Age conditions

The Thames Valley Region was only rarely invaded by ice sheets during the Quaternary. The most widespread invasion of the past few million years occurred during the Anglian cold phase 450,000 years ago, when ice reached the London Basin and diverted the course of the ancestral River Thames. The more local effects of the Anglian glaciation on the London Basin are discussed further in the Area accounts.

Although most of the Region has not been covered by ice sheets, it has still been severely affected by the periglacial (near-glacial) climate. For most of the time the land was treeless tundra, with a permanently frozen subsurface layer of soil and bedrock. At the surface, soil and bedrock were frozen in winter but thawed every summer, an effect which, combined with the snow-fed spring meltwater, created fast-flowing and highly erosive rivers. The 'dry valleys' of the Chalk were carved at this time: chalk is naturally porous because it is highly fractured, but the frozen subsurface blocked the fractures and prevented water from draining away through the chalk as it did during warmer times. Instead the water flowed across the surface, carving valleys that are visible today.

Other cold-climate effects on the scenery were land-slumping and land-slipping, accelerated by freeze–thaw cycles. These created characteristic indents in hill ranges (see Areas 10 and 12) and concentrated Sarsen Stones in valley floors (see Area 10). Glacial processes also modified the earlier, river-created landscape, for example in south Essex in Area 12.

The River Thames was severely affected by the Ice Ages. Before the great Anglian glaciation the Thames entered the London basin from the west approximately where it does now, but then flowed northeastwards along the Vale of St Albans, some 30 km north of its present course. It then turned northwards in the Chelmsford area and flowed across north Essex and Suffolk, eventually joining the Rhine somewhere in the area now covered by the southernmost North Sea (see Area 11). Just under half a million years ago, the advance of the Anglian ice from the north extended across the course of this ancestral Thames, locally damming the river and deflecting it progressively southwards to finally take up its present path. The hill ridges of south Essex, the Valley of Romford and the estuaries of the Blackwater and Crouch are all likely to have been shaped during episodes when the Thames or its immediate tributaries flowed in that direction.

Coastlines and sea-level rise

The coastline of the Thames Valley area is one of the youngest features of the landscape, since it has been profoundly affected by the dramatic rise in sea level over the last 10,000 years. At the end of the most recent cold phase of the Ice Age, the River Thames and its tributaries flooded seasonally over wide, braided floodplains. The rise in sea level flooded the Channel, turning the lower river valleys of the Thames and its tributaries into tidal estuaries. The sea level did not rise continuously, however, and small drops in sea level are marked by layers of peat in the sediment. The peat layers are the remains of plants which colonised the exposed mud flats when sea level dropped, only to be buried by silt and clay when the sea level resumed its rise once more. The last peat layer dates from the third or fourth century AD, when sea-level rise destroyed several Roman forts built on the coast.

Away from the estuaries, most of the coastline consists of large expanses of mud flats and salt marshes, although much of the original marsh has been drained for agriculture. The coast between Southend-on-Sea and Dengie (30 km to the northeast) is typical: salt marsh is separated from intertidal mud flats by chenier ridges. These are raised ridges almost totally composed of seashells, which can be up to 3 m high and 25 m wide. They mark the transition between land and shore, since they are formed when shells are thrown up onto the salt marshes by storm-whipped waves. The ridges are moving landward at up to 8 mm a year due to continuing sea-level rise in this area.

Sea-level rise poses an important problem for the London area. Due to a combination of subsidence and global sea-level rise (estimated at ~1–2 mm a year since 1900), levels are rising in the Thames estuary by about 60 cm a century, relative to the land.

After the 1953 flood of the east coast and Thames Estuary, when some 300 people were killed, it was decided to build the Thames Barrier (Fig. 185). This is situated at Woolwich and has six moveable gates which can be raised in minutes if needed. It was built between 1972 and 1984, and was designed to be effective until at least 2030. Many longer-term solutions to protect London are also being considered. One recent proposal is for a 16 km ("ten-mile") barrier from Sheerness in Kent to Southend in Essex, in order to protect a much more extensive section of the Thames Estuary (Fig. 180).

FIG 185. The Thames Barrier. (Copyright Dae Sasitorn & Adrian Warren/www.lastrefuge.co.uk)

AREA 10: THE COTSWOLDS TO READING

Area 10 straddles the main topographic and drainage divide of Southern England (Figs 186 and 187). About half of it is part of the Thames catchment and drains eastwards, via London, to the North Sea, while its western areas form parts of the Bristol Avon and Severn catchments, which drain into the Bristol Channel, and its southern part (Salisbury Plain) drains southwards towards the South Coast (Fig. 188).

The Area can be divided into four Landscapes based upon the presence of particular bedrocks immediately below the surface blanket (Figs 189 and 190). The large-scale features of the bedrock pattern, as shown by the locations of the Chalk hills, have already been explained in the general introduction to this Region. The more detailed pattern has been created largely by river erosion, which has modified the gently sloping limbs of the London Downfold and transported material to the east. In particular, the locations of the Chalk Edges are entirely due to the interaction of earth movements and landscape erosion over the past 60 million years, influenced especially by climate change.

FIG 186. Location map for Area 10.

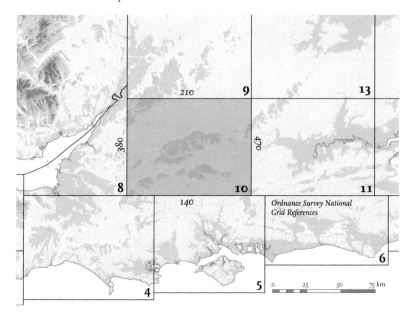

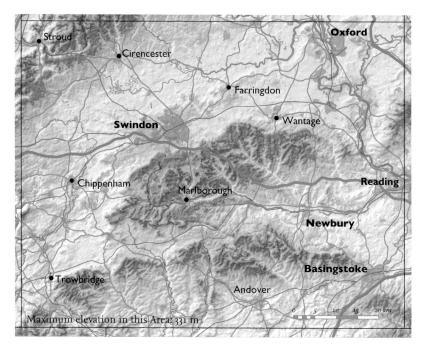

FIG 187. Natural and man-made features of Area 10.

The bedrock of Area 10 ranges from Jurassic to Early Tertiary in age (Fig. 189), and the distinctive patterns of hills and valleys in each of the four Landscapes correspond directly to the different bedrocks that underlie them. Each Landscape is considered in turn below.

Landscape A: The Cotswold Hills of Middle Jurassic limestone

The upper Thames and Avon valleys are bordered in the northwest by the Cotswold Hills, which trend roughly northeast from Bath (see Area 8), across the corner of Area 10 towards Northamptonshire (see Area 9). The Cotswolds are formed of Middle Jurassic layers, often oolitic and shelly limestones with an average thickness of about 100 m. They dip very gently southeast, forming a series of rolling plateaus or 'wolds' dissected by narrow, wooded valleys. To the southeast the valleys widen and the landscape becomes gentler as the limestone layers slope very gently beneath the clays of Landscape **B**. In Area 10, Stroud and Cirencester are the main Cotswolds towns, and they were important centres of the wool industry during the Middle Ages. The fine, honey-coloured Cotswold

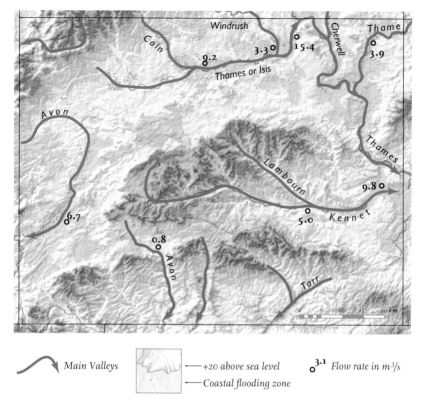

Main Valleys

+20 above sea level

Coastal flooding zone

$o^{3.1}$ Flow rate in m³/s

FIG 188. Main river pathways and flow rates for Area 10.

Stone houses can still be seen in town centres today, along with fine 'wool churches', built in the late Middle Ages when the economy of the region was very strong.

Around Stroud it is remarkable how much of the highly sloping landscape of the Cotswold Edge appears to conceal large masses of limestone that have become displaced and moved down-slope, under gravity, as the slopes have been evolving by erosion. The most vigorous of these collapse movements are likely to have taken place during the Ice Age under periglacial conditions, when freeze–thaw processes were most active.

Landscape B: The Mudstone Lowlands of Late Jurassic to Early Cretaceous bedrock

The Wiltshire and Oxfordshire Clay Vales form much of the northernmost part of Area 10, extending roughly from Trowbridge, via Cirencester (**b1**), to Oxford

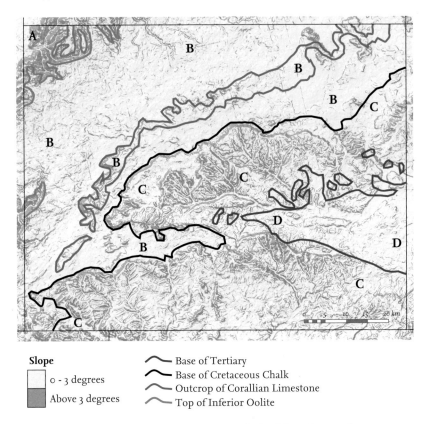

Slope

☐ 0 - 3 degrees

▨ Above 3 degrees

⌒ Base of Tertiary
⌒ Base of Cretaceous Chalk
⌒ Outcrop of Corallian Limestone
⌒ Top of Inferior Oolite

FIG 189. Slope map of Area 10, showing important bedrock boundaries and Landscapes **A** to **D**.

(**b3**) along the path of the Thames. The Vales consist of a broad belt of open, relatively low-lying, gently undulating farmland underlain by blue-grey Oxford and Kimmeridge Clays of Late Jurassic age They are part of a larger belt of clay-dominated lowlands that link eastwards with the Cambridgeshire Late Jurassic–Early Cretaceous Greensand–Gault belt (Landscape **B** of Area 13). The clays of the Vales weather into heavy, wet, slightly calcareous soils which support wide expanses of hedge-lined pasture.

The centre of the Oxfordshire Clay Vale is dominated by the valley of the River Thames, flanked by Quaternary gravel deposits derived from the Cotswolds. The largest towns tend to have grown on these free-draining gravels. The surrounding floodplain consists of Jurassic clay mantled by a

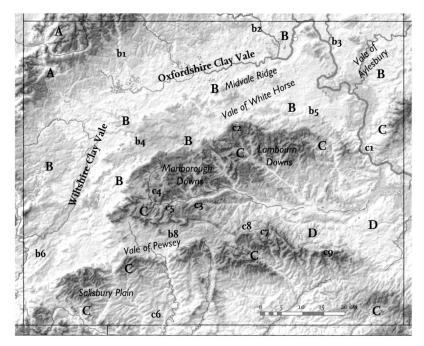

FIG 190. Landscapes, Downs, Vales and localities (**b1, b2** etc.) of Area 10.

substantial layer of more recent river sediments, providing excellent arable farmland. Over the past few hundred years farmers have planted hedges and pollarded willows to divide the area into a very distinctive patchwork pattern of fields, thought to have inspired Lewis Carroll's 'chessboard' landscape in *Through the Looking-Glass*.

As well as offering ideal ground for building, the Quaternary gravel deposits have also been exploited as a ready source of aggregate for road building and the construction industry. In the regions south of Cirencester (**b1**), southeast of Whitney (**b2**) and north of Oxford (**b3**), active gravel workings and flooded former gravel pits have become locally extensive features of the landscape. These gravel pits are clearly visible on the maps, particularly south of Cirencester, where an area some 7 km across has been designated as the Cotswold Water Park. Many of these areas of man-made lakes are now being managed as nature reserves, or have been turned into lakeside housing developments.

The character of the River Thames has changed dramatically over the last 2.6 million years of Quaternary time. Like all rivers that are only constrained by resistant bedrock in a few localities, it has changed its course many times, switching back and forth across a floodplain that is also continually changing. By studying the record of these changes preserved in the Thames terrace gravels, geologists have been able to reconstruct the later drainage history and climate of the Quaternary for much of Southern England. The evidence shows that the Thames was a much greater river at times in the past than it is today. There are also indications that, prior to the uplift of the Cotswolds, its headwaters may once have drained wider areas of the West Midlands and even north Wales (see Chapter 6). During cold episodes of the Ice Age, when sea level was much lower than it is today, the river also extended eastwards over what is now the floor of the North Sea, following the axis of the London downfold to join the Rhine, before flowing southwards and westwards along the valley of what is now the English Channel (see Chapter 2).

At least nine distinct gravel terraces, each at a different height above sea level, have been identified in the Thames Valley generally (see Area 11), and attempts have been made to link these terraces to the climate record inferred from oxygen isotope data (see Chapter 2, Fig. 13). The dating of individual terraces remains controversial, but a recurrent cycle of climate change and terrace formation is generally assumed, consisting of alternating cold and warm episodes:

Cold episodes: High river flow rates, at least during spring melts, lead to down-river transport of coarse gravel sediment and channels with high erosive power. The river is able to build up gravel on its floodplain or cut downwards into its floodplain, depending on elevation, which is determined by the sea level at the time.

Warm episodes: Lower flow rates and less powerful rivers, associated with temperate climates, deposit finer-grade sediments. A relative rise in sea level, due to the warming climate and melting of ice sheets, results in flooding of the lower parts of river valleys and the deposition of estuarine and marine sediments. The lower reaches of the river become clogged up with silt. As the next cold phase begins, there is an increase in river discharge and erosion, and the river begins to cut down into its floodplain.

In addition to the vertical movements of the river and floodplain surface described above, the upper Thames has also switched its course back and forth across the Vale of Oxfordshire, constrained by the Cotswold Hills to the north and the Midvale Ridge to the south. The gravel terraces are therefore widespread, distributed horizontally as well as vertically, and their ages vary.

The River Thames now drains eastwards along the Oxfordshire Clay Vale before turning north and then south as it cuts through the Midvale Ridge at Oxford, entering the Vales of White Horse and Aylesbury. In this area, the patchy

FIG 191. The Goring Gap (Fig. 190, C1), looking north (upstream) along the Thames from near Pangbourne. (Copyright Dae Sasitorn & Adrian Warren/www.lastrefuge.co.uk)

nature of the oldest (and highest) Quaternary gravels has, in places, protected the underlying Oxford Clay from further erosion, resulting in a series of scattered tabular hillocks rising above the present-day floodplain. The Thames then cuts through the Chalk Downs at Goring Gap (C1; Fig. 191), which was probably initiated when a tributary of the middle section of the Thames cut through the northern Chalk rim and intercepted the drainage of the ancestral northern clay vales. It is generally believed that the Thames was constrained within the Goring Gap half a million years ago, when its course much further downstream in the St Albans area was deflected southwards to its present position by the arrival of the Anglian ice sheets.

In the west of Area 10, the Wiltshire Clay Vale occurs between the dip slope of the Cotswolds to the west and the Marlborough Downs to the east. To the south the Vale extends past Trowbridge and Frome (Area 8) to join with the clays of Blackmoor Vale and the Vale of Wardour, described in Area 4.

The Wiltshire Clay Vale is primarily underlain by the Late Jurassic Oxford Clay, which gives the area a subdued, undulating topography and heavy, wet soils. In the west, substantial outcrops of rather older sandy bedrock (called *Kellaways Sand*) produce rich, free-draining soils that are highly valued as arable farmland. The centre of the Vale is dominated by the wide, level floodplain of the Bristol Avon, which, despite modern agricultural development, still retains traces of an ancient pattern of flood meadows. Surface sediments include river deposits of fine-grained alluvium and terrace gravels. The eastern margin of the Vale is marked by a resistant band of Late Jurassic Corallian Limestone and Early Cretaceous Greensand – equivalent to the Midvale Ridge of Oxfordshire – which is backed by the Late Cretaceous Chalk scarp of the Marlborough Downs.

The market towns and villages of the area are particularly distinctive. A number of valuable building stones are available locally, from the warm, yellow Middle Jurassic Cotswold Stone in the northwest to the rough, brown Late Jurassic Corallian Rag from the east. Ancient towns such as Malmesbury, Chippenham, Melksham and Trowbridge, all of which became wealthy due to the thriving post-medieval wool trade, have made full use of these attractive stones, and their town centres are filled with beautiful historic buildings.

At Wootton Bassett (**b4**), south of the M4 motorway and just southwest of Swindon, the clays of the Wiltshire Clay Vale region have produced a geological phenomenon that is extremely rare in Britain – a series of mud-springs. The springs are situated in a small wood called Templar's Firs, and were first described as three domed 'blisters' some 10 m long by 5 m wide by 1 m high. The skin of the blisters was formed by matted vegetation and contained a core of liquid mud which oozed out of any fissure in the skin and into a nearby brook. The blisters have since been burst by inquisitive visitors, but the springs themselves remain. Surveys have shown that the vents contain liquid mud down to a depth of at least 6 m, and that the volume of the underlying mud chamber is much larger than originally anticipated: local farmers have stories of cattle drowning in the springs and, in 1990, in an attempt to block up the main spring for safety reasons, a local contractor dumped 100 tonnes of quarry rubble into the main vent. Within half an hour the stone had disappeared without a trace and the displaced mud spilled out over the surrounding countryside, blocking a nearby stream. The area has since been fenced off and warning signs posted.

The exact cause of the Wootton Bassett springs is controversial, but they appear to result from a combination of local bedrock structure and particular rock types. The springs emerge through the Late Jurassic Ampthill Clay Formation. Underlying this clay is a layer of permeable Corallian Limestone, which acts as an aquifer in which water migrates to the lowest part of a local downfold, where it escapes upwards when the water pressure is sufficient. When the water emerges at the surface it moves the surrounding muddy material upwards with it.

Further east, the Midvale Ridge forms a southern limit to the Oxfordshire Clay Vale. It can be traced from southwest to northeast, running from Chippenham, through Swindon and on towards Oxford. The ridge is formed mainly of sandy Corallian Limestone of early Late Jurassic age, although locally there are also patches of latest Late Jurassic Portlandian sandstones and limestones. These hills are in places capped by a layer of Early Cretaceous Lower Greensand, which has prevented the weathering and erosion of the limestone below, forming prominent sandy knolls. Broadly speaking, the ridge has a tabular profile and, in contrast to the surrounding clay vales, the soils are sandy, light and free-draining, home to scattered woodlands interspersed with sandy pastures.

The Midvale Ridge has a long history of human settlement, and there are a number of important Roman sites located on prominent areas of higher ground. More recently, the small villages and hamlets typical of this region have been built upon spurs and subsidiary low ridges, using locally occurring Corallian Limestone as the main construction material. The area is attractive and offers fine, commanding views over the clay vales to the north and south.

To the south of the Midvale Ridge is the Vale of White Horse. As with much of Area 10, the rocks here dip gently to the southeast, exposing Late Jurassic Kimmeridge Clays along the northern sides of the Vale, followed by Early Cretaceous Gault Clay a little to the south. These rock types produce typical low-lying clay-vale scenery, though this is punctuated in places by prominent-weathering outcrops of Portland limestone. The southern margin of the Vale, immediately north of the Chalk scarp of the Lambourn Downs, is underlain by Early Cretaceous Upper Greensand (mudstones and sandstones), which supports rich orchards in the vicinity of Harwell (**b5**).

The Vale of White Horse drains generally eastwards to join the Thames at Abingdon. Like that of the Thames, this floodplain offers fertile arable farmland and frequent gravel deposits, upon which many of the area's towns were first settled. Buildings in the Vales of the Upper Thames are often brick-built, reflecting the widespread use of local clay as a building material. This contrasts with the Wiltshire Vale to the west (see page 248), where local limestones were extensively used as building stones.

The City of Oxford (Fig. 192) probably started to grow because of the strength of the local farming economy and its role as a transport hub, located where the River Thames cuts through the Midvale Ridge. Its ancient heart rests on a tongue of Quaternary gravels that have formed terraces where the Thames and its tributary the Cherwell run parallel to each other before joining.

It is interesting to compare landscape features of Oxford with those of England's other ancient university town, Cambridge (see Area 13). Oxford's large eastern and southern extension from Headington to Cowley is relatively new, and reflects major industrial development in the early twentieth century that largely passed Cambridge by. There is also a considerable difference in the scale

FIG 192. Looking northwards across the City of Oxford, with the Thames (or Isis) flowing from left to right across the foreground. Beyond that is the ancient centre of the city, with Christ Church Great Quad acting as a landmark, with grass in the quad and Tom Tower on its left side. (Copyright Dae Sasitorn & Adrian Warren/www.lastrefuge.co.uk)

of the development of the ancient parts of the two cities, perhaps due to the importance of the river link with London in the case of Oxford. However, it also seems to reflect the difference in scale of the rivers and the terraces that have provided the frameworks for growth. The Thames some kilometres north of Oxford has a mean flow rate of 15.4 m^3/s, draining 1,609 km^2 of catchment (Fig. 188), whereas the Cam in Cambridge has a much smaller mean flow rate of only 2.8 m^3/s from 762 km^2 of catchment (see Chapter 8, Fig. 230). So the altogether smaller size of the Cam, both in flow rate and in the size of its catchment, has strongly influenced the size and number of branch water courses constructed, and the scale of the terrace and bedrock hill topography.

The Vale of Pewsey (**b7**) separates the Marlborough and Lambourn Chalk Downs from the Chalk of Salisbury Plain to the south. The Vale is characterised by lush orchards and meadows and gently undulating lowlands, in contrast to the Chalk scarps and uplands to north and south. The Vale is aligned roughly parallel to a broad upfold or anticline running from Trowbridge (**b6**) eastwards, formed during the mid Tertiary. Following this crustal movement, the Chalk at the crest of the anticline has been eroded away, exposing the Early Cretaceous Upper Greensand. Subsequent erosion has focused on the relatively softer Greensand, carving a broad, gentle valley with fertile, sandy soils.

Landscape C: The Downs of Late Cretaceous Chalk
The Marlborough and Lambourn Downs, stretching across north Wiltshire and Berkshire, are a region of high, rolling hills underlain by Late Cretaceous Chalk. The Chalk dips gently to the south and southeast and has a dramatic northern edge overlooking the Vale of White Horse. In most cases along this northern edge the upper Chalk appears to have provided more resistance to erosion than the lower Chalk materials, so that it forms the lip of the steep slopes. However, particularly in the Marlborough Downs and just south of Harwell (**b5**), hill features of intermediate height have also been eroded into the lower Chalk levels.

Within the Chalk hills, a complex network of dry valleys or 'coombes' seems to have formed during glacial times, when the subsurface was permanently frozen to a depth of several metres. The ice sealed the fractures that normally make the Chalk such a permeable bedrock, resulting in poor surface drainage, slope collapse and erosive surface streams. The dry valleys may be divided into two types: *edge valleys* that cut into or across the Chalk edge itself, and *dip-slope valleys* that dissect the Chalk down-slope, away from the edge. Edge valleys show the greatest variability in size and shape, ranging from shallow depressions to deeply incised cuts. They are generally aligned approximately perpendicular to

FIG 193. The Manger (Fig. 190, **C2**), a dry valley in the Chalk scarp at Uffington. (Copyright Dae Sasitorn & Adrian Warren/www.lastrefuge.co.uk)

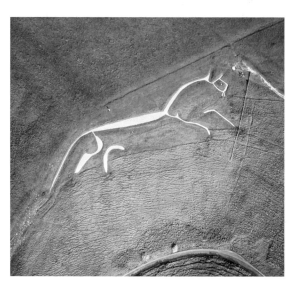

FIG 194. The White Horse (Fig. 190, **C2**) at Uffington. (Copyright Dae Sasitorn & Adrian Warren/ www.lastrefuge.co.uk)

the Chalk edge, and their morphology is controlled principally by the width of the escarpment. Complex, multi-branching systems tend to develop where the zone is broad, while straight, simple coombes tend to be found where the scarp is high, straight and steep. Dip-slope coombes are typically longer than those on the scarp face and often form well-developed, branching valley networks. Near the edge, the dip-slope valleys are shallow and gentle, and the resulting landscape smooth and rounded. Further down dip, as the streams on frozen ground increased in volume and power, the valleys became deep coombes with steep sides. Both classes of dry valley have a broadly U-shaped cross-section.

When the ground thawed after the last (Devensian) cold phase of the Ice Age, the streams that carved these valleys soaked away into the permeable Chalk bedrock and the valleys were left dry. The lower portions of many of these valleys are considered too steep to be worth farming, and it is here that the last remnants of the original chalk grassland can be found, sometimes supporting several species of rare orchids. Perhaps the most famous dry valley in this area is the Manger (c2), with distinctive flutes on its slopes where the chalk has slumped downwards (Fig. 193). The White Horse at Uffington (Fig. 194) is nearby, and according to local folklore the Manger is the spiritual abode of the white horse, which on moonlit nights would travel here to feed. Up until recently, the steep valley sides were also the venue for local cheese-rolling competitions, held during a two-day festival once every seven years called the 'Scouring of the White Horse'. The floor of the Manger contains thick deposits of Chalk rubble and silt that slumped and washed down-slope under freeze–thaw climate conditions. Careful dating of similar sediments elsewhere in Southern England (see Area 7) has shown that steep Chalk slopes like these were last active during the warming times after the Devensian cold episode.

In general, the Chalk produces light, free-draining, thin soils supporting wide expanses of open chalk grassland. This helps to explain why the area around Lambourn in the Berkshire Downs has become one of England's main centres for race-horse training, with exercise 'gallops' and stables scattered over much of the Landscape.

Over much of the dip-slope of the Chalk, the surface is underlain by a layer of Clay-with-flints, an insoluble, clayey residue with flints left behind after the upper layers of the Chalk had been dissolved by chemical erosion. Clay-with-flints gives richer, more acidic soils than the surrounding chalk grassland and is capable of supporting large tracts of woodland. An example is Savernake Forest (c3), to the southeast of Marlborough, which is believed to be very ancient.

Another common feature of these Downs are the scattered sarsen stones or *greyweathers* (Fig. 195). It has been suggested that the sarsen blocks are relics of

FIG 195. Sarsen stones on Fyfield Down (Fig. 190, c5).
(Copyright Landform Slides – Ken Gardner)

local patches of Early Tertiary sandstone which developed a hard silica cement and so resisted erosion while the surrounding, less-cemented and softer sandstones were worn away. These isolated blocks of weathered Tertiary sandstone are often found incorporated into ancient burial mounds or into the foundations of the area's oldest houses. Glacial *solifluction* processes have transported these blocks downhill, and they are often seen to be concentrated in lines at the bottoms of dry valleys. The sarsens are thought to have come from the Tertiary Reading Formation, a greyweathering sandstone which outcrops as bedrock in a narrow band in the east of Area 10. The wide distribution of sarsen stones across the Chalk Downs suggests that Tertiary sediments used to be much more widespread than they are today across Area 10, but have since been eroded away.

Area 10 has a long and archeologically important history of human settlement, often strongly influenced by the bedrock geology. The Marlborough Downs region includes many of the most spectacular ancient sites (such as Avebury, c4) linked together by the Ridgeway, an ancient travellers' route from Dorset to the Wash running along the top of the northern Chalk escarpment. This route has been in more or less constant use since at least Neolithic times, around 5,000 years ago, and was presumably chosen because the permeable and well-drained Chalk offered a more direct and reliable all-weather route than the neighbouring clay vales, which were probably densely wooded and marshy. Today the Ridgeway is maintained as a popular long-distance walking path running from Avebury to the northeast, providing an excellent route through some of the most spectacular chalk downland scenery in Southern England.

North of the village of Pewsey, on the southern edge of the Marlborough Downs, is Fyfield Down (**c5**), an easily accessible area of chalk downland with one of the highest concentrations of sarsen stones in the country (Fig. 195). Stones from this area have been used in the construction of Avebury stone circle (**c4**) and in megalithic monuments at the famous Stonehenge (**c6**).

To the south of the Vale of Pewsey is Salisbury Plain, the largest single piece of unimproved chalk grassland left in northern Europe. Since the early part of the twentieth century, much of the Plain has been reserved by the Ministry of Defence for military training purposes, while the surrounding downlands have been extensively modified by agricultural intensification. The downland landscape is of vast, rolling arable fields and unimproved chalk grassland, punctuated by small hill-top woodlands of beech and conifer. The northern and western margins of the Plain are clearly marked by a steep, near-continuous edge overlooking the Upper Greensand of the Vale of Pewsey and the clay vales of the River Avon. As with the Marlborough Downs, a patchy blanket of Clay-with-flints mantles the Chalk in places, often supporting scattered stands of woodland. The Late Cretaceous Chalk slopes very gradually (slightly more than 1 degree) to the southeast, away from the upfold in which the Vale of Pewsey has been eroded.

For the most part, Salisbury Plain is without surface water, providing the typical open scenery associated with the Stonehenge area (**c6**). There are, however, a few streams, such as the Hampshire Avon, that drain the plateau. These streams are often deeply incised into the Chalk, with valley bottoms that are lined with gravels and alluvium sourced from the Plain and large numbers of regular side valleys, giving a distinctive branching pattern on the slope map (Fig. 189). Trees have taken advantage of the nutrient-rich soils along these valleys, and the contrast between open chalk grasslands and occasional wooded river valleys is a striking characteristic of this region.

North of Andover and east of Salisbury Plain, the further continuation of the Chalk hills is called the Hampshire Downs. Their northern margin forms a very clearly defined edge that includes Walbury Hill (**c7**), which, at 297 m, provides clear views to the north across the Early Tertiary bedrock of Landscape **D**. Close to the edge of this Tertiary material, local upfolds at Shalbourne (**c8**) and Kingsclere (**c9**) have brought Early Cretaceous bedrock upwards to be level with

FIG 196. The River Thames just upstream from Reading and downstream from Pangbourne. (Copyright Dae Sasitorn & Adrian Warren/www.lastrefuge.co.uk)

the Late Cretaceous Chalk. These upfolds can be regarded as a continuation of the Vale of Pewsey structure further west.

Watership Down, made famous as the title of Richard Adams' 1972 book, is a north-facing Chalk edge south of Newbury, on the southerly-sloping (at about 3 degrees) fold limb of the Kinsclere Upfold (**c9**). The northern limb of the upfold slopes more steeply, at about 25 degrees to the north, showing that the general movement there was down towards the north. This sense of local movement is consistent with the movement that might be expected on the northern edge of the large London Basin downfold (Fig. 182).

Landscape D: The Kennet Valley with Early Tertiary bedrock

The final Landscape of Area 10 is defined by its bedrock of Early Tertiary sediments, marking the western end of the London Basin downfold (Figs 180 and 182). The town of Reading has grown where the River Thames emerges from its valley incised into the Chalk to the north and first meets these Tertiary sediments (Fig. 196). The sediments are largely flat-lying except locally, along the southern margin of the Basin, where they have been tilted by folding in the Kingsclere upfold (c9). The River Kennet is the central drainage feature of most of this Landscape, although further west its headwaters and tributaries (particularly the Lambourn) drain large valleys with numerous dry side branches in the Chalk Downs.

The Early Tertiary sediments consist of between 100 and 200 m of muddy and sandy sediment. Some of this was deposited by streams and in swamps, but most of it, particularly the London Clay, accumulated in what appears to have been an arm of the sea occupying the London Basin.

To the south, topographic surfaces in the Chalk Downs have been suggested to represent coastal erosion *peneplains* formed at about 200 m above sea level about 5 million years ago (Late Miocene or Pliocene), but the definition of the surfaces, and their age, are very speculative.

Many of the slopes visible in the slope map (Fig. 189) on the valley floors in this Landscape are clearly the result of river erosion into Early Tertiary or Chalk bedrock. In some cases they may be fragments of earlier river floodplains now represented as terraces. These have been mapped and correlated with the 'staircases' of terraces identified in the middle and upper Thames (See Fig. 192 and Landscape **B** respectively). It is relatively easy to distinguish some of the higher floodplains as dating from the Anglian glacial (about 470,000 years old), and lower ones as post-Anglian, representing episodes in the Late Pleistocene history, although local correlations are difficult to confirm in many cases. Despite the difficulties, the way the River Kennet has generally cut downwards through time and climate cycles is clear.

AREA 11: LONDON

One hundred years ago, more people lived in London (Figs 197 and 198) than in any other city on Earth. Although London now rates as only fifteenth in a recent survey of the populations of the world's cities, it is indisputably still one of the greatest in terms of its historical and economic importance. In fact, a recent report based on the 2001 British census suggests that, in economic and social terms at least, the whole of Southern England can be regarded as fringing Greater London!

The proportion of the ground covered by buildings, roads and railways in London is so great that it often obscures the local landscape (Fig. 199). It is

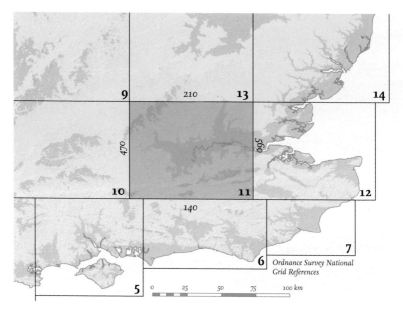

FIG 197. Location map for Area 11.

therefore necessary, in the maps, to take away the layers of man-made 'cover', in order to see the natural features beneath.

As Figures 200 and 201 show, London has grown in the natural basin created by the Chiltern Hills to the northwest and the North Downs to the south. The centre of this basin, including most of Greater London, is dominated by the River Thames and its floodplain, along with a number of isolated hills. In spite of the remarkable growth of Greater London, the river still dominates the scenery at its heart, and has created most of the local slopes and hilly viewpoints. Towards the west end of the basin, around Bracknell, are the Thames Basin Heaths, while to the east the River Thames broadens out into a wide estuary (Area 12). The Thames and its estuary have been key factors in London's remarkable growth and development.

I have divided this Region into seven Landscapes, indicated by the letters **A** to **G** on Figure 201.

Landscape A: The Vale of Aylesbury

This Landscape is defined largely by its low elevation relative to the Chiltern Hills to the southeast. The bedrock consists of largely Late Jurassic mudstone (mainly Kimmeridge Clay and Portland Beds) covered by mudstones of the Early

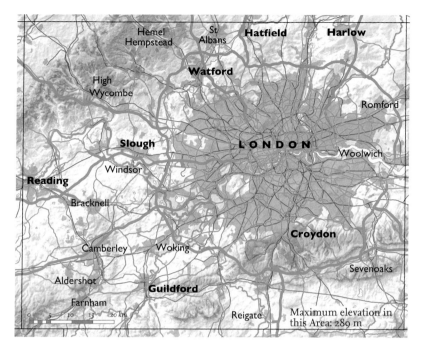

FIG 198. Natural and man-made features of Area 11.

Cretaceous Gault Clay, so it is not surprising that the land is relatively low-lying and lacks obvious topographic features. This Landscape links with more mudstone lowlands to the west (Landscape **B** of Area 10) and with the Clay–Greensand–Gault belt to the northeast (Landscape **B** of Area 13).

Landscape B: The Wealden margin

South of the spectacular Chalk hills of the North Downs, there is a distinct belt of hills formed because of the resistance to erosion of the Lower Greensand of Early Cretaceous age. The Greensand is rich in quartz grains held together by mineral cement, and seems to have resisted erosion more effectively than the overlying and underlying mudstones. In fact, the Greensand has resisted erosion so well in this Area that Leith Hill (**b1**) has an elevation of about 290 m – distinctly higher than the Chalk hills of the North Downs (Landscape **D**), which reach a height of only 173 m at Box Hill (**d4**). The Greensand has again resisted erosion to the east of the River Mole, south of the M25 and M26 motorways, and the resultant hills reach over 200 m in elevation south of Sevenoaks.

FIG 199. View from Westminster over central and eastern London, looking along the Thames towards the sea. (Copyright London Aerial Photo Library)

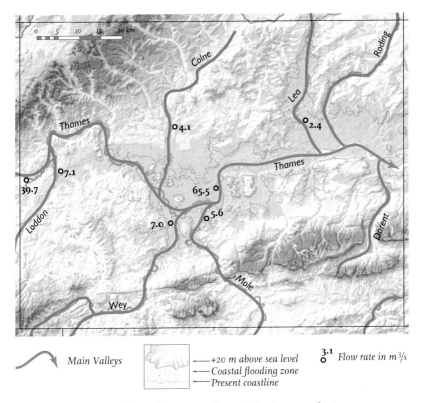

Main Valleys

——+20 m above sea level
——Coastal flooding zone
——Present coastline

3.1
o Flow rate in m³/s

FIG 200. Main river pathways, flow rates and coastal flooding zone for Area 11.

South of the Lower Greensand ridge, earlier Cretaceous bedrock has again influenced the topography, particularly towards the centre of the Weald Uplift. Here the tough, sandstone-rich Hastings Beds create more hilly topography, surrounded by the more readily eroded Weald Clay. As described more fully in Area 6, the hills here are prominent, but lack the linear pattern of the Lower Greensand ridge to the north.

Landscape C: The Chiltern Hills

The Chilterns are the northeasterly continuation of the Marlborough and Berkshire Downs (Landscape C of Area 10). The Chalk bedrock that has produced the Chilterns slopes gently downwards to the southeast beneath the London Basin and has been eroded to produce distinctive features in the Chiltern scenery. The first of these is the Chiltern Edge (**c1**), which faces to the northwest

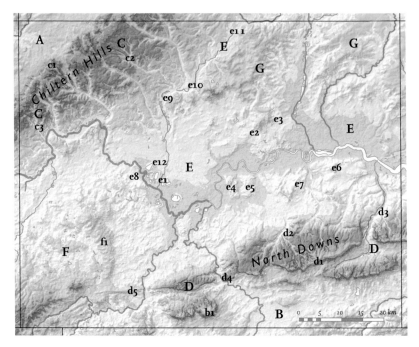

FIG 201. Map of Area 11, showing Landscapes **A** to **G** and localities (**b1**, **c1** etc.) mentioned in the text.

and results directly from the greater strength of the chalk material, in the face of river erosion, compared with the older and weaker underlying mudrocks. Southeast of the scarp, the Chiltern plateau (**c2** and **c3**) dips very gently to the southeast and is divided into distinct sectors by a remarkable series of branching, largely dry valleys, picked out beautifully in Figures 201 and 208. These dry valleys were formed during Ice Age times when freezing of the ground mobilised the near-surface Chalk and prevented water from soaking away, creating surface streams that cut downwards into the plateau. Railways and roads heading northwest from London make good use of these valleys to take travellers across the Chilterns, avoiding the steepest slopes and highest ground.

The Chiltern plateau is unlike other Chalk uplands in that it is often very heavily wooded, lacking the airy, open character of the Berkshire Downs a short distance to the southwest. Indeed, the region supports the most extensive beech woodland in the country, including examples of 'hanging woodlands' where trees thrive even on the steep slopes of dry valleys. This difference is due to a combination of natural and human factors. Firstly, ice sheets never extended from the north to cover the Chiltern plateau, although further east they did extend well into the London Basin. This means that the Chilterns were able to develop and preserve a thick weathering blanket of Clay-with-flints, covering the plateau with soils that have encouraged vegetation more actively than the typically thin Chalk soils in other areas. Secondly, during the eighteenth and nineteenth centuries, beech trees were planted and managed here in order to supply the rapidly growing furniture industry then developing in London. This contrast between thick forests and more typical Chalk grassland gives the Chilterns a very distinctive charm.

Landscape D: The North Downs, Hog's Back and Greensand

The North Downs form the southern limb of the London Basin Syncline or downfold (Fig. 202). Here the upper surface of the Chalk slopes gently to the northwest, just as the Chilterns form the northern limb and slope to the southeast. Otherwise the Chalk hills of the North Downs have much in common with the Chilterns, though there are some important differences. In the east they are broad – similar in width to the Chilterns – extending further east into Area 12 and ultimately reaching the coast between Folkestone and Deal. To the west, the hills narrow dramatically, and there is a very distinctive scarp facing southwards (e.g. at Botley Hill, **d1**). These features reflect the form and position of the Chalk bedrock layer that underlies the Downs, influenced by its long history of folding and faulting.

FIG 202. The Chalk scarp of the North Downs, as seen from Box Hill near Dorking (Fig. 201, **d4**). Denbies Vineyard is on the south-facing slope beneath. (Copyright R. C. Selley, 2004. *The Winelands of Britain*, Petravin Press)

The clearly branched dry valley patterns cut into the Chalk hills are similar to those of the Chilterns. Two very clear examples are the valley that provides the main railway and road route across the scarp between Croydon (**d2**) and Reigate, and, further east, the large valley of the River Darent (**d3**), now paralleled by the M25.

A very distinct difference compared with the Chilterns is the presence of a second clear scarp to the south of the Chalk scarp, due to erosion of a bedrock layer lower than the Chalk in the bedrock succession. This Lower Greensand layer is part of Landscape **B**, just described above.

In the western part of the area, particularly west of the centre of Guildford, is the Hog's Back (**d5**), a remarkably straight Chalk ridge that separates the Thames Basin in the north from the Wealden area in the south. The crest of the ridge rises up to 70 m above the ground to the north and is capped by the A31 road. The ridge is an eroded stepfold or monocline that represents the transition between two major asymmetric folds: the London Basin downfold or syncline to the north, and the Weald Uplift or anticline to the south (Fig. 203). The reason for

FIG 203. Sketch sections showing (A) the location of the Hog's Back monocline in the overall fold pattern and (B) more detailed pattern of folding and faulting around the Hog's Back.

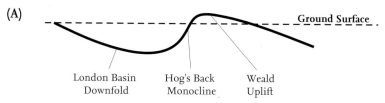

(A)

Ground Surface

London Basin
Downfold

Hog's Back
Monocline

Weald
Uplift

North

South

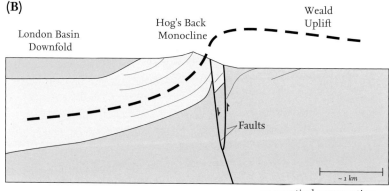

(B)

Weald
Uplift

Hog's Back
Monocline

London Basin
Downfold

Faults

~ 1 km

2.5 x vertical exaggeration

the narrowness and the straightness of the Hog's Back ridge is the presence of large faults beneath this region, separating the London Basin from the Wessex Basin (see the general introduction to this chapter). Movement along these faults, combined with compressional folding, has rotated the strong Chalk layer so that, in places, it is now sloping at up to 55 degrees to the north. As a result of this, the Chalk outcrops at the surface in a long, narrow band cut by straight fracture surfaces. Because the Chalk is strong, and sloping in this way, it has resisted river erosion more successfully than the softer material to the north and south, so producing this prominent ridge.

Landscape E: The Thames Valley and the London hills

In the Early Tertiary, sands and marine muds were deposited over the Chalk in the centre of the London Basin downfold, forming bedrock deposits such as the London Clay and Bagshot Beds that underlie much of London. Later crustal compression in Middle Tertiary times involved further gentle movements of the downfold, along with steep folding over a few localised faults, which produced structures such as the Hog's Back.

Landscape erosion then picked out the harder Chalk on the north and south edges of the basin, creating the Chilterns and North Downs. This created a drainage network that focused river erosion on the central part of the basin. In time, the ancestors of the Thames, Colne and Lea developed to form the main stems of today's branching river pattern (Fig. 200). These rivers have cut progressively downwards into the Tertiary bedrock, forming floodplains with alluvial sediment at a variety of different levels, often described as a 'staircase' of river terraces. The staircases provide a record of the river history of the London Basin over the past million years or so.

The terraces form much of the flat land upon which Greater London is built. Slough (**e12**), for example, has been constructed upon the ancient Boyn Hill Terrace and sits above the level of the present-day floodplain. The terraces also contain extensive deposits of sand and gravel that have long been worked and used as a source of aggregate. The abandoned gravel pits (**e1**) have often filled with water and in time become valuable wetland habitats, recreational parks and water treatment works, such as those in the vicinity of Heathrow Airport (**e1**), and between Windsor (**e8**) and Richmond Hill (**e4**). The Quaternary terraces of the Thames Valley are amongst the best studied in the country and provide an excellent record of the switching of the River Thames back and forth across its floodplain. In addition, the terraces in the lower reaches of the Thames record the most recent rise in sea level associated with the end of the last (Devensian) cold episode, which flooded the lower Thames Valley to form the Thames Estuary.

Each terrace deposit is the remains of a sheet of old floodplain material that formed when the river was flowing at the level of the terrace. Each step of the staircase reflects an episode of downward cutting by the local river channel, while the succession of steps, from highest and oldest down to lowest and youngest, shows how the rivers have cut downwards into the landscape as time has passed (Fig. 204). It has sometimes been possible to suggest ages for the terraces in terms of the stages of the oxygen isotope timescale (see Chapter 2, Fig. 13). The youngest and lowest terrace material was deposited during the rise of sea level that has occurred over the last few thousand years.

Figures 201 and 208 help to pick out the scattered, isolated hills that are distinctive features of the London Basin. Examples include Parliament Hill on Hampstead Heath (**e2**; Fig. 205) and Highgate Cemetery (**e3**) to the north of the Thames. To the south of the present Thames are Richmond Hill (**e4**), Wimbledon Common (**e5**), Shooter's Hill (**e6**) and Crystal Palace (**e7**). Most of these hills are features that became isolated and left behind as the staircase of river terraces was being formed. The importance of these upstanding river-terrace hills is enormous in providing present-day Londoners with a sense of natural landscape, wildlife and recreation.

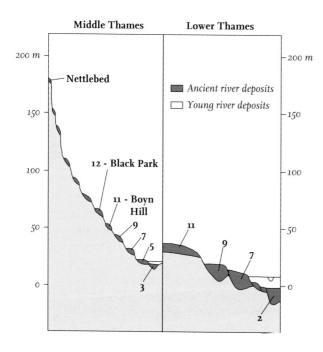

FIG 204. Diagram representing the terraces in the middle (Nettlebed to Slough) and lower (Area 12) parts of the Thames valley, with their ages in terms of oxygen isotope stages.

FIG 205. Looking eastwards over Highgate Ponds and Parliament Hill on Hampstead Heath (Fig. 201, **e2**). (Copyright London Aerial Photo Library)

At the western end of the Thames Valley Basin, northeast of Bagshot Heath (**f1**), the present-day Thames flows past another isolated hill. This one is crowned spectacularly by Windsor Castle (**e8**), the largest fortified castle in the world that is still inhabited by the (royal) family that owns it. This hill owes its existence to the presence of strong Chalk that was raised up as a small anticline or upfold above faults in the bedrock, probably during the Middle Tertiary (Fig. 206). The fold is relatively narrow and angular, meaning that the Chalk outcrops at the surface over an area only about 1 km across, creating a prominent, isolated hill and an ideal location for a castle (Fig. 207).

About 470,000 years ago, the Anglian cold episode resulted in ice sheets reaching their furthest southern position, leaving a distinctive mark on the London area. It was the only cold episode in the last 2 million years when ice extended as far south as London. As the ice advanced, it deposited a glacial *till* of

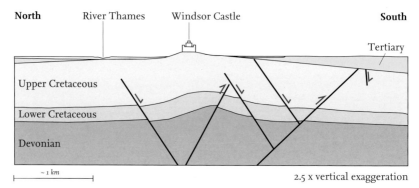

North   River Thames   Windsor Castle   **South**

Tertiary

Upper Cretaceous

Lower Cretaceous

Devonian

~ 1 km   2.5 x vertical exaggeration

FIG 206. The geological structure under Windsor Castle (Fig. 201, **e8**).

FIG 207. Looking westwards over Windsor Castle (Fig. 201, **e8**) and the River Thames. (Copyright London Aerial Photo Library)

boulders, sand and clay. In places, this till is closely associated with river-deposited gravels, showing that material was often transported locally by meltwater streams that ran beneath and in front of the ice. It is the presence of the till that indicates how far south the ice sheets came.

Investigations of Quaternary deposits in the Vale of St Albans (**e9**) have identified glacial till overlying gravel deposits that appear to have been laid down by an ancestor of the River Thames. This suggests that, rather than flowing generally eastwards as it does today, the early River Thames used to flow in a generally northeasterly direction towards Essex and Suffolk. When the Anglian

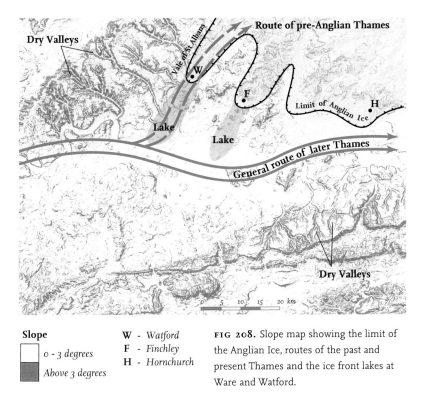

Slope

☐ *0 - 3 degrees*

■ *Above 3 degrees*

W - *Watford*
F - *Finchley*
H - *Hornchurch*

FIG 208. Slope map showing the limit of the Anglian Ice, routes of the past and present Thames and the ice front lakes at Ware and Watford.

ice later advanced into the area from the northeast, the path of the original Thames was deflected to approximately its present-day position some 30–40 km to the south, creating two glacial lakes at the ice front as it did so (Fig. 208). The evidence for these lakes is found in a series of finely laminated silts and clays in the Ware and Watford (**e10**) areas north of London. The laminations in these sediments are known as varves, and they are typically formed by annual freeze–thaw cycles experienced by large lakes in cold regions. By counting the number of cycles, sedimentologists have been able to establish that the lakes must have existed for several hundred years.

With the Thames diverted to the south, a number of large outwash streams developed at the ice front, flowing southwards into the new Thames. As the climate became milder at the start of the next interglacial, these rivers became charged with large volumes of meltwater, cutting valleys to eventually form the rivers Colne and Lea as we know them today. Flow rates in the Thames itself also increased and a number of very coarse gravel deposits date from this time, carried into position by the fast-flowing waters. Examples include the coarse gravel beds of the Black Park terrace (Fig. 204).

As the climate warmed further and the ice retreated, large blocks of ice buried within the till melted, causing subsidence and eventually creating a number of small lakes known as *kettle holes* (Fig. 209). Over the course of the subsequent interglacial, these small lakes were filled with peat and silt, as well as pollen from the surrounding vegetation. They therefore provide an excellent record of climatic conditions during the warm phase, and so are often of considerable interest to climatologists. A number of kettle holes were discovered during construction work at Hatfield north of London (**e11**) where they appear as isolated patches of interglacial sediment set within the surrounding glacial till.

Landscape F: The Thames Basin Western Heaths
The Tertiary fill of the London Basin has influenced the landscapes mainly in the areas surrounding Landscape **C**, with its river floodplains and their terraces.

FIG 209. Diagram illustrating the processes of kettle-hole formation.

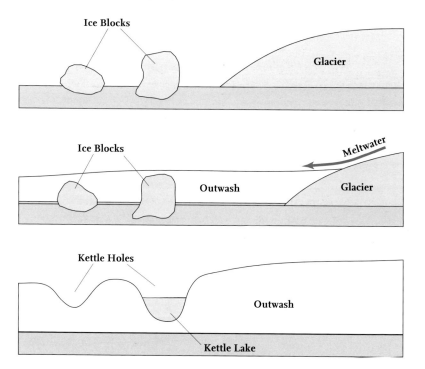

The Bagshot Beds (Fig. 181) are sandy deposits which overlie the London Clay in parts of the Basin, especially in the southwest, where they define Landscape **F**. The sand content of the bedrock here gives rise to nutrient-poor, acidic soils that favour heathland vegetation and pasture, and are of little use for agriculture. The Bagshot Beds mostly outcrop around the Reading–Aldershot–Woking area, also known as the Thames Basin Heaths. The area has been widely taken over for military training purposes, particularly around the Sandhurst and Aldershot military centres, in the valley of the Blackwater river. The waters of the Blackwater flow northwards into the River Loddon beside the hills of Bagshot Heath (**fi**) and enter the Thames to the east of Reading.

To the south, where the Chalk scarp of the Hog's Back meets the lower-lying Heaths, water stored within the higher Chalk strata escapes to the surface in a series of freshwater springs. These springs are commonly associated with ecologically important natural habitats, and also seem to have had an influence upon early human settlement patterns in this area.

The Bagshot Beds also outcrop on Hampstead Heath in north London, and around Brentwood and Rayleigh in south Essex (see Area 12).

Landscape G: The Hertfordshire Plateau
The Hertfordshire Plateau, between the rivers Colne and Lea, extends northwards into the southern part of Area 13. It is underlain by Tertiary bedrock, most widely the London Clay, with a cover of Quaternary alluvium. Historically it was heavily cultivated, growing a variety of crops including hops and wheat to sustain London, making Hertfordshire famous as the best corn county in England. Over the last 50 years urbanisation has crept north from London, and the area is now a zone of commuter homes and new towns.

As with other Landscapes in this Area, the scenery in Landscape **G** has been strongly influenced by an episode when the pre-Anglian Thames flowed through it, leaving spreads of gravel at high levels on the Hertfordshire Plateau. The arrival of the edge of the Anglian ice sheet, with lobes extending down the Vale of St Albans and as far as Finchley and Hornchurch (Fig. 208), must have modified the landscape considerably, and the subsequent history of ice-sheet front lakes and kettle holes has been mentioned already.

AREA 12: THE THAMES ESTUARY

The general introduction to this Region has explained how Greater London occupies the centre of a wide and gentle downfold in the bedrock. The formation of this downfold began more or less at the same time as this Area (Figs 210 and 211) first emerged from the sea, after a long episode of Chalk accumulation. In Early Tertiary times, marine sediments started to accumulate in the Area once again, though this time they were limited to the large embayment of the sea formed by the continuing downfolding of the basin. This sedimentation ceased in mid-Tertiary times, and was followed by a long episode of erosion by rivers that has created much of the present-day landscape of low-lying ground intersected by estuaries (Fig. 212). The River Thames has been the central feature of this erosion, and has also been the main reason for London's remarkable growth to become the commercial hub of England.

This Area, centred on the Thames Estuary, represents a continuation of the London Basin downfold that we have examined in Areas 10 and 11, although its

FIG 210. Location map for Area 12.

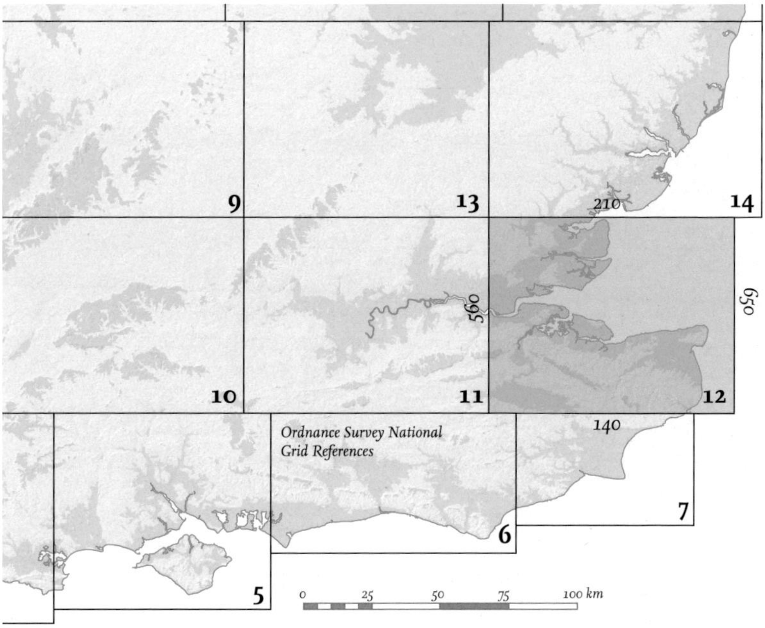

geometry changes eastwards from the simple downfold structure that cradles Greater London. The southern margin of the downfold is still clearly defined in Area 12 by the North Downs, but the northerly Chalk margin curves off first to the northeast and then to the north as it crosses East Anglia (see Chapter 2, Fig. 9). As a result, the northern half of Area 12 is underlain by Early Tertiary bedrock, marking the centre of the London Basin downfold. This pattern in the bedrock (Figs 213 and 214) provides the best division for more detailed examination of local scenery, and forms the basis for dividing the Area into four Landscapes, marked **A** to **D** in Figure 215. Whereas the main features of the Landscapes in the southern part of Area 12 reflect the different resistance to river erosion of the Greensand and Chalk bedrock, the features of the northern parts directly reflect the recent history of river and coastal movement.

Landscape A: The Northern Weald

At the beginning of this chapter I introduced the Weald as being exposed within a large uplift, created by upward movement of the Cretaceous bedrock. In the area around Maidstone, the northern Weald succession can be seen ranging

FIG 211. Natural and man-made features of Area 12.

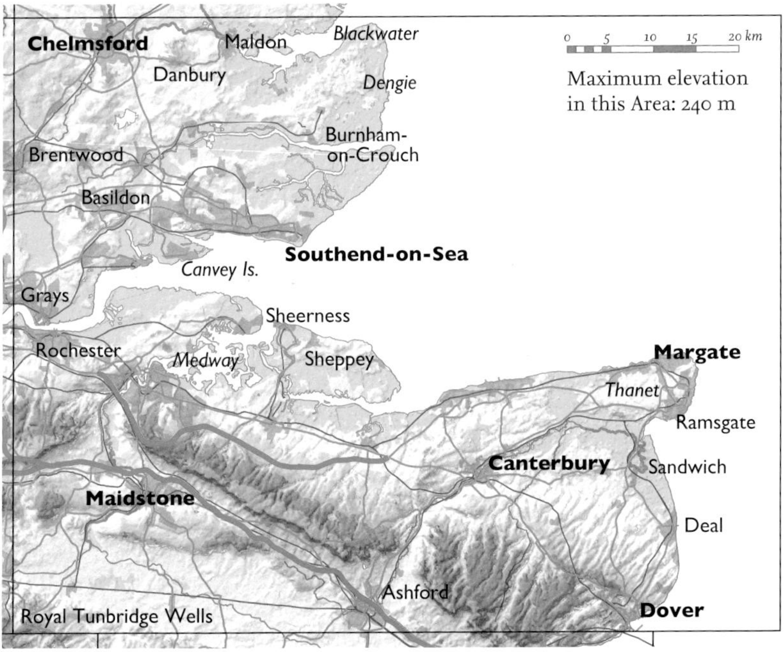

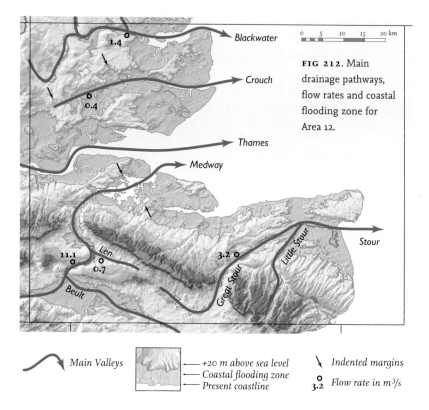

FIG 212. Main drainage pathways, flow rates and coastal flooding zone for Area 12.

Main Valleys · +20 m above sea level · Coastal flooding zone · Present coastline · Indented margins · Flow rate in m³/s

southwards from Late Cretaceous Chalk in the North Downs, to the Early Cretaceous Hastings Beds around Royal Tunbridge Wells.

South of the North Downs Chalk hills (see Landscape **B**), there are a number of hills and valleys that correspond to Early Cretaceous resistant sandstones and weaker mudstones respectively. Moving southwards corresponds to working downwards in the rock succession because of the gentle northward slope of the bedrock. The following features can be observed:

1. A low-lying linear bench that tends to have been eroded in the Early Cretaceous Gault Clay, south of the North Downs scarp. Some parts of the M26 and M20 motorways follow this feature. The low ground has been eroded at least partly by the River Len, a tributary that joins the Medway in Maidstone (**a1**), and by the Great Stour upstream of the valley it has carved through the North Downs.

2. A ridge of hills eroded from the Early Cretaceous Lower Greensand, which is about 100 m thick in the Maidstone area but thins easterly, resulting in lower

Ages (millions of years)   **Rock types & names**

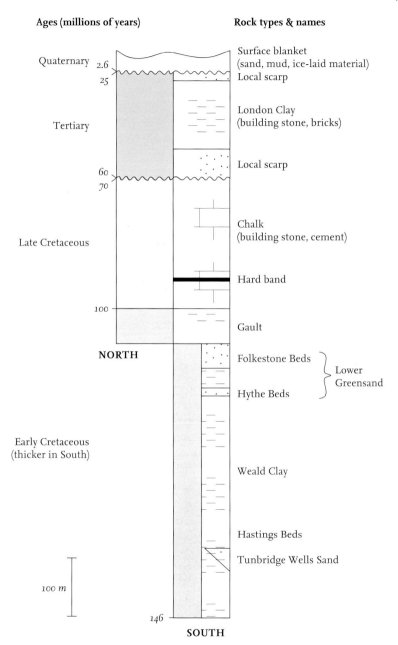

FIG 213. Bedrock succession for Area 12.

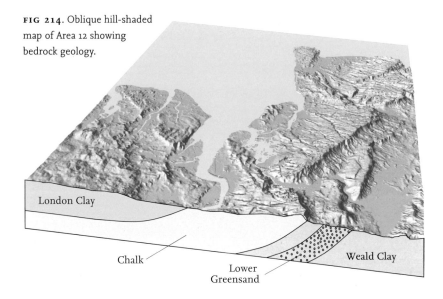

FIG 214. Oblique hill-shaded map of Area 12 showing bedrock geology.

London Clay

Chalk

Lower Greensand

Weald Clay

elevations of the hills. At locality **a2**, 5 km south of Maidstone, the Lower Greensand scarp has a particularly distinctive relief of about 100 m.

3. A further belt of low ground (**a3**) that has been eroded preferentially in the relatively weak Weald Clay by the upper Medway and its tributary the River Beult.

4. A general area of hilly country around Royal Tunbridge Wells (**a4**). Here the bedrock is the more erosion-resistant Tunbridge Wells Sandstone, which forms part of the Hastings Beds (see Area 6). Unusual sandstone bluffs have weathered out to produce features similar in form to the granite tors of Southwest England, which are much prized by outdoor groups and rock climbers.

The Weald Uplift continues south and west of this Area, and is examined in more detail in Areas 6, 7 and 11. The origin of the Wealden bedrock as a southerly-building Early Cretaceous delta is discussed in Chapter 5, Area 6.

Landscape B: The North Downs and Isle of Thanet

The North Downs are the most clearly defined and easily followed topographic feature of this Area. The Downs rise to heights of over 190 m above sea level and have the typical shape of a hill range formed by erosion of a tilted layer of resistant bedrock: the north slope of the Downs is relatively gentle, following the

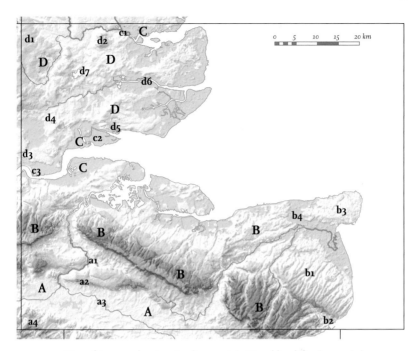

FIG 215. Map of Area 12, showing Landscapes **A** to **D** and localities (**a1**, **a2** etc.) mentioned in the text.

northerly dip of the Chalk layers, while the southerly slope is a steep scarp, because here the Chalk has tended to collapse along internal fracture surfaces, which are often steeply inclined.

Another feature of the North Downs, clearly seen in Figure 215, is the way that the northerly slope is covered with distinct valleys running directly down-dip. In some areas, for example at locality **b1**, just north of Dover, the regularity and parallel trend of the valleys is remarkable, even though the down-slope dip is only about 1 degree. Figure 216 looks northwestwards up the well-defined large valley that cross-cuts the linear valleys developed on the high Chalk ground that it has traversed. This suggests that the main valley has been carved very vigorously compared with the linear, parallel, higher valley features, and this may have been caused by pulses of sea-level lowering. The White Cliffs of Dover are also shown in the photograph, but represent a much younger episode of erosion: the way in which they spectacularly cut across the fortifications of the castle shows just how recently the carving of the cliff has been active.

FIG 216. The White Cliffs of Dover (Fig. 215, **b2**) with their fortifications, castle and Roman lighthouse. (Copyright Dae Sasitorn & Adrian Warren/www.lastrefuge.co.uk)

Further west in the North Downs, the Chalk valleys are more branched and appear to have formed by backwards erosion of upper valley ends, which were shaped by multiple collapse events creating the branches. All the valleys appear to have been carved and enlarged under Ice Age conditions when the subsurface was permanently frozen, as today most of the valleys are dry and so could not have been carved under modern climatic conditions. Many of the valleys contain *head*, the name given to a mixture of Chalk blocks and chalky mud produced by Ice Age slumping and land-slipping of the bedrock down-slope.

Only two rivers cut right across the North Downs in Area 12. To the west, the Medway flows through Maidstone before passing through the Medway Gap and entering its extensive estuary (see Landscape **C**). To the east, another breach in the North Downs has been cut by the Great Stour branch of the Stour, flowing through the Downs and then on to Canterbury and the sea south of Ramsgate.

The resistant Chalk ridge of the North Downs has, throughout history, provided a key transport route between London and the shortest sea crossing to continental Europe. The shortest crossing, only some 30 km in length, runs from the resistant Chalk cliffs of Dover (**b2**) and Folkestone (Area 7) on the English side, to the similar landscape of Calais and Boulogne on the French side. On the English side, the North Downs have provided the obvious inland routes because they separate the flat lands and estuaries of the south shore of the Thames from the heavily wooded and often wet country of the Weald (Landscape **A**) to the south.

For example, the Pilgrim's Way from Winchester to Canterbury (Fig. 217) is a historically important route that runs along the southern slopes of the North Downs, avoiding the highest plateau edge. King Henry II is sometimes regarded as the first to undertake the pilgrimage to Canterbury, after hearing of the murder there of Archbishop Thomas Beckett in 1170.

North of the main North Downs lies the Isle of Thanet (**b3**; Fig. 218), an isolated and distinctive Chalk landscape feature of the East Kent coastline. Here the Chalk layers have been moved into an upfold that has been eroded and now forms a gentle range of hills up to 50 m in elevation. The layering in the Chalk slopes at almost 10 degrees along the southern margin of the Isle. Between the North Downs and Thanet, the Chalk has been downfolded, and is buried under soft-weathering Tertiary sediments, forming the low-lying lands of the Sandwich–Pegwell Bay area.

The Isle of Thanet was a true island up until very recently. In Roman times the Wantsum Channel (**b4**) separating it from the mainland to the west was up to 3 km wide, and the Vikings were able to sail into Canterbury in the eighth century. Over time, the channel has silted up, aided by the land reclamation

FIG 217. Canterbury Cathedral, with Roman and medieval city and walls. (Copyright Dae Sasitorn & Adrian Warren/www.lastrefuge.co.uk)

FIG 218. Looking northwestwards across the Isle of Thanet (Fig. 215, **b3**) and Ramsgate on the Chalk cliffs. (Copyright Dae Sasitorn & Adrian Warren/www.lastrefuge.co.uk)

efforts of the Church in the twelfth and thirteenth centuries, and by the sixteenth century the channel had ceased to be navigable. The Great and Little Stour now flow out to the sea eastwards to the south of the Isle of Thanet (Fig. 212).

Landscape C: The Thames and tributary estuaries

The intricate pattern of tidal channels and islands that is so typical of this Landscape extends from the Blackwater Estuary in Essex (Fig. 219) to the Medway and the Isle of Sheppey in Kent. The Landscape has formed by the flooding of river valleys by the recent (Flandrian) rise in sea level. The bedrock of the estuary is London Clay, but this is buried under large thicknesses of recent marine, estuarine and freshwater muds.

Sea level has risen by over 100 m worldwide in the last 20,000 years, since the end of the last (Devensian) cold episode of the Ice Age. Sea-level rise relative to the local land surface may have been even higher in this particular area, due to a seesaw effect between the northwest and the southeast of Britain: northern and western Britain have been rising since they are no longer being depressed by the weight of the ice sheets; meanwhile, south and east England, on the other end of the 'seesaw', have been gradually subsiding.

FIG 219. Maldon (Fig. 215, C1) on the upper Blackwater estuary. (Copyright Dae Sasitorn & Adrian Warren/www.lastrefuge.co.uk)

The idea that this area may recently have been tilted eastwards at the same time as worldwide sea level was rising is supported by the sedimentation pattern of the region. Over the last 10,000 years, more than 30 m of marine and estuarine sediment has accumulated where Canvey Island (C2) now is, whereas at Tilbury (C3), 20 km further up the Thames, only 10 m of sediment has accumulated. During the last 10,000 years, a number of peat beds formed further up the Thames, representing distinct phases of swampy river conditions. Similar beds have not been found further downstream, suggesting that downward movement and marine conditions were more continuous there.

One fascinating feature of the shoreline of this Landscape is the Medway Estuary, which is remarkable for its width and its large number of islands. Most of the islands appear to have grown recently as mud and sand have been brought

FIG 220. The Medway river and estuary, with Rochester castle and cathedral. (Copyright Dae Sasitorn & Adrian Warren/www.lastrefuge.co.uk)

into the estuary by the tides, creating isolated salt marshes and other expanses of intertidal sediment. The width of the estuary suggests that it formed under Ice Age conditions, prior to the recent rise in sea level, as an extensive, flat-lying lowland. This lowland area may have grown in size through freeze–thaw slumping of its hilly margins, similar to the areas of south Essex described below (Landscape **D**). In the aerial photograph (Fig. 220), Rochester's Norman castle and cathedral can be seen in the foreground, overlooking the River Medway.

The rising sea level did not just flood valleys and streams. Sea storms moved large quantities of soft sand and mud, which were then deposited against the new coastlines. The ancestral Thames and its associated tributaries also supplied large quantities of mud and sand to the coastline, transported from further upstream. Plants stabilised the sediment, and eventually it developed into wide expanses of salt marsh and estuarine mud flats.

The efforts of humankind have also had a large impact on the estuary: man-made sea walls encourage the deposition of sand and mud, accelerating the growth of the salt marshes and mud flats. The new land is reclaimed from the sea and new sea walls are built further seaward as the process of reclamation continues. The Romans were the first to drain the wetlands for agriculture, although the fields largely returned to marshland when the empire crumbled. Since the early Middle Ages, land has been systematically reclaimed from the sea and protected by sea banks. Historically the land was used for farmland, especially wet pasture. During the last century, the land has been further used for oil-storage depots, military training ranges and tourism (yachting, marinas, water and jet-skiing) as well as for intensive arable farming on the fertile loamy soils.

Landscape D: South Essex and the Northern Thames Basin

Most of South Essex is underlain by flat-lying horizontal layers, mainly mudstones of Tertiary age. Patches of the sandy Bagshot Beds underlie Ice Age deposits in the northwest corner (**d1**), but most of the region is underlain by London Clay that is covered by Quaternary river and ice-laid deposits. Around Tilbury (**c3**), near the River Thames, the older Chalk layer is exposed at the surface, as shown in Figure 214.

Much of the landscape of Essex does not directly reflect contrasts in the erosional strength of the underlying bedrock. It has a distinctive topography that reflects most obviously the variety of processes that have shaped it over the last few million years. The River Thames has been the primary influence on the shape of this Landscape, accounting for much of the erosion of south Essex, although deposition by the Anglian ice has also played an important role. Consideration of the landforms can help to work out which processes have been involved.

An undulating plateau (Fig 215 **d1**), sometimes reaching 100 m above sea level, forms the corner of this Landscape, northwest of the Brentwood–Chelmsford A12 trunk road. Much of this plateau is underlain by Anglian ice-laid material, and the undulations may reflect surface-blanket topography left by the melting ice, although it must have also been modified later by small stream systems.

To the southeast of the plateau there are more distinctive ridges and slope features, mostly trending southwest–northeast. The first of these hilly features is a knoll centred on Danbury (**d2**), which is linked to a ridge continuing northeast towards Tiptree in Area 14. The slopes and ridges were carved by the Thames or one of its branches before the arrival of Anglian ice, which seems to have extended southeastwards only as far as this Danbury–Tiptree Ridge.

Southeast of the Danbury–Tiptree Ridge, the next distinct topographic feature is a series of lowlands that extend all the way from Thurrock (**d3**), near the Thames in the southwest, to Maldon (**c1**) in the northeast. This is the Valley of Romford, another old course of the River Thames, with very distinct margins to the northwest and southeast (Fig. 221). The northwest margin is a strongly indented southeast-facing scarp which forms the edge of the Hanningfield Plateau (**d7**), whereas the southeastern margin is the Rayleigh–Dengie Ridge. The lowlands are also crossed by distinctive smaller ridges at Purleigh (northwest of **d6**) and the Langdon Hills (**d4**). The northwestern margin of these lowlands contains a series of arcuate hollows which probably formed when freeze–thaw processes in the largely clay bedrock triggered land-slipping down slopes. On a more general scale, the lowlands appear to have encroached on the

FIG 221. Slope map of Area 12, showing the extent of Anglian ice, along with former and present drainage pathways.

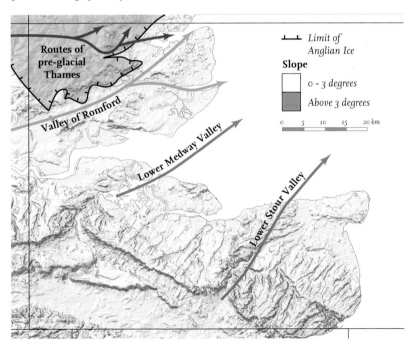

surrounding hills by a combination of Ice Age land-slipping processes and removal of the slumped mud by river action.

To the southeast of the Valley of Romford, erosion has picked out slopes that are often capped by the more sandy Claygate Member, which forms the uppermost part of the Early Tertiary London Clay Formation. Hadleigh Castle (**d5**), shown in Figure 222, has been built on a particularly distinctive point of the 70 m high Southend scarp. It is from here that John Constable captured remarkable light effects in his views towards the mouth of the Thames Estuary (see Area 14).

An interesting insight into more recent landscape development comes from the flat Dengie and Rochford peninsulas, north and south of the Crouch Estuary (**d6**). Field boundary patterns, apparently dating from Iron Age times, about 2,000 years before the present, show a remarkably parallel alignment on the two sides of the tidal Crouch Estuary. This observation, along with evidence of early bridging and fording of the channel, confirms that a very recent rise in sea level must have taken place, drowning ancient fields and crossing places to form today's 400 m wide estuary.

FIG 222. Hadleigh Castle (Fig. 215, **d5**), 7 km west of Southend-on-Sea. (Copyright Dae Sasitorn & Adrian Warren/www.lastrefuge.co.uk)

CHAPTER 8

The East Anglia Region

GENERAL INTRODUCTION

E AST ANGLIA (Fig. 223) is famous for its spectacular skies, partly because they often lack the distractions of horizons dominated by mountains or hills. Indeed, one of the most intriguing features of East Anglian scenery is its general flatness.

The East Anglian Region as a whole shows remarkably little variation in topography, being some 200 km from west to east and 150 km from north to south, but with the highest hill top lying only 256 m above sea level. Furthermore, within the Region are landscapes such as the East Anglian Fens and the Broads, which are flat to the extent that traverses of many kilometres often contain no changes in surface elevation of more than 2 m. These areas represent the extremes of flatness in Southern England.

Why is the landscape of this Region so flat compared with other British regions? The bedrock and surface-blanket history help us to answer this question.

Bedrock structure and early history

Most cross-sections prepared to represent the Earth's uppermost crust in detail show very little unless their vertical scale is greatly exaggerated. In Figure 224 we can compare the same cross-section of East Anglia with no exaggeration, and with the vertical scale exaggerated ten times and 100 times. Exaggeration gives a false impression of the angles of slopes or tilts in the bedrock, but it does help us to understand the relationships between different rock units.

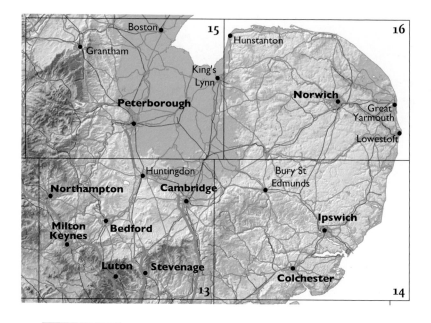

FIG 223. The East Anglia Region.

Beneath the near-surface layers of the bedrock of East Anglia, there is older bedrock that can be examined only in boreholes, and by remote geophysical methods. This has revealed evidence for an important geological episode some 300 million years ago, during latest Carboniferous or earliest Permian times. Before this, the geography of the Region was very different to that of the present, with sediments accumulating in some areas while hills had formed elsewhere due to movements of the crust. Approximately 300 million years ago, the whole Region became a land area of general erosion, and part of the area was uplifted to become what we now call the London Platform.

Since that time, younger sediments have been deposited and turned into bedrock. Initially they only accumulated in the northwest of the Region but then, in Jurassic and Early Cretaceous times, the area of deposition extended further southeast towards the London Platform. Eventually, in Late Cretaceous times, the whole Region was submerged and covered by accumulating Chalk. After this, during the Tertiary, the surface was moved upwards and tilted, so that sediment accumulation became confined to the southeast of the Region.

Although none of these sedimentary layers is uniform across the Region, the

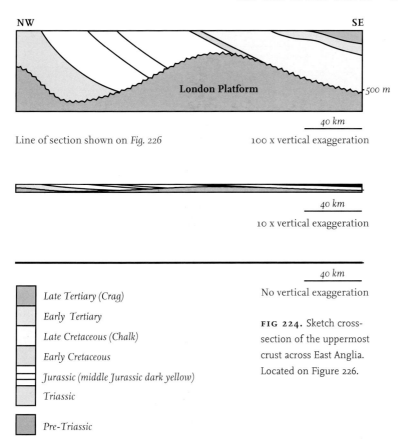

NW   SE

London Platform

500 m

40 km

Line of section shown on *Fig. 226*

100 x vertical exaggeration

40 km

10 x vertical exaggeration

40 km

No vertical exaggeration

Late Tertiary (Crag)

Early Tertiary

Late Cretaceous (Chalk)

Early Cretaceous

Jurassic (middle Jurassic dark yellow)

Triassic

Pre-Triassic

FIG 224. Sketch cross-section of the uppermost crust across East Anglia. Located on Figure 226.

fact that the 300-million-year-old landscape (labelled pre-Triassic in Fig. 224) is still so close to the present surface shows that little vertical movement of the crust (less than ~500 m) has taken place since that time. Its younger bedrock cover provides key information about the environments in which the sediments formed, and these are all consistent with unusual stability and lack of crustal movement.

The type of bedrock appearing near the surface in different parts of the Region has a major influence upon the scenery, at least locally. The succession shown in Figure 225 generalises the thickness of the main layers and the time of their deposition over the last 230 million years.

The earliest information comes from the northwest of the Region, where the bedrock, of Triassic age, consists largely of red mudstones deposited by rivers

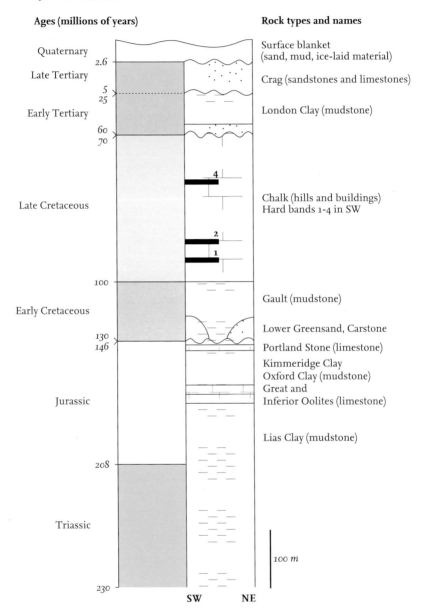

Ages (millions of years)

Rock types and names

Quaternary
2.6

Late Tertiary

5
25

Early Tertiary

60
70

Late Cretaceous

4

2

1

100

Early Cretaceous

130
146

Jurassic

208

Triassic

230

SW   NE

Surface blanket
(sand, mud, ice-laid material)

Crag (sandstones and limestones)

London Clay (mudstone)

Chalk (hills and buildings)
Hard bands 1-4 in SW

Gault (mudstone)

Lower Greensand, Carstone

Portland Stone (limestone)
Kimmeridge Clay
Oxford Clay (mudstone)
Great and
Inferior Oolites (limestone)

Lias Clay (mudstone)

100 m

FIG 225. Generalised near-surface bedrock succession for the East Anglian Region.

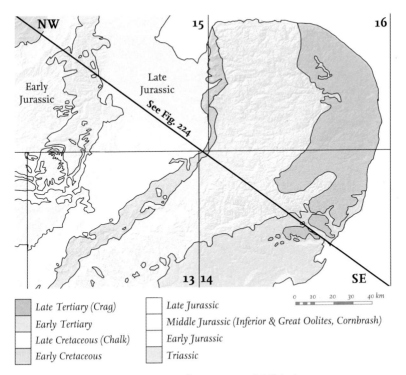

FIG 226. Bedrock map of the East Anglian Region with hillshade.

and streams in low-lying ground between low hills (Fig. 226). At this time, the area to the southeast consisted of a landscape of uplands made of London Platform bedrock, more than 300 million years old, where sediments did not accumulate. This same platform feature can be traced below the surface under the southern North Sea and the Low Countries, and is often referred to as the London–Brabant Landmass (Brabant is an old name applied to the land roughly equivalent to present-day Belgium.

About 200 million years ago, as Jurassic times began, the sea invaded East Anglia and established a marine gulf between the London Platform to the southeast and other areas of low hills in Wales and the West Country to the north and west (Fig. 227). The position of this Jurassic gulf is now marked by the presence of bedrock of Jurassic age extending from the North York Moors, across the East Midlands and East Anglia, to the Cotswolds, Hampshire, Dorset and the South Coast. Most of the marine sediments are mudstones, but there are limestones of mid-Jurassic age that are particularly important in terms of the

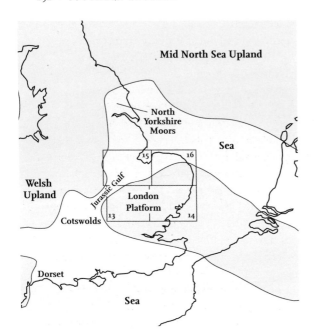

FIG 227. The land and sea pattern during the Middle Jurassic, with Areas 13–16 outlined.

scenery. When these limestones were later uplifted and eroded, they proved to be more resistant than the mudstones and so have produced distinctive limestone topography. It is also because of their toughness that these Middle Jurassic limestones became a common building material in the west of this Region, from Northampton towards Peterborough and up to Grantham. This building stone gives villages and towns an attractive appearance that is better known further southwest, in and around the Cotswold Hills. The Late Jurassic mudstones have also proved to be nationally important as sources of oil and materials for brick-making.

Early Cretaceous sediments were again largely limited in their deposition to a gulf similar in its position to the Jurassic gulf, though there were episodes of no sedimentation and sedimentation by streams and rivers rather than the sea. The thickness of the sands deposited varies from place to place, as represented by the present bedrock of the Lower Greensand (very obvious in Bedfordshire), and the Carstone (in West Norfolk), but the variations still involved very low slopes. Subsequent erosion has picked out the relative strength of these sandstones enough to form local hill features. In some areas the sandstones have been valued as local building stones, particularly where they have been hardened by the addition of iron minerals (often now rust-coloured) formed in the sands after they were deposited.

In Late Cretaceous times, a distinctive episode began in which the entire London Platform became submerged and unusually uniform marine sedimentation extended across it. The sediment deposited at this time was to become the particularly pure, fine-grained, white limestone known as Chalk. This unique material, made largely of the very small plates of floating microscopic plants, was deposited widely across the floor of a shallow sea (perhaps 200 m in depth) that extended over most of the British Isles. The compact and homogeneous nature of the Chalk has yielded the scenery of steep escarpments, rounded hills and dry valleys that are typical of the Chalk hills of East Anglia. The white Chalk has been an important local building material, particularly when certain unusually hard bands have been quarried. It has also been an important source of the generally black and very strong flint nodules that have grown within it, by precipitation of silica dissolved in the groundwater. Flints have been quarried locally from the Chalk, but more commonly collected from coastal beaches and river gravels for use in buildings and as tools by early humans.

There is a time gap in the bedrock succession representing an episode in the lower Cretaceous from which no deposits have been preserved. In the East Anglian Region, this episode involved uplift and eventual abandonment of the Late Cretaceous Chalk sea. Rather later, deposition began again in the London area, which started to subside to form the London Basin or downfold. This Early Tertiary deposition culminated in the deposition of the London Clay.

In mid-Tertiary times faulting and folding of the Earth's crust became quite widespread across the southern parts of Southern England, although only gentle tilting of bedrock layers occurred in East Anglia. By this time, some 25 million years ago, the East Anglian Region was largely land and subject to widespread river erosion. Indeed, this time saw an important change from general sinking of the East Anglian surface as sediment accumulated, to general uplift and erosion of the surface due to tectonic processes. This was the time when the main pattern of the present-day bedrock map started to form.

In general terms the bedrock pattern consists of a simple series of slightly curved belts (Fig. 226), each providing outcrops of one of the main layers of the bedrock succession. This map pattern is very simple compared with the pattern of other parts of Britain, because it is the result of the erosion of a gently tilted succession that was broadly uniform across the whole Region. The curvature of the zones is due to a change in the tilt direction of the rocks, from easterly in the north of the Region, to southeasterly in the south of the Region, where the rocks slope towards the London downfold. Over the extent of the whole Region (between 200 and 150 km depending on the direction) the bedrock has been tilted downwards – relative to its original position – by about 700 m, so a quick calculation shows that the overall amount of the tilt is less than 1 degree.

In latest Tertiary times, further downward movement taking place in the southern North Sea caused the eastern edge of East Anglia to sink slightly once again, depositing a thin veneer of sandstones and limestones. The general term *Crag* has been given to these deposits.

Surface blanket and more recent history

The surface blanket of softer material that rests upon the bedrock contains evidence for episodes that have occurred during the Quaternary (the last 2.6 million years at most). There is debate about the number, the timing and the areas covered by the ice-sheet invasions associated with this time period, but it is generally agreed that the most extensive glaciation was due to the advance of the Anglian Ice Sheet about 450,000 years ago (see Chapter 2, Figs 13 and 14). At this greatest extent, ice covered the whole Region except for the area of the higher Chalk hills southwest of Luton.

Both before and after this Anglian cold episode, East Anglia lacked ice-sheet cover and was subjected to very varied but predominantly cold conditions. There is evidence that the ground was often frozen, and that seasonal melting created conditions of widespread river erosion and deposition, along with highly active slumping of slopes and melt-induced movements of the soils.

Much more recently, the worldwide sea-level rise that has followed the melting of the last ice sheet (see Chapter 2, Fig. 13) has been responsible for much of the sedimentation in the very flat areas of the Fens and the Broads, as well as widespread sedimentation in most of the main river valleys. Local features that are the results of these episodes will be picked out in the Area discussions that follow.

East Anglia's flatness

Although a plot of the bedrock succession, generalised for the whole of the East Anglian Region (Fig. 225), shows some 800 m of bedrock, it must not be thought that layers accumulated to this total thickness at any one place. Indeed, as described above, the succession shows that gentle movements of the Earth's surface caused the thickest accumulations of each of the main layers to move through time from the northwest to the southeast (Fig. 224), so that the layers rest on the ancient London Platform foundation rather like overlapping plates in a plate rack.

The presence of the London Platform foundation only a few hundred metres below the East Anglian landscape, and its relatively uniform cover by sediments since, is evidence that movements of the Earth in this Region have been very limited compared to those taking place in other regions. Most of the near-surface bedrock has therefore avoided the deep burial within the Earth that causes rocks to harden, so it has remained soft enough to be readily eroded by rivers, ice sheets and the sea. With this in mind, it is perhaps not so surprising that East Anglia lacks high ground to such an unusual degree.

The erosion of the East Anglian landscape has worked to create large areas of very little topography at or close to present-day sea level, and ready to receive sediment from the very recent (Flandrian) sea-level rise. These sediments have filled what few hollows there were in an already flat landscape to produce areas of extreme flatness such as the Fens and the Broads.

AREA 13: NORTHAMPTON TO CAMBRIDGE

In the general introduction to this chapter we saw how movements of the Earth's crust in the East Anglian Region over the last 300 million years have been limited to very gentle tilting (less than 1 degree across the Region as a whole). In terms of the present scenery, this means that most of the natural features of Area 13 (Figs 228 and 229) are predominantly due to surface processes (driven by rivers, ice, tides and storms) that have progressively modified the landscape since these minor crustal movements took place.

FIG 228. Location map for Area 13.

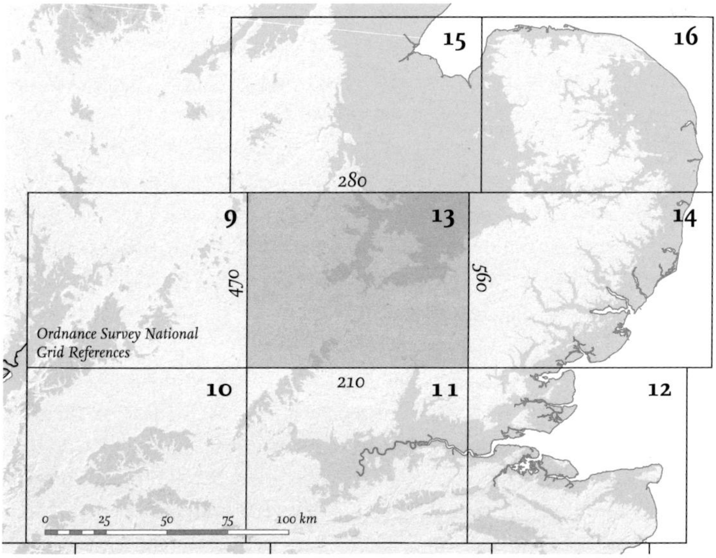

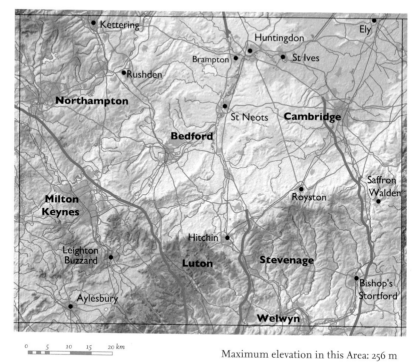

Maximum elevation in this Area: 256 m

FIG 229. Natural and man-made features of Area 13.

We will examine Area 13 by considering firstly the present-day river and coastal systems and then, secondly, the way in which the bedrock pattern has influenced them.

Comparison of the main valley pattern of the Area with the bedrock pattern makes it clear that the drainage divide provided by the Chalk hills is one of the most important scenic features. The largest valleys tend to be parallel to the bedrock belts of different ages, with tributaries and lesser valleys perpendicular to this trend, most obviously on the southeastern slope of the Chalk hills (Fig. 230). Northwest of the Chalk hills the main rivers flow northeasterly, towards the coastal zone represented by the edges of the Fens.

I have chosen five Landscapes as convenient divisions for the discussion of this Area (Fig. 231). Landscapes **A** to **D** are defined by their underlying bedrock and form a series of southwest-to-northeast trending zones, each reflecting the persistent, though very gentle, tilt of the bedrock layers downwards towards the southeast. Landscape **E** is a feature of the surface blanket, rather than the

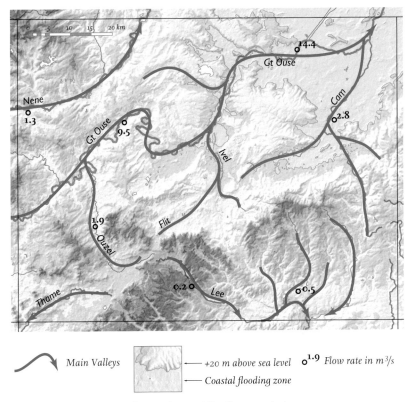

Main Valleys | +20 m above sea level | $o^{1.9}$ Flow rate in m³/s
—— Coastal flooding zone

FIG 230. Main drainage valleys and coastal flooding zone in Area 13.

bedrock, and reflects recent coastal flooding of the lowest areas. For the sake of more detailed examination of certain aspects of Landscape **B** and **C**, I have introduced three sub-areas, labelled in Figure 231 as I, II and III.

Landscape A: Jurassic limestone hills

Landscape A extends across the northwestern part of Area 13, from the northern edge of Milton Keynes, via Northampton to Rushden. It is underlain by bedrock ranging from Triassic to Middle Jurassic in age, though the Middle Jurassic limestones provide most of its distinctive hill scenery. It is drained by the River Nene, which has a mean flow of only 1.3 m³/s near the western edge of Area 13, but then increases in flow northeastwards as its tributaries converge and it enters the Fens in Area 15. Large gravel workings from Northampton downstream reflect the Nene's much greater activity during the Ice Age,

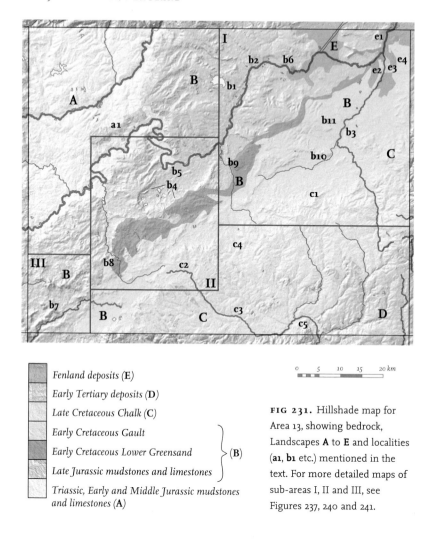

Fenland deposits (**E**)

Early Tertiary deposits (**D**)

Late Cretaceous Chalk (**C**)

Early Cretaceous Gault

Early Cretaceous Lower Greensand   } (**B**)

Late Jurassic mudstones and limestones

Triassic, Early and Middle Jurassic mudstones
and limestones (**A**)

0   5   10   15   20 km

FIG 231. Hillshade map for
Area 13, showing bedrock,
Landscapes **A** to **E** and localities
(**a1**, **b1** etc.) mentioned in the
text. For more detailed maps of
sub-areas I, II and III, see
Figures 237, 240 and 241.

when its spring melt flow rate was sufficient to deposit large floodplains
of gravel.

The Early Jurassic mudstones (the Lias, Fig. 225) contain a thin occurrence of
the Marlstone Rock Bed – although, compared to Area 9 further west, this bed
has little importance in Area 13, either topographically or economically. The
Early Jurassic is overlain by Middle Jurassic sandstones, mudstones and
limestones belonging to the Inferior and Great Oolite Series. These Jurassic

strata slope very gradually downwards to the southeast, at much less than 1 degree overall, although there are local variations in tilt and small faults, often due to the settling of the bedrock as the edges of valleys have been eroded.

The present scenery in the northwest of Area 13 consists of valleys eroded into these Triassic and Jurassic materials, with Middle Jurassic sandstones and limestones capping hills between valleys that are floored by earlier mudstones. On top of many of the hills are sheets of Anglian glacial deposits, often with river sands and gravels that may have been closely linked to ice sheets. Much of the 100 m relief of the valley topography has been created since the glaciation by erosion into and through this surface blanket. A plateau of this material forms the Yardley–Whittlewood Ridge (a1) between the Nene and Great Ouse valleys (Landscape B). An important conclusion is that much of the scenery of this Landscape has been formed since the departure of the Anglian ice, some 400,000 years ago. In this erosional work, the main agents have been the rivers and their tributaries: reaches of the Nene tend to have a wide valley – often over 1 km across – and are typically fringed by river terraces, representing episodes in the evolution of the river during the varied climatic fluctuations since the Anglian cold episode.

Landscape B: Clay–Greensand–Gault belt

This belt extends diagonally across Area 13, containing Milton Keynes, Bedford (b5), Huntingdon (b2) and Cambridge (b3). It is underlain by mudstones of Late Jurassic age (e.g. Oxford, Ampthill and Kimmeridge Clays), as well as sandstones (Lower Greensand) and mudstones of Early Cretaceous age (Gault). Because the local topography is complicated by these bedrock variations and by the patchy presence of large amounts of Anglian ice-laid sediment, it is worth selecting some parts of this Landscape for more detailed treatment. I shall first outline some of the features of the Great Ouse and Cam drainage system, and then examine more closely the patterns of hill slopes in the three sub-areas (I, II and III) marked in Figure 231, from northeast to southwest along the Clay–Greensand–Gault belt.

The Great Ouse is the largest river of the Area, and it is interesting to examine information on its flow rate. The Great Ouse has a mean flow of only 10.4 m³/s at Bedford, where it is draining an upstream catchment of 1,460 km². Further downstream at Brownshill Staunch (about 8 km from St Ives, b6) and just before the Great Ouse becomes tidal, its mean flow rate is 14.4 m³/s from a catchment of 3,030 km², reflecting its drainage of much of Area 13 and some of Area 9. For comparison, the mean flow in a downstream reach of the largest river of Southern England, the River Severn, is 106 m³/s from a wetter catchment of 9,900 km².

FIG 232. Looking northwards over the Great Ouse and Bedford
(Fig. 231, **b5**; see Fig. 240 for a better idea of the location). (Copyright Aerofilms)

The photograph over Bedford (Fig. 232) shows a relatively wide reach of the Great Ouse, but this is the result of the raising of the local river level by engineering structures. The medieval town lay north of the river, but new roads have been created to allow for modern traffic. More recent development has greatly extended the city, and has created radial patterns of development north and south of the Great Ouse.

Considerably downstream from Bedford at St Ives (**b6**; Fig. 233), the medieval markets and lanes are beautifully preserved, as well as the ancient bridge incorporating a chapel. In the further distance the numerous lakes are the result of flooding gravel pits that mark the deposits of the ancestral Great Ouse, which deposited large quantities of gravel at the end of the last (Devensian) glaciation.

FIG 233. Looking eastwards across the Great Ouse and the town of St Ives (Fig. 231, **b6**; see Fig. 237 for a better idea of the location). (Copyright Cambridge News)

Not far downstream from St Ives, the Great Ouse enters an area that may be called the Cottenham Flatlands. They appear to have been formed where the River Cam emerges from the valley that parallels the front of the Chalk hills, and joins the Great Ouse (Fig. 230). In the surroundings of Cambridge, the alluvial terraces of the Cam have been studied and their ages have been estimated using their fossil content. The sketch map (Fig. 234) shows the radial arrangement of the successive pathways of the river over the last 300,000 years of great climate fluctuation, using a simplified scheme in which three episodes of river activity are recognised, each with its distinct pathway and climatic signature.

The fan arrangement reflects the freedom of the river to shift laterally once it reached the open country downstream from the confining higher ground to the west and east. The deposits of each of these main phases of Cam activity occur at progressively lower elevations as the river continued to lower the local landscape. Indeed, old river deposits of sand and gravel appear to have resisted erosion to form high ground that was then avoided by later floods, diverting younger rivers to new courses.

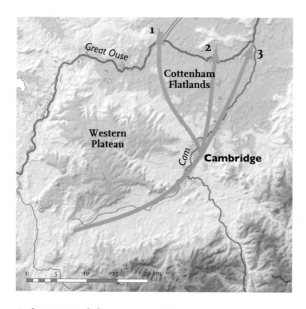

FIG 234. Former courses of the River Cam.

Red arrows mark former river pathways
1) 300, 000 years ago (upper terrace level). Cold
2) 150, 000 years ago (middle terrace level). Cold, then warm.
3) 30, 000 years ago (lower terrace level). Cold.

The River Cam and its upstream tributary, the Rhee, flow some 50 km northeast to join the Great Ouse a few kilometres south of Ely, running parallel to (and draining) the northwestern face of the Chalk hills. During the general lowering by erosion of the landscape, this face of the Chalk hills must have migrated southeastwards, down the direction of the gentle tilt. This will not have been a steady process and, particularly during the Anglian glaciation, the presence of ice (and meltwater) will have influenced the pattern of erosion by the rivers. An example of this is the way the Rhee–Cam river flows generally on Early Cretaceous (Gault) bedrock, except for some areas near Cambridge where it crosses the earliest Late Cretaceous (lower Chalk) that now extends across its valley to the Harlton (**b10**) and Madingley (**b11**) ridges. In this area, interglacial (Ipswichian) gravels have provided evidence that valley erosion was active just south of the Harlton ridge some 120,000 years ago. The width of the valley of the Rhee and Cam here is evidence for the erosional effectiveness in the past of what now seems to be a minor river: the present mean flow rate of ~1.2 m^3/s from a catchment of 30 km^2 would not be sufficient to produce a valley of this size. It seems likely that periglacial processes of slope erosion, as outlined in Chapter 2, also played an important role in the southeastern migration of the Chalk hills. As an aside, the Ipswichian gravels from this area have also yielded some remarkable fossils, including the Barrington Hippo now in the Sedgwick Museum, Cambridge.

In the foreground of Figure 235, the River Cam (yellow arrow) flows away from the camera across its floodplain, which can be picked out as a curving belt of college gardens and parks, swinging to the left and then following the large bend in the river to the second yellow arrow, where the river leaves the right-hand edge of the view. The only place where the floodplain has been built over – repeatedly – is the area beside the earliest bridge over the Cam (now Magdalene Bridge), in the top left of the photo (starred). This area, where Chalk bedrock has been preserved and the curve in the River Cam has been constrained, saw development and fortification by the Romans and the construction of the older colleges and churches of medieval Cambridge. Away from the present-day floodplain, slopes lead upwards to flat terraces that are fragments of older floodplains formed as the river carved its valley downwards to its present level.

A recent reversal of the general down-cutting of the River Cam is represented in Figure 236, a cross-section of the river and its floodplain in the grounds of King's College, at the centre of Cambridge. Shallow drillings in this area show that the present channel is flowing at a higher level than an earlier channel, which appears to have cut a small valley when sea level was low during the Devensian cold phase (~20,000 years ago). This valley was subsequently filled

FIG 235. Looking northeastwards across Cambridge.
(Copyright London Aerial Photo Library)

with sediment as the Devensian ice melted and sea level rose, and the present-day channel has been cut into this sediment infill. The filling with sediment of a previously incised valley is a common result of the recent Flandrian sea-level rise around Southern England.

Having looked at aspects of the histories of the main rivers, we now consider the pattern of slopes in the three sub-areas identified in Figure 231, all of which include this Landscape.

Southeast of the valleys of the rivers Rhee (or Ashwell Cam) and the lower Cam, the slopes of the Chalk hills are well defined, particularly west of the Royston area (Fig. 237, **c1**). Most of the steeper slopes in the outer or northwestern face of the Chalk hills are the direct result of the presence of erosionally resistant (hard) layers in the Chalk succession (see Landscape **C** for further details).

Southeast of these outer Chalk hills, the tops of the inner hills are largely underlain by upper (younger) levels in the Chalk, and they tend to have the form of a tilted plateau sloping very gently to the southeast. Much of this tilted plateau has a cover of Quaternary deposits, mainly those left by the Anglian ice. Many of the local valley slopes are capped by this material. The slopes, therefore, have

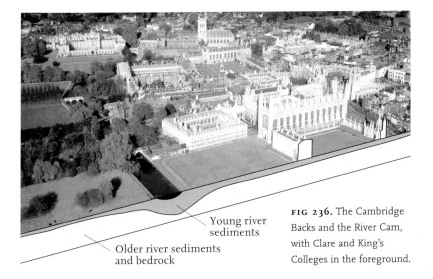

Young river sediments

Older river sediments and bedrock

FIG 236. The Cambridge Backs and the River Cam, with Clare and King's Colleges in the foreground.

probably been eroded during the last 400,000 years since the deposits were left by the Anglian ice sheets.

In the northern half of sub-area I, between Grafham Water (**b1**) and Harlton (**b10**), the scenery eroded into the mudstone bedrock consists of well-developed tributary valleys separated by narrow, often near-parallel ridges. The ridges are generally capped by a sheet of Quaternary (Anglian) ice-laid material. Similar uplands, with clearly defined tributaries and valley slopes carved into Anglian ice-laid material and Late Jurassic mudstones, occur north of the Ouse near Huntingdon (**b2**) and east of the Ouse near St Neots (**b6**), where they make up part of the 'Western Plateau' of Cambridge. Central parts of the plateau are about 70 m above sea level. Below its surface, its cover of Anglian ice-laid deposits has filled earlier valleys, and new patterns of slopes have been eroded, completely changing the shape of the earlier scenery. Parts of the plateau margin display incised valleys that have been cut into the ice-laid deposits since the Anglian. They have been further eroded when their slopes collapsed due to freeze–thaw mobilisation during subsequent cold spells. Iron-rich concretions in the Lower Greensand of Cambridge's Western Plateau have given rise to a surprisingly long history of local iron smelting.

The Greensand ridge behind Sandy (**b9**) overlooks the River Ivel valley, and the typical rusty-weathering of the sandstones is visible in a number of quarries. The ridge extends more widely across Area 13, forming the northwestern edge of the Early Cretaceous, though it varies from under a few metres in thickness in

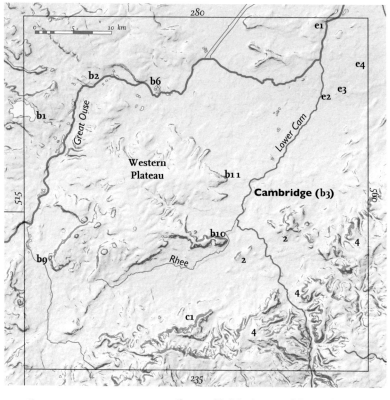

Slope

0 - 3 degrees

Above 3 degrees

FIG 237. Slope and hillshade map of the Sandy–Cambridge sub-area (I) of Area 13 (located on Fig. 231), showing localities (**b1, b2** etc.) and, towards the southeast, two hard layers within the Chalk (see under Landscape **C**, below): **2**, Melbourn Rock; **4**, base of upper Chalk.

the northeast of the Area to a much more important 70 m in thickness in the southwest, near Leighton Buzzard (Fig. 240, **b8**). In this thicker development in the southwest, the Lower Greensand has been quarried extensively as a source of sand, which has been most prized where the iron minerals that are often present have been removed by solution in the groundwater to yield a pure quartz sand. In some localities the quarries reveal stratification patterns typical of sandbars that ranged up to several metres in height, migrating under the action of the Early Cretaceous tides (Fig. 238). The variation in thickness of the Lower Greensand is probably due to episodes of non-deposition and very gentle

FIG 238. Old quarry face near Sandy Warren, showing stratification formed by migrating sandbars. (Copyright Peter Friend)

movement of the Earth's surface, before and after deposition on the floor of the Early Cretaceous sea.

A Greensand Ridge Walk has been established along the length of this feature, linking a number of estates and nature reserves where the acid-soil vegetation and fauna are distinctive.

Northeast of Sandy, under the Cambridge Western Plateau, and further northeast across the rest of Area 13, the Lower Greensand below the surface blanket becomes thinner and has only rarely produced low ridges, being generally completely obscured by Anglian ice-laid material or younger alluvium.

The rest of the Early Cretaceous succession, above the Lower Greensand, consists of mudstones of the Gault, about 75 m in thickness. The Gault tends to be a uniform, relatively soft material, so topographic slopes that occur within the area underlain by Gault bedrock are generally due to valley incision or slope retreat, rather than to the picking out of bedrock material contrasts.

Phosphate-rich *coprolites* caused an economic boom in Cambridgeshire, particularly in the nineteenth century, when they were extracted from the Cretaceous rock at a number of different levels. One of these, labelled the

FIG 239. Coprolite digging in the late nineteenth century, between Orwell and Barrington, 11 km southwest of Cambridge. (Photo held at the Sedgwick Museum, Cambridge)

Cambridge Greensand, occurs at the junction between the Gault and the Chalk, where a few metres of chalky material contain a scatter of black and grey fossils, pebbles and nodules that are enriched in phosphate and valuable as agricultural fertilisers. Some of the phosphate is the result of mineralisation in the groundwater of the excreta of Cretaceous organisms, particularly fish. This phosphate-rich material was named coprolite, for polite purposes, using a word from classical Greek (*kopros*, faeces). Areas of low-lying Cambridgeshire, wherever the Cambridge Greensand, Gault or Lower Greensand were found to be rich in coprolites, were subjected to a coprolite 'rush' (Fig. 239). Open-cast digging and washing of the coprolites involved large numbers of local and imported workers.

The Great Ouse upstream from Bedford (Fig. 240, **b5**) has a particularly sinuous course which must have developed before it cut down into the Jurassic bedrock, incising and fixing the meanders.

Southwest of Bedford is a remarkable topographic feature that I refer to here as the 'Bedford Bite' (**b4**), though it is also sometimes referred to as the Marston Moretaine Basin. The floor of this feature is underlain by Late Jurassic Oxford Clay that has been extracted in large amounts for brick-making around Marston

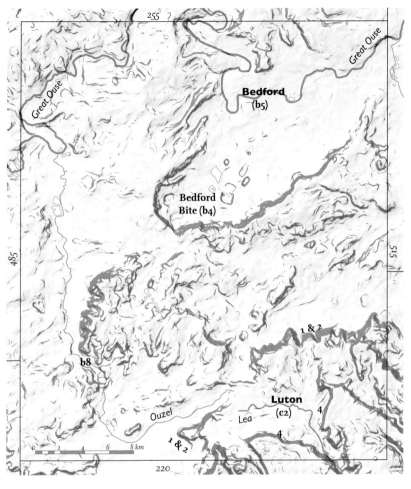

FIG 240. Slope and hillshade map of the Bedford sub-area (II) of Area 13 (located on Fig. 231), showing localities and hard Chalk layers **1**, **2** and **4** (see Landscape **C**).

Slope

0 - 3 degrees

Above 3 degrees

Moretaine and Stewartby. The slope map shows small slopes edging some of the rectangular brick pits, but also the much larger curved slopes that face into the Bite as a continuous edge to the southeast, south, west and northwest. Some of the southern sector of this edge is capped by Early Cretaceous sandstone (Lower Greensand), but the rest of it, to the east and west, is made of slopes capped by

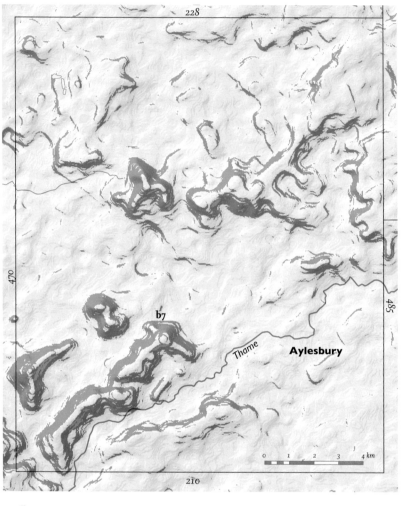

Slope

0 - 3 degrees	
Above 3 degrees	

FIG 241. Slope and hillshade map of the Aylesbury sub-area (III) of Area 13 (located on Fig. 231).

Anglian ice-laid material, which has draped the Early Cretaceous or Late and Middle Jurassic bedrock. The clear definition and curved shape of the bounding edges of this Bite, along with the flatness of its floor, suggest that the edges have retreated backwards as they slumped under the very varied climatic conditions since the Anglian. The slumped material may then have been cleared from the floor of this large feature by freeze–thaw processes, before finally being carried downstream by the ancestors of the Great Ouse.

Southwest of the Bedford Bite, the next extensive slopes are in the Brickhill area (**b8**), where they have been carved into the Lower Greensand and look out over the valley of the River Ouzel to the west.

In the southwest corner of Area 13, west of Aylesbury (Fig. 241, **b7**), is an area of flat-topped hills with well-marked marginal slopes (sub-area III). These hills and slopes have been carved from the youngest Jurassic sediments visible in the whole of East Anglia, which consist of several metres of sediment dominated by the limestones of the Portland Formation. These are the time equivalent of the limestones that form the famous building stone that is quarried on the Isle of Portland in Dorset (Area 4). The hills in Area 13 are clear examples of the way that the general lowering of a landscape underlain largely by mudstone can produce distinctive hills simply because of the presence of a few metres of erosionally strong limestone.

Landscape C: Chalk hills and valleys
The Chalk hills stand out on the map (Fig. 230) as the largest and most clearly defined topographic feature of the southern part of Area 13. They are highest and most clearly defined in the southwest, around Luton, but extend northeast via Hitchin, Stevenage, Royston and Saffron Walden. These hills are the relicts left behind as erosion acted on the gently tilted, 250 m thick Chalk layer. The orientation of the Chalk hills is the result of their tilt to the southeast, and their present location is due to the level presently reached by the processes of landscape erosion.

Even though the tilt is so gentle, it still gives rise to a contrast between the northwestern flank of the Chalk hills, where erosion has cut through successive levels within the Chalk, and the southeastern flank, where well-defined valleys have been eroded a few tens of metres into the tilted upper surface of the Chalk (Fig. 230).

The greatest elevations in the Chalk hills of Area 13 are in the southwest, near to Luton and Whipsnade, where elevations of 250 m occur. In this area the Chalk edge is unusually distinct, making it a very popular launch site for paragliders keen to explore the lower ground to the north. Elevations tend to decrease southeastwards, following the tilt of the upper surface of the Chalk layer. Further northeast in Area 13, Chalk hill elevations rarely exceed 100 m and the Chalk edge facing northwestwards is much less distinct. In this area, the Rhee branch of the Cam is joined by the Cam and Granta streams just upstream from Cambridge.

These drain the Saffron Walden and Linton valleys in the Chalk Hills, where the Chalk edge is particularly far to the southeast. These lower elevations may reflect erosion by Anglian ice in this eastern area, because it appears that the higher edge in the Luton area (c2) was never surmounted by the Anglian ice sheets.

The lowest part of the Chalk is often called the Chalk Marl, because it is richer in clay than more normal Chalk, which is almost entirely calcite. During the erosion of the landscape the Chalk Marl has tended to behave in a similar way to the underlying Gault mudstones: both usually form rather low ground, in contrast to the rest of the Chalk, and may have been subject to widespread periglacial mobilisation of near-surface material, producing low, rounded hills and hollows that are typical at this level.

Within the main Chalk layer there are a number of hard bands (Fig. 225), each a few metres thick, which have often resisted general landscape erosion to produce distinct escarpments in the topography (Figs 237 and 240). The hard bands tend to vary from place to place, and they rarely all produce slope features in the same area, but the following number system is used to refer to the most distinctive: (1) Tottenhoe or Burwell Rock; (2) Melbourn Rock; (3) Middle Chalk; (4) Base of Upper Chalk. The hardness of the bands appears to reflect changes in the environment of the original Chalk seas, but it may also reflect differences in the precipitation of calcite within small pores in the Chalk after its burial. Spring lines are also features of the landscape caused by these hard bands, for example at Ashwell, where the Cam (Rhee) rises.

In the southeastern corner of sub-area II (Fig. 240) the slope map shows two different slope features forming the northwest face of the Chalk hills. The Chalk hard bands (1, 2 and 4) have produced the steeper slopes as well as the gently sloping surface to the southeast, where valleys have eroded parallel to the tilt of the Chalk bedrock through a cap of several metres of Clay-with-flints and Upper Chalk bedrock. The Clay-with-flints is a soil-like deposit resulting from solution and weathering of Chalk. It forms a capping layer rich in the flints that were present as nodules in the original Chalk. More generally, this special material has Anglian ice-laid material on top of it in places, and must therefore have formed at least partly before the ice sheet arrived some 450,000 years ago. The solution and weathering probably took place under the warmer climatic conditions that existed in the millions of years before the Ice Age.

The upper, southeasterly surface of the Chalk Hills has a cover of Anglian ice-laid material, except southwest of Luton (c2), where the hills do not seem to have been overwhelmed by the ice. Another area lacking ice-laid material is the intriguing northwesterly face of the Chalk hills, which seems to have had an important influence on the location of historic travel and trade routes. It seems most likely that ice-laid deposits did cover this face when the Anglian ice sheet melted, but that they have been stripped off by river and slope erosion over the subsequent 400,000 years.

One of the greatest environmental changes in the Chalk hills landscape was the arrival of the Anglian ice sheet. Southwest of the upper Lea Valley (c3) and Luton (c2), the lack of ice-laid deposits is evidence that the elevation of the Chalk topography was sufficient to prevent the further spread of the ice sheet in that direction. Northeast of this ice margin, ice-laid material was deposited over the whole of the southeasterly surface of the Chalk Hills and influenced the form of the valleys later eroded into it.

The patterns of southeasterly- and southerly-flowing river valleys eroded into the Chalk are striking, particularly on the slope maps, where the paired valley margins are picked out, clearly contrasting with the flatter valley floors (Figs 230 and 237). Most of these Chalk valleys now lack a permanent stream, because rainfall runoff percolates through fractures in the Chalk instead of flowing over the ground surface. It is believed that these valleys were eroded under Ice Age conditions, when rivers flowed vigorously for at least part of the year because their water could not percolate through the near-surface zone of permanently frozen bedrock.

The Hitchin–Stevenage gap (c4) is a funnel-shaped hollow in the face of the Chalk hills, some 10 km wide in the north and narrowing southwards. It contains the A1 trunk road and the main East Coast railway line from London (King's Cross) to Scotland. The development of Hitchin, Baldock, Letchworth and Stevenage is further evidence of the importance of these transport routes to local settlement.

The floor of the gap is underlain by a complex of Anglian ice-laid material with sands and gravels deposited by rivers. An unusual feature of these surface-blanket sediments is that they have often been deposited as material plugging a system of branching valleys up to 100 m deep (Fig. 242). Valleys that have been almost completely filled with glacial and later sediment are an intriguing feature of many areas of Chalk hills. Some of the present open valleys may have been cut under similar conditions, then plugged with material, and then emptied again by later river action. It is now believed that much of the erosion of these valleys took place by meltwater flow active under the Anglian ice sheets. Most of the buried valley floors slope southwards, indicating drainage flow in that direction, but local reversals in valley slope do occur. These northward-sloping valleys seem to result from situations where the rivers were forced to flow up local gradients under the ice sheet, like water in an enclosed pipe.

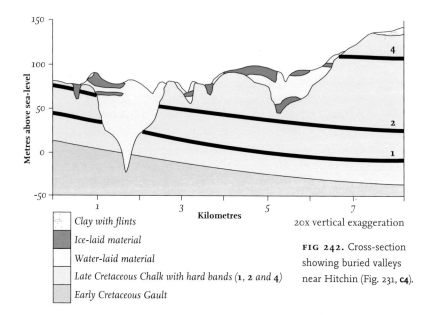

Clay with flints

Ice-laid material

Water-laid material

Late Cretaceous Chalk with hard bands (1, 2 and 4)

Early Cretaceous Gault

20x vertical exaggeration

FIG 242. Cross-section showing buried valleys near Hitchin (Fig. 231, **c4**).

Some of the southeastern Chalk-slope valleys have eroded into the Upper Chalk, but not cut deeply enough to expose hard band 4. Much of the erosion of these shallow valleys is relatively young and has taken place into Anglian ice-laid material since it was deposited about 400,000 years ago. The valleys often show beautiful branching patterns of their tributaries, which probably result from the distinctive behaviour of the muddy ice-laid material when the heads of the tributaries cut back into it. Good examples of these patterns are the valleys that flow from the north into the Lea trunk river on the southern edge of Area 13 (**c5**).

Landscape D: Bishop's Stortford Clay hills

This Landscape occupies the southeastern corner of Area 13, where it is defined by the occurrence of Early Tertiary sediments below the surface blanket. Up to 17 m of sandy Woolwich and Reading Beds are overlain by some 65 m of London Clay, all deposited in an arm of the sea during Early Tertiary times.

Above the bedrock, the surface blanket contains river sands and gravels which are thought to have been deposited by an ancestor of the River Thames (Areas 10 and 11).

Some 450,000 years ago, the Anglian ice sheet covered – at its maximum extent – the whole of this Landscape, deflecting the ancestral Thames to its present more southerly route. When the Anglian ice sheet melted, it left up to

30 m of ice-laid deposits. Most of the natural topography of the present-day Landscape is the result of river erosion, which has cut shallow valleys through this and into the Early Tertiary mudstones.

Landscape E: The Fen edge

In the northeast corner of Area 13, the wide, shallow valleys of the Great Ouse and Cam slope very gently towards the sea. The covering of the lower parts of these valleys with mud and peat during the recent Flandrian rise of sea level has produced local arms of very flat Fenland that is more fully described in Area 15.

The Fens surround the Isle of Ely (**e1**), a low upland that has been carved in Late Jurassic mudstones capped by Early Cretaceous Lower Greensand, an extension of our Landscape **B**. Other local fenland features in the Cam valley are due to a patch of Late Jurassic limestones a few kilometres across near the village of Upware (**e2**), and a ridge of Anglian ice-laid material on which the village of Wicken (**e3**) stands.

FIG 243. Former area of Soham Mere, just southeast of Ely (Fig. 237, **e4**). (Photography held at Cambridge University Collection of Air Photographs, Unit for Landscape Modelling)

Wicken Fen (**e3**) is a nature reserve famous as one of the first places in the country where determined efforts were made to preserve a rapidly disappearing natural environment. It was purchased as a small sample of Fen wetland environment at a time when aggressive draining of the surrounding farmland was threatening its existence. The present development plan for the Fen involves the enlargement of the reserve to include some surrounding farmland, which will then be allowed to revert to natural wet land, acting as a recreational 'green lung' for the highly developed Cambridge area.

Before the engineered drainage of the Fens, more-or-less permanent lakes were local features, particularly around the edges of the Fenland, where groundwater tends to flow from the neighbouring uplands. Soham Mere was a good example of one of these lakes, and the outline of the drained lake is still clearly visible in aerial photographs (Fig. 243). The extent of the former mere is now marked by a patch of lighter soil that contrasts strongly with the surrounding fields of darker peaty soils. The lightness is the result of chalk-like limey deposits made by single-celled plants that lived in the lake. The plants made use of the 'hard' water which emerged as springs through the limestone and chalk of the surrounding uplands, producing calcium carbonate that then collected on the bottom of the lake as the plants died and sank.

AREA 14: SUFFOLK AND NORTH ESSEX

In the general introduction to the East Anglian Region, I stressed the open feel of the scenery and the absence of high hills, explaining these to be the result of the unusual lack of movement of the Earth's surface in this Region over the last 300 million years. Other results of this lack of movement are that the bedrock succession formed during this time varies only slightly across the Region, so that a single, generalised bedrock succession (Fig. 225) is adequate to represent the bedrock pattern across all four Areas of the Region (Fig. 226), and the bedrock layers have a very gentle tilt and simple pattern.

The scenery of Area 14 (Figs 244 and 245) is largely the result of relatively recent river and coastal processes acting upon earlier landscapes. In broad terms, the valleys of the Area consist of a small northwesterly-flowing group draining to the Fenland coastal zone, and a more extensive southeasterly group draining towards the coasts of north Essex and Suffolk (Fig. 246). These rivers have fairly small catchments, with their headwaters in the nearby Chalk hills, an area which receives relatively little rainfall compared to other areas of Southern England. Consequently the mean flow rates for these rivers are rather small.

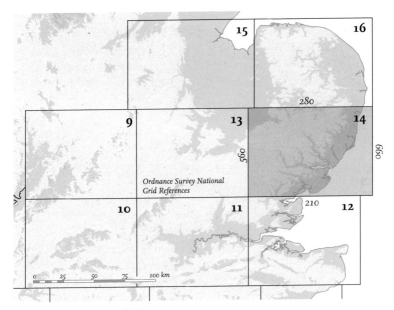

FIG 244. Location map for Area 14.

FIG 245. Natural and man-made features of Area 14.

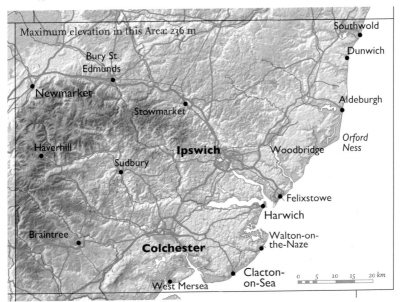

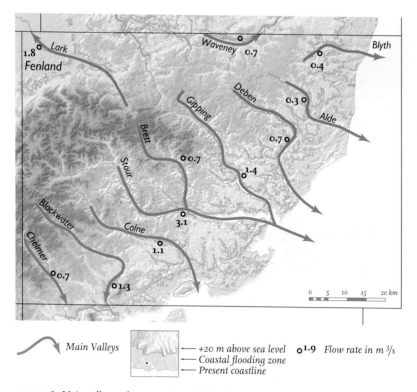

FIG 246. Main valley pathways and coastal flooding zone in Area 14.

Apart from the erosion pattern of the drainage valleys, the other major factor in determining the local scenery is the distribution of the underlying bedrock. This reflects movements of the Earth's surface which, although very minor, have still caused some areas to rise and others to subside, exposing bedrock of different ages near the surface across the Area (Fig. 247).

I have divided Area 14 into four Landscapes, labelled **A** to **D** (Fig. 247). This division is based largely on the bedrock that underlies the surface blanket, and it may be helpful that these four Landscapes are similar to the 'character areas' used by the Countryside Agency.

Landscape A: The Fen-edge Claylands (Late Jurassic and Early Cretaceous)

This Landscape in the northwest corner of Area 14 is defined by its bedrock of Late Jurassic age (Kimmeridge Clay) and Early Cretaceous age (Lower Greensand and Gault). The scenery carved into this bedrock has been formed by the Fenland

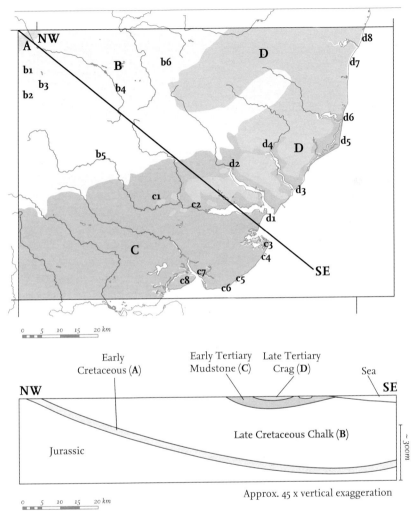

FIG 247. Bedrock pattern, structure, Landscapes **A** to **D** and localities (**b1, b2** etc.) in Area 14.

rivers more fully described under Areas 13 and 15, where this landscape is more extensive.

The tilt of the bedrock layers in this area is uniformly less than 1 degree to the southeast; there is no measurable difference between the Late Jurassic and the Early Cretaceous tilt, despite a time gap of some 16 million years. This implies an absence of tilting movement during this period, before the formation of the thin (up to 20 m thick) Lower Greensand and the thicker Gault. In scenery terms, the Lower Greensand has often produced slightly higher ground than the mudstones below and above, demonstrating its greater resistance as the landscape was being eroded.

Landscape B: The Chalk Hills (Late Cretaceous)

This Landscape is defined by the near-surface presence of Late Cretaceous Chalk. The erosion of the Chalk hills is being carried out now by rivers flowing in two very different directions. In the north and northwest of Area 14, the River Lark drains northwestwards towards the Fens (Area 15). However, the vast majority of the Chalk hills are drained to the east coast by rivers such as the Waveney, Deben and Stour.

In the northwestern part of this Landscape, because of the southeasterly tilt of the Chalk, the surface is underlain by the lowest layer of the Chalk, which has produced generally low ground with gentle slopes. This reflects the mud content of the lowest layers of the Chalk succession, which makes them easy to erode compared with the higher Chalk to the southeast. Views around the Cambridgeshire Fen-edge villages (for example Burwell, **b1**) and Newmarket (**b3**) provide good examples of this low-lying, but undulating, Chalk-edge landscape. They lie centrally in a distinctive belt of country that runs along the north and west edge of the Chalk hills right across East Anglia. The belt is several kilometres across and runs between the higher Chalk hills to the southeast, with their surface blanket of Anglian ice-laid material, and the low wetlands of the Fens to the northwest. Why the Chalk-edge belt lacks ice-laid material is a puzzling question, but may simply reflect the way river erosion has stripped cover from the edge of the Chalk hills, leaving the main Chalk landscape still covered with ice-laid material. It may also reflect the way this mud-rich bedrock has been particularly prone to mobilisation under freeze–thaw Ice Age conditions, perhaps even involving thaw-lake processes (see Chapter 2). The muddy ice-laid material mantling the higher Chalk to the southeast has made it very difficult to farm, leading to a history of thick tree cover in contrast to the open character of the Chalk-edge belt to the northwest. Because of this, the Chalk-edge belt became important in prehistoric times as an area for settlement and a pathway for long-distance travel. The name Icknield Way has been applied for centuries to the series of ancient roads linking settlements along the Chalk-edge belt, in recognition of the regional importance of a through-route here.

Several Anglo-Saxon boundary markers extend across the Chalk-edge belt, perpendicular to its length. The Devil's Dyke (**b2**) near Newmarket is the most completely preserved of these. On the July Racecourse, the horses race up a gentle but steady incline underlain by the lower part of the Late Cretaceous Chalk and forming the Chalk-edge hills (Fig. 248).

FIG 248. The Devil's Dyke in the foreground, with the July Racecourse (Fig. 247, **b2**), near Newmarket, behind.

Between Haverhill, Newmarket and Bury St Edmunds, the Chalk hills reach their greatest elevations in Area 14 at about 120 m above sea level. South and east of Newmarket (**b3**), north-facing scarps are the result of hard bands in the Chalk resisting erosion. In the rest of this higher area of the Chalk hills, the slopes are the sides of valleys carved in the surface blanket of Anglian ice-laid material, and so must have formed during the last half-million years since that glaciation.

The town of Bury St Edmunds was laid out in the early 1100s around the precinct of the great Abbey Church and shrine to St Edmund, which owes its location to the River Lark (Fig. 249) and stands on a terrace with a gentle slope facing the floodplain of the river.

In contrast to the Lark, most of the seaward-draining valleys in the Chalk hills landscape flow generally towards the southeast, but some show distinct doglegs, which seem to parallel the mapped boundary with the Early Tertiary landscape (Landscape **C**) to the south (Fig. 246). These doglegs may have formed when the downward-eroding rivers met changes of erosional strength at the boundary between the Early Tertiary bedrock and the underlying Chalk. As the landscape subsequently eroded downwards, the valleys may have maintained their dogleg plan, following the boundary between bedrock units by moving several kilometres southwards, down the gentle tilt of the bedrock layers.

FIG 249. The Abbey precinct in Bury St Edmunds (Fig. 247, **b4**). The River Lark flows just in front of the red-roofed building. In the lower right corner is St Edmundsbury Cathedral, to which a magnificent Millennium tower has been added since the photograph was taken. (Copyright Aerofilms)

One of the most obvious doglegs is in the upper reaches of the Stour valley (**b5**), which links the famous Suffolk villages of Clare, Cavendish and Long Melford. These villages are famous for the preservation of large numbers of beautiful houses and churches, reflecting the fifteenth-century peak of prosperity in the wool and textile trade in this area. Flints from the Chalk have been widely used in building here, and the timber frames, often painted and ornamented into surface patterns (pargetting), along with their Chalk-based plaster work, are particularly attractive.

Northeastward of the A14 trunk road and the Bury St Edmunds to Ipswich railway (Fig. 245), the Chalk hills landscape of north-central Suffolk (**b6**) is a southern extension of the Breckland, discussed further under Area 16. The landscape here is lower than the Chalk hills to the southwest, and is widely covered by a gently undulating sheet of Anglian ice-laid material, locally eroded by valleys that penetrate to the Chalk bedrock.

Landscape C: The Essex Claylands (Early Tertiary)
This Landscape is defined by the Early Tertiary age of the bedrock underlying it. The hill-shaded elevation maps (Figs 245 and 246) make it clear that the size and form of the hills and valleys is remarkably little influenced by the change of bedrock, which continues to be capped widely by Anglian ice-laid material.

As with the southern part of the Chalk hills (Landscape **B**), present-day erosion of this Landscape is being carried out by a number of rivers draining southwards and eastwards towards the sea. At locality **c1** in Figure 247 there is a second major dogleg on the River Stour, in one of the most clearly developed of these widened valley systems. It has steep valley walls, cut through Anglian ice-laid material resting on Early Tertiary mudstone bedrock. In the case of both materials, undermining by the river will have tended to cause collapse, which has produced the steep slopes that form the valley walls. Another feature is the presence of small, steep-sided branch valleys, often with their own branches. These are probably due to local collapses of the valley heads under the freezing and thawing conditions that existed during much of the Ice Age.

Figure 250 shows an early pen and watercolour drawing made by John Constable in 1800, when he was only 24. It is a beautifully careful representation of the coach road leading across the flat floodplain of the Stour valley, the distinct northern wall of which is visible in the background. The present view from this locality is obscured by large trees, and the entire valley crossing at this point has now been heavily engineered to reduce gradients on the busy A12 trunk road running between Colchester and Ipswich. Constable's drawing shows very clearly the distinctive slopes of the valley walls to north and south compared to the flatness of the floodplain floor (Fig. 251), although he probably had no idea that the flat valley floor is the result of recent (Flandrian) sea-level rise.

John Constable (1776–1837) was born in East Bergholt (**c2**), a village 3 km downstream from Stratford St Mary on the Stour, near to the present crossing of the A12 trunk road. He was the fourth child in a family whose successful milling and river transport business on the Stour dominated John's early years, providing the basis for his life as an artist. His delight in the challenge of portraying river-bank scenery and activities – often under highly variable light and changing skies

FIG 250. The Valley of the Stour with Stratford St Mary in the distance.
(Copyright J. Constable/V&A Images/Victoria and Albert Museum)

– was highly original. Most previous artists had tended to invent landscapes as incidental backgrounds to portraits of individuals, or to historical or religious scenes. Much of his work shows scenes in the 20 km stretch of the lower Stour valley that is now known as Constable Country, and he built much of his reputation on this work. Remarkably, Thomas Gainsborough (1727–88) came from further up the same Stour valley of Suffolk, though he was born some 50 years earlier, and is most famous for his portraits.

Over the whole of the southern part of this Landscape, the gently hilly scenery is dominated by the presence of the coastline. There are two rather distinct kinds of coastal scenery here, each reflecting a different response to the Flandrian rise in sea level that has taken place since the last important cold episode of the Ice Age. The first of these consists of cliffs where low hills (now 10–30 m above sea level) have been attacked by storm waves. These cliffs occur from the Naze (**c3**), via Walton, to Frinton-on-Sea (**c4**) and Clacton (**c5**) and, to a minor extent, at Jaywick (**c6**). Most of these cliffs have been cut in material of the Early Tertiary London Clay, but small amounts of Late Tertiary Crag deposits exist on top of this at, for instance, the Naze. Surface-blanket layers of younger sand and gravel have also locally been cut into small cliffs.

The second kind of coast scenery has formed where the rising sea level has invaded a flat and low-lying land surface, causing the sea to deposit mud on a

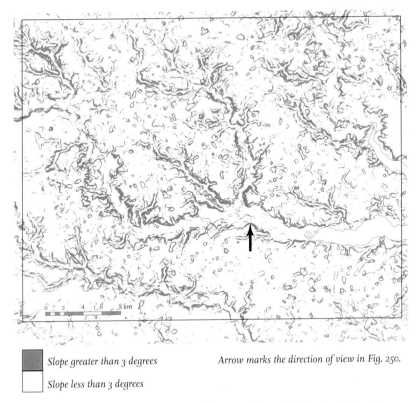

Slope greater than 3 degrees

Slope less than 3 degrees

Arrow marks the direction of view in Fig. 250.

FIG 251. Slope map of the Stour and neighbouring valleys, also showing the location and direction of Constable's drawing (Fig. 250).

tide-dominated coast with mud flats and tidal channels. Good examples of this second type are around Brightlingsea (c7) and Mersea Island (c8), with the Colne tidal estuary between. The River Colne estuary extends across the whole of the view shown in Figure 252, its drowned valley running inland towards Colchester. The mud flats in the foreground of the photograph show very beautifully the winding patterns formed by small tidal flood-and-ebb channels on muddy foreshores.

Landscape D: Suffolk Coast and Heaths (Late Tertiary)
The presence of the Late Tertiary Crag bedrock is used to define the extent of this Landscape, which is dominated by the coast and the estuaries that have been formed by the Flandrian flooding of valleys draining the inland parts of Area 14. The Orwell Bridge (Fig. 253) spans one such drowned valley.

FIG 252. Looking westwards from Brightlingsea Creek (Fig. 247, c7) to Mersea Island (c8) in the distance. Cindery Island is visible in the foreground and, in the bottom right-hand corner of the picture, the mud flats just east of Brightlingsea can be seen. (Copyright Aerofilms)

Harwich Harbour (d1) is a remarkable natural haven where the Stour and Orwell valleys join, sheltered behind the coastal ridge that extends through Felixstowe to Landguard Point (Fig. 254). Both of the main valleys have been carved, over long periods of changing conditions, by freshwater streams, and have been flooded recently by the Flandrian rise in sea level since the last cold episode of the Ice Age.

Over the last 30 years, the Port of Felixstowe (north of d1; Fig. 255) has been built on the flat ground behind the main coastal gravel barrier. The port is one of the largest commercial developments in Southern England over the last few years, and has been specifically engineered to handle international container transport.

FIG 253. Looking northwestwards up the tidal estuary of the Lower Orwell (Fig. 247, d1).
The Orwell Bridge spans the estuary in the distance, carrying the A14 trunk road to
connect the industrial Midlands with Felixstowe container port, and some of the
buildings of Ipswich can be seen beyond the bridge on the right-hand side of the
picture. Orwell Park House is in the middle distance on the right, on one of the steep
20–30 m high shoulders typical of the drowned valleys of Suffolk, and the marina near
Pin Mill is visible rather further away on the left. (Photography held at Cambridge
University Collection of Air Photographs, Unit for Landscape Modelling)

It is interesting to note that the Early Tertiary layer just below the surface
between Felixstowe and Ipswich yields phosphate mineral material (generally in
the form of coprolites) that has been commercially important in the past, and
helped to develop the fertiliser industry in this area. These coprolites are
younger than the Early Cretaceous coprolites of Cambridgeshire (Area 13), which
also strongly influenced local commercial development. The Early Tertiary
London Clay has also yielded valuable materials that have given rise to local

FIG 254. Landguard Point and the Port of Felixstowe. (Copyright Dae Sasitorn & Adrian Warren/www.lastrefuge.co.uk)

FIG 255. Felixstowe container quay. (Copyright Suffolk County Council)

industries. *The Harwich Cement Stone* came from one bed – less than a metre thick – that occurs on the foreshore. On heating, this stone was found to produce excellent Portland cement able to set strongly even in the presence of water. The Harwich *Copperas Stones,* also collected from the foreshore, and often originating as fossil wood, provided a source of sulphate important in tanning and the dyeing of textiles.

FIG 256. Looking southeastward from Ipswich down the Orwell estuary. Medieval Ipswich is to the left of the river, in the middle distance. Two more geometrically planned suburban areas have been built on high plateaus that form the shoulders of the valley: California and Rosewell (left, middle distance) and Chantry (right, foreground). (Copyright Aerofilms)

Ipswich (Fig. 256) developed in the first area upstream from the open estuary of the Orwell where a river crossing was relatively easy. So the position of Ipswich is a direct result of the last great (Flandrian) rise of sea level, which flooded the Orwell valley up to this point. Three kilometres downstream, the Orwell Bridge (completed in 1982) was built to allow the A14 trunk road from the Midlands and northern England to bypass Ipswich, taking container and other traffic to and from Felixstowe Port.

Excavations in the Ipswich area (**d2**) reveal bedrock of Late Cretaceous Chalk, Early Tertiary mudstones (mainly London Clay) and Late Tertiary Crag deposits. Rivers must have been eroding valleys during the time between the formation of these layers, but the evidence of these rivers is largely missing. The surface layer above the bedrock, however, tells us quite a lot about the conditions in the Ice Age. Deeply eroded valleys – many of them tens of metres deep – were cut into the Chalk before being filled with Ice Age sediment. The load-bearing properties of such sediment infills are generally poor, and one of these valleys caused engineering problems during construction of the Orwell Bridge. Some of the valleys were cut more than 50 m below present-day sea level, confirming that the sea must have been much lower when the valleys were eroded. Anglian river sands and gravels representing the ancestral Thames were spread widely over this area, covering the flat plateau picked out in the aerial photograph (Fig. 256). The Anglian ice-laid material was then deposited, marking the farthest extent of these ice sheets. In the 400,000 years since this cold spell, the present valley system of the Gipping and Orwell has been eroded and partly filled with sediment, most obviously related to the Flandrian rise of sea level since the end of the Devensian glacial.

FIG 257. Felixstowe Ferry crossing over the River Deben, between Felixstowe Ferry, in the foreground, and Bawdsey Manor, on the far side (Fig. 247, **d3**). The coast continues to the northeast, where Orford Ness (**d5**) forms the prominent bulge in the far distance. (Copyright London Aerial Photo Library)

At the mouth of the River Deben (Fig. 257) the passenger ferry crossing is only about 200 m wide between Felixstowe Ferry and Bawdsey Manor (**d3**), famous as a key site for radar experimentation during World War II. On the outer coast near the woods of Bawdsey Manor, outcrops of Early Tertiary London Clay and Late Tertiary Crag form low cliffs that have been cut since sea level rose following the last glacial.

The estuary of the River Deben extends inland for some 12 km from Felixstowe Ferry and the sea to Martlesham Creek (the right branch in the photo, Fig. 258) and the town of Woodbridge (**d4**). The tidal reach of the Deben, up to 1 km wide, is a marvellous example of a river valley with well-developed bends that has been drowned by the rise of sea level since the Devensian. The 10–20 m shoulders of the valley define its edges clearly, even though mud has been gathering along the inside of many of the river's bends, which have sometimes been embanked and drained. At Sutton Hoo, on the slopes of the Deben Valley opposite Woodbridge, the body of the Anglo-Saxon warrior King Raedwald was buried in about AD 625, along with a ship and one of the most remarkable treasures so far found in Britain. The site and visitor centre have been developed by the National Trust.

FIG 258. Looking southeastwards from Woodbridge (Fig. 247, **d4**) down the River Deben to Felixstowe Ferry and the sea. (Copyright Aerofilms)

FIG 259. Northeastward view from the settlement of Shingle Street, along Orford Beach to Orford Ness, the outward bulge some 10 km away from the end of the spit, in the far distance (Fig. 247, **d5**). (Copyright Aerofilms)

Further north along the coast, the long, finger-like spit of Orford Beach (Fig. 259) has been constructed by storm waves and has grown several kilometres from Orford Ness (**d5**). At the southern end of the spit, a complicated pattern of linear ridges records former outlines of the spit as it has changed its position and shape with time.

Orford Beach and Orford Ness together form one of the largest coastal accumulations of gravel on the east coast. Although the exact timing of the growth episodes of the Orford Beach spit is not known, it is clearly the result of powerful waves from the northeast driving sand and gravel southwards along the coast (Fig. 260). The growth of the gravel and sand barrier has created a back-barrier of salt marshes and flats, which have accumulated muds in waters that are still strongly tidal, but sheltered from storm waves. Valleys entering this sheltered back-barrier have been topped up with fine mud-flat sediments, as is the case in the Norfolk Broads (Area 16) or the Fens (Area 15). The Butley River can be seen in the middle distance in Figure 259, joining the River Ore to flow parallel to and behind the spit.

FIG 260. Episodes in the evolution of the coast from Aldeburgh (Fig. 247, **d6**) southward, past Orford Ness (**d5**).

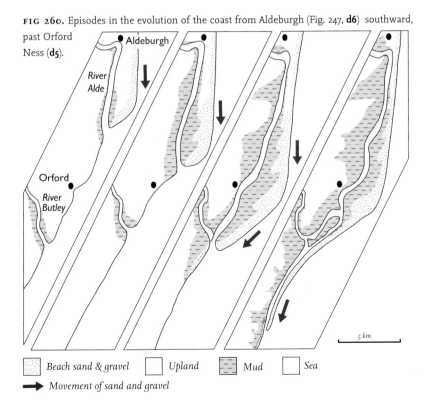

Beach sand & gravel · Upland · Mud · Sea

Movement of sand and gravel

FIG 261. Looking southwards across Southwold (Fig. 247, **d7**) towards Walberswick. (Copyright Aerofilms)

At the northeastern corner of Area 13, Southwold (Fig. 261) is attractively located on small cliffs carved into Crag deposits of the Late Tertiary. This material is preserved in a plateau between the low ground of the River Blyth valley to the south, and the low ground immediately to the north, where Buss Creek enters the sea at Sole Bay.

Southwold (**d7**) and Dunwich (**d8**) provide another beautiful example of the way natural coastal processes, in this case storm wave activity, can change the shape of the coastline on a historical timescale (Figs 262 and 263). Over the last

FIG 262. Episodes in the evolution of the coastal scenery of Southwold (Fig. 247, **d7**) to Dunwich (**d8**).

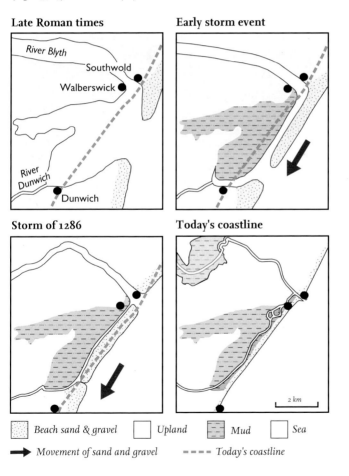

Late Roman times

River Blyth
Southwold
Walberswick
River Dunwich
Dunwich

Early storm event

Storm of 1286

Today's coastline

2 km

Beach sand & gravel   Upland   Mud   Sea

➤ Movement of sand and gravel   ----- Today's coastline

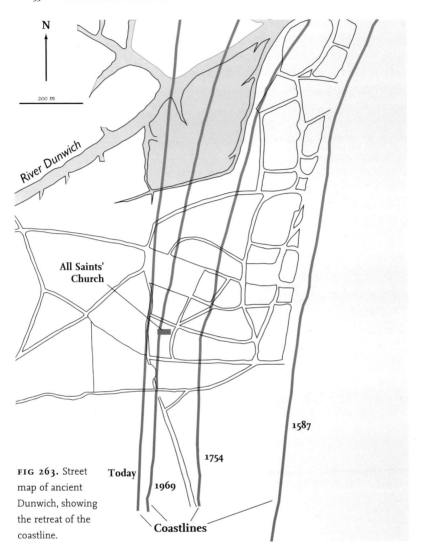

N

200 m

River Dunwich

All Saints' Church

1587

1754

FIG 263. Street map of ancient Dunwich, showing the retreat of the coastline.

Today

1969

Coastlines

1,600 years, since the end of the Roman period, the position of the outer coast at Southwold has moved inland by more than 1 km. This coastal retreat simply measures the success of storm wave attack in removing Late Tertiary Crag material from the landscape during this recent period, which was long after the sea reached approximately its present level as a result of the Flandrian sea-level rise. Some of the sand and gravel moved by the storm waves at Southwold must have contributed to the filling-in of the large bay that existed at the end of Roman times between Southwold and Dunwich.

The history of Dunwich during this time is dramatic and famous. By the year 1300, Dunwich was one of the most important ports in eastern England, with many parishes and churches, an extensive merchant shipping trade and two members in Parliament. However, it was already suffering from the problem of cliff erosion, and the filling-up of its north-facing harbour with sand and gravel driven southwards along the coast during storms. The average rate of cliff erosion in this area has been well over 1 m per year for at least the past 1,000 years, but this figure gives a misleading impression of steady movement: in practice, retreats take place suddenly as responses to infrequent and particularly violent storms. Until recently, gravestones from the churchyard of All Saints' were visible on the cliff top, but now even these have gone (Fig. 264).

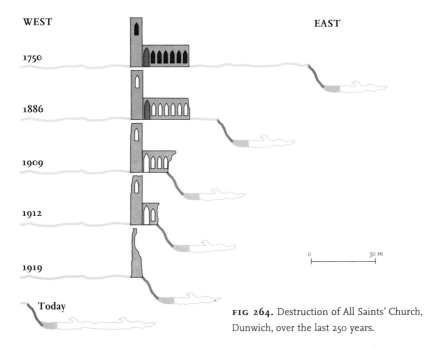

FIG 264. Destruction of All Saints' Church, Dunwich, over the last 250 years.

AREA 15: LEICESTER TO THE FENS

In the west of Area 15 (Figs 265 and 266) the scenery consists of low hills and open valleys in Leicestershire and Nottinghamshire, whereas the eastern scenery is dominated by the spectacular flatness of the Fens. We shall be considering why the scenery is so different in these two parts of the Area.

The bedrock history of Area 15 is similar to that of the other three Areas of the East Anglian Region, so the general bedrock succession (Fig. 225) and distribution map (Fig. 226) provide a perfectly good introduction.

The coastal zone and the inland river system are the active sites of present-day change to the scenery, so it is useful to start by summarising their map pattern (Fig. 267). The ways these coasts and valleys are related now, and how they have interacted with the bedrock, will help us to understand the long-term development of the scenery.

The coastal zone of this Area – defined as the ground lying less than 20 m above sea level – is mostly part of the Fenland Basin (Fig. 268, Landscape C), which owes its exceptional flatness to the thin cover of sediment that has accumulated on the flat bedrock surface during the last few thousand years of

FIG 265. Location map for Area 15.

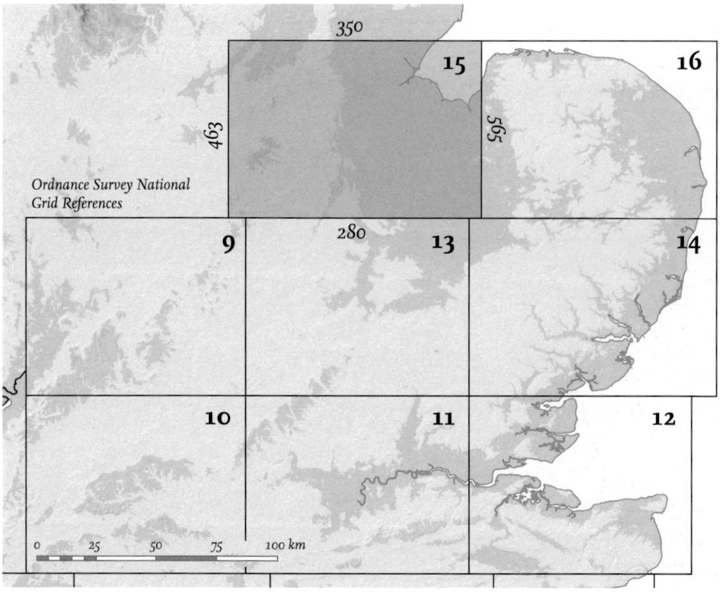

Flandrian sea-level rise. Knowledge of this and earlier sea-level changes suggests that some of the present-day slopes at the edges of the Fens have been carved into the bedrock at times when they formed the shoreline of the sea or short-lived lakes.

The drainage pattern of the Area is complicated, and not immediately obvious to the casual traveller because of the gentleness of the slopes and the open nature of the landscape (Fig. 267). In the extreme southwest corner of the Area, southwest of Market Harborough, small streams drain westwards to eventually join the Avon and Severn and flow into the Bristol Channel. Ground elevations here are only 170 m above sea level – remarkably low for one of the main drainage divides in the whole of Southern England.

Further north, the River Trent, one of the main rivers of central England, drains the hilly northwestern corner of Area 15. Considerably to the west of this Area, the Trent flows southeasterly through Stoke-on-Trent in the Potteries, then past the Burton-on-Trent breweries before passing the Trent Bridge cricket ground in Nottingham, just beyond the western boundary of this Area. Further downstream, to the north of Area 15, the Trent runs through Newark-on-Trent (90.5 m³/s mean flow) before joining the Humber estuary some 70 km north of this Area. In the west of this Area, the Melton Mowbray hills drain westwards, ultimately into the Trent, via the Rivers Eye and Wreake.

FIG 266. Natural and man-made features of Area 15.

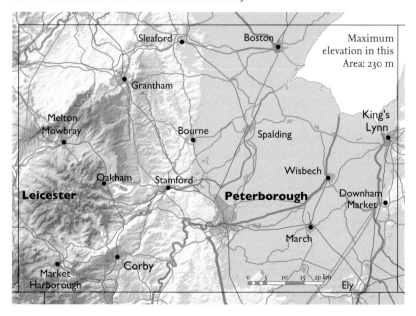

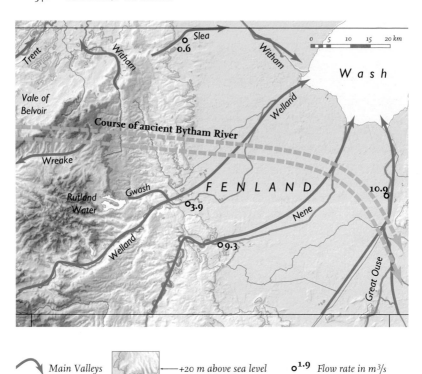

Main Valleys — +20 m above sea level $o^{1.9}$ *Flow rate in m³/s*
— *Coastal flooding zone*
— *Present coastline*

FIG 267. River pathways and coastal flooding zone in Area 15.

All of the other rivers in this Area drain into the Wash via the Fenland, where they have been considerably rearranged by centuries of engineering work. From southeast to northwest, the main rivers are the Great Ouse (10.9 m³/s), Nene (9.3 m³/s) and Welland (3.9 m³/s), where the mean flows have been measured at the stations marked on Figure 267.

Along with the present-day pattern of rivers and coasts, the other major factor determining the local scenery is the underlying bedrock. I have divided Area 15 into four Landscapes (labelled **A** to **D** in Fig. 268), basing the division largely on the bedrock or its surface blanket.

Landscape A: Triassic bedrock and the River Trent
This Landscape is defined by the presence of Triassic bedrock below the surface blanket in two small patches in Area 15 (Fig 268). This bedrock consists of layers of red mudstone that were deposited in an inland basin supplied with mud and

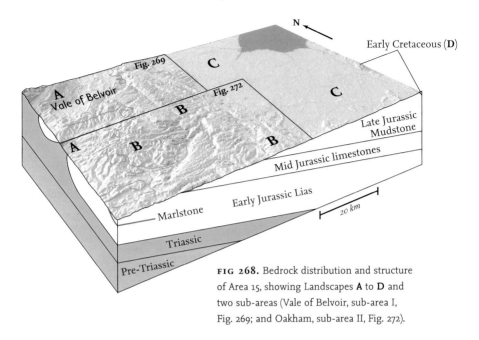

FIG 268. Bedrock distribution and structure of Area 15, showing Landscapes **A** to **D** and two sub-areas (Vale of Belvoir, sub-area I, Fig. 269; and Oakham, sub-area II, Fig. 272).

occasional sand by rivers over 200 million years ago (Fig. 225). Thin gypsum layers were deposited periodically in lakes or arms of the sea when they dried out in the arid climate of that time. The landscape here has been shaped by recent erosion into a gently undulating surface, except where the thin bedrock sandstones have resisted recent river erosion to produce low escarpments.

The River Trent flows across this corner of Area 15 within a distinct floodplain, which is 2–3 km wide, remarkably straight and constrained between steep valley walls that are generally about 50 m high. The last events in the retreat of these valley walls probably eroded the Triassic bedrock during times of low sea level since the Anglian glaciation, and some of the floodplain has been constructed during the recent Flandrian sea-level rise. However, the Trent has a well-developed series of river terraces (see Chapter 2, Fig. 11), and this suggests a long and varied early life from pre-Anglian times.

The northerly part of Landscape **A** only contains small relict patches of Anglian ice-laid material, probably because the rest of the cover has been removed by the Trent as it shifted its course widely during its early history. The southern part of Landscape A, near Leicester, has a more extensive cover of Anglian material, along with distinctive incised valleys that have been carved in the 400,000 years since it was deposited.

Landscape B: Jurassic hills and valleys

This Landscape encompasses the area of low hills immediately west of the Fens. Its Jurassic bedrock is reviewed first.

The closing episode of Triassic times was marked by the flooding of this landscape by the sea and the deposition of the Rhaetic layer of distinctive limestones. This flooding heralded the opening of the Jurassic and Cretaceous seaway (Fig. 227), which lasted for more than 100 million years. These Rhaetic limestones have locally resisted recent erosion to produce small escarpments in the scenery. The limestones were followed by a general accumulation of Early Jurassic sediments, mostly the mudstones and thin limestones collectively known as the Lias. These do not usually produce distinctive scenery, except in the case of the Marlstone Rock Bed. This remarkable layer – never more than 10 m thick – consists of iron-rich limestones and sandstones that have been widely

FIG 269. Map of slopes in the Vale of Belvoir, sub-area I, showing localities mentioned in the text (**b1**, **b2** etc.), Marlstone Rock Bed of the Early Jurassic (**mr**) and Middle Jurassic bedrock (**mj**). Located on Figure 268.

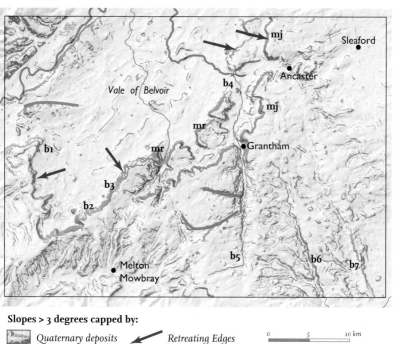

Slopes > 3 degrees capped by:

Quaternary deposits		Retreating Edges	
Bedrock		Faulted Slope	

0   5   10 km

quarried across the western parts of Area 15, often using a network of local railways. Its unusual materials, formed in a distinctive chemical episode during the life of the Jurassic seaway, have made it resistant to recent landscape erosion, so that it forms a clear escarpment in the western part of Area 15 (Fig. 268).

The Marlstone Rock Bed (Fig. 269, **mr**) underlies the eastern edge of the Vale of Belvoir, the largest and most distinctive scenic feature in the northwest of Area 15. In contrast, the less well-defined southern and western edges of the Vale are carved in Anglian ice-deposited material.

Above the Marlstone Rock Bed, the Jurassic succession includes more of the Early Jurassic (Lias) mudstones, carved into hilly terrain. However, the next major slopes in the scenery are the result of resistant bedrock materials, particularly limestones, of the Middle Jurassic. Because of the generally uniform tilt of the bedrock layers at less than 1 degree to the east-southeast, the slopes in the scenery due to the Middle Jurassic units (Fig. 269, **mj**) generally lie to the east of those due to Late Triassic and Early Jurassic units. In the early days of geological exploration, the Middle Jurassic succession was divided by William Smith (Chapter 6, Area 9) into an Inferior Oolite unit and a Great Oolite unit. The Inferior Oolite lies below the Great Oolite, but there is much variation from place to place in the detailed nature of these bedrock materials. Limestones, of particular importance in producing steep slopes in the scenery, alternate in the successions with mudstones and sandstones. Special mention should also be made of the Northampton Sandstone layer (forming the local base of the Middle Jurassic), in which ironstones have been of great importance economically, particularly in the southwest of Area 15 around Market Harborough and Corby. This variable package of Middle Jurassic bedrock, rarely more than 50 m thick in total, has been eroded into isolated hills in the west but forms whole valley sides further east, where the tilt has brought it down to lower elevations. Many of these incised valleys have rather parallel sides and trend roughly east–west, a pattern that may indicate that the early streams formed on easterly sloping surfaces.

Rutland Water, near Oakham, was created in 1977 by the construction of a dam across two such easterly-trending branches of the River Gwash. The Gwash has eroded downwards through the Middle Jurassic limestones into the underlying Northampton Sandstone and Early Jurassic mudstones. The limestone has been used in building the older houses in the village of Edith Weston, shown in the foreground of Figure 270.

The Middle Jurassic limestone has also provided stone for many of the buildings throughout Landscape **B**, whether in villages or stately mansions. The building of Burghley House (Fig. 271) was begun in 1555, largely using the locally quarried Lincolnshire Limestone of Middle Jurassic age. It has been the home of the Cecil family ever since.

FIG 270. Northwesterly view across Rutland Water from the village of Edith Weston. (Copyright Aerofilms)

North of Stamford, between Bourne and Sleaford, a number of low hills are underlain by Late Jurassic Oxford Clay, often capped by Anglian ice-laid material. Erosion here has carved numerous 30–40 m deep valleys, cut through the Anglian material and into the Oxford Clay beneath. These valleys must have formed since the end of the Anglian glaciation about 400,000 years ago.

In pre-Anglian times, perhaps 600,000 years ago, a large eastward-draining 'Bytham River' is thought by some to have flowed across this Area (Fig. 267). The evidence comes from sediment grains found in the far east of Area 15, which appear to have originally come from bedrocks in the West Midlands and Wales. This river must have flowed at a higher level than most of the present surface, because its course bears little relationship to present valleys or to the flow directions of present rivers.

FIG 271. Burghley House, near Stamford.

The slope map of sub-area I, around the Vale of Belvoir (Fig. 269), helps us recognise some further episodes in the formation of the landscape. The key to this is the realisation that some parts of the local area are characterised by slopes that are capped by – and largely cut into – the bedrock, whereas in other parts the capping material is largely sediment left by the Anglian ice sheets. These deposits cover large parts of the landscape, capping some of the highest elevations and carpeting some of the low areas in the southwest. The western edge of the Vale of Belvoir (**b1**) consists of Anglian material, still not removed by later erosion. The southern section of the southeastern edge is largely capped by Early Jurassic lithologies, except for two places (**b2** and **b3**) where pre-Anglian valleys, plugged by ice-laid deposits, have been cut across by later erosion. To the north of this, Early and Middle Jurassic layers form the double edge of the Vale, and have been stripped of Anglian material. To the east of the Vale of Belvoir is the Ancaster Gap (**b4**), now used for road and rail transport (via Sleaford) through the Middle Jurassic scarps. It appears to be large enough to have been carved by early ancestors of the River Trent, which may have been the agents for the general removal of the Anglian cover from the floor of the Vale and its southeastern edge.

In the southeast of Figure 269, the pattern of shallow valleys of the Witham (**b5**) and the West and East Glen (**b6** and **b7**) is remarkably rectangular, suggesting some fracture pattern in the bedrock, perhaps due to stresses linked to earth movements.

Similar ideas, based on the distribution of Anglian material, can be applied to sub-area II, around Oakham (Fig. 272). Here the cover of Anglian material is general except for a large part of the northeast, where the larger rivers (for example the ancestral Welland and Nene) have eroded widened valleys and may be largely responsible for the removal of the cover of Anglian ice-laid material.

Local slopes must have been modified and moved by slumping and collapse under Ice Age conditions of frequent freezing and thawing. Some of the flatter surfaces in this Landscape may have formed during cold, but not ice-covered, periods of the Ice Age via the removal of sediment by meltwater streams.

On the edge of the Fens south of Peterborough, the slope bounding the Fens may have been formed, at least partly, by coastal erosion during high-stands of the sea, perhaps during the Ipswichian interglacial just over 100,000 years ago. Another suggestion that has been made is that a Fenland lake existed here when the Devensian ice was melting, and that shoreline erosion at the margins of this lake may have been responsible for the Fen-edge slope line.

FIG 272. Map of slopes in the Oakham area, sub-area II. Located on Figure 268.

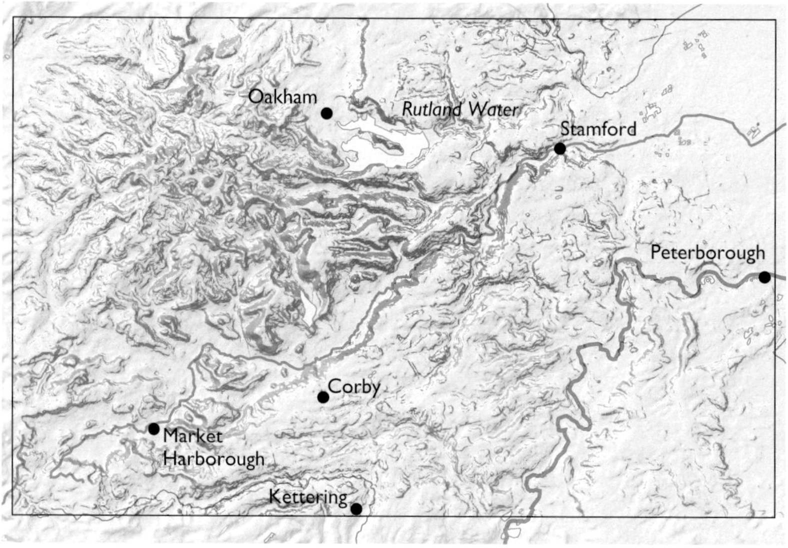

Slopes > 3 degrees capped by:

Quaternary deposits

Bedrock

Recent examination of the shapes of some of the depressions in the Jurassic upland bedrock surface, to the west and south of this Fen edge, has suggested that the depressions may have formed as thaw lakes that grew on the surface when the ground was frozen (Fig. 273). These features, generally 1 km or so in diameter, have been recognised as the probable products of *thermokarst* processes (because of the key roles of heat and ice-melting – see Chapter 2), and they provide a valuable insight into the mechanisms that have led to the lowering of these clay flat-lands.

Landscape C: The Fens

The Fenland Landscape is defined by the presence of a remarkably flat and extensive surface blanket of silts and peats that date from the last few thousand years (Fig. 274). This surface blanket was deposited during the Flandrian rise of

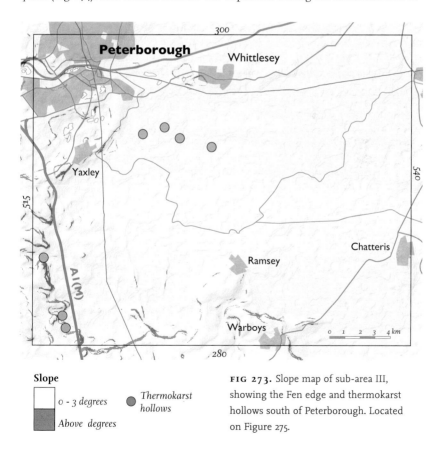

Slope

☐ 0 - 3 degrees   ● *Thermokarst hollows*

■ *Above degrees*

FIG 273. Slope map of sub-area III, showing the Fen edge and thermokarst hollows south of Peterborough. Located on Figure 275.

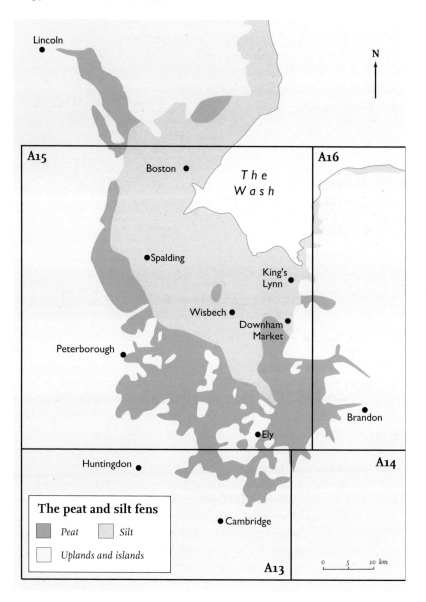

FIG 274. The Fenland.

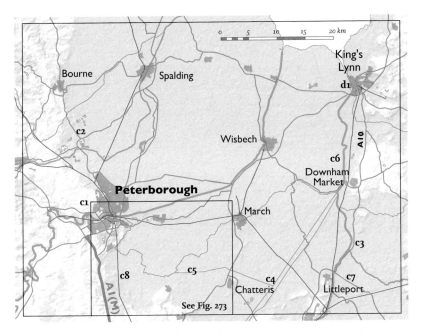

FIG 275. Central Fenland, showing locations (**c1**, **c2** etc.) mentioned in the text.

sea level following the worldwide melting of ice that marked the end of the last cold phase of the Ice Age. Below this cover of surface blanket is Late Jurassic bedrock (Fig. 268). The Oxford Clay and the Kimmeridge Clay are the best-known layers in the Late Jurassic succession, which consists primarily of mudstone. The relative ease with which this mudstone has been eroded during the late Tertiary and Quaternary, particularly by rivers but also by the Anglian ice, explains why this Fenland Landscape is never more than a few metres above or below sea level. In the south, islands of marginally more resistant bedrock are surrounded by younger Fen deposits, for example at Ely.

Numerous gravel pits in the surface blanket of the Fens near Peterborough (Fig. 275, **c1**) and Stamford (**c2**) mark the location of fans of gravel brought into the Fenland basin by the ancestral Nene and Welland, as they carved the hill and valley landscape to the west. Some of the gravel was deposited simply because the rivers were slowing as they emerged from their valleys and flowed into the flat lands of the Fens. In other cases, the gravel was moved around by storm waves at times when the sea – or perhaps a lake – was standing several metres higher than the present water level.

The Fens are the largest expanse of really flat land in Britain. The remarkable flatness of their present-day surface is the result of a very young infilling or 'topping-up' process illustrated in Figure 276. In a situation where the sea level is rising, low-lying areas are increasingly prone to flooding because they are drowned repeatedly by high river or storm waters. Each flood leaves deposits of muddy particles behind, topping up the surface towards the level reached by the highest floods.

The parts of the Fens nearest to the sea are known as the Silt Fens (Fig. 274). Their sediment has been deposited largely by wave and tidal action in the coastal zone as the land was built upwards and outwards into the embayment known as the Wash. Former coastlines (back to the Middle Ages) can be seen on the 1 : 50,000 Ordnance Survey maps (e.g. *Landranger* 131), where they are marked by former sea walls, now more than 1 km inland from the present sea defences. This retreat of the sea has been encouraged by the building work undertaken by people, because the construction of walls helps to pond up tidal waters, leading to the deposition of fine coastal muds. This man-made build-out of the coastline over the past few hundred years is a reversal of the drowning of the Wash–Fenland Basin caused by Ice Age melting over many thousands of years (see Chapter 2, Figs 20 and 21).

The Silt Fens have been farmed since medieval times. With their ancient churches and intricate pattern of tracks, roads and field boundaries, they provide an isolated example of the 'ancient countryside' described in Chapter 2 (Fig. 26). It is also interesting to realise that the early concentration of farming activity here will tend to increase the supply of mud to rivers and storms, thus accelerating the recent retreat of the sea.

FIG 276. Infilling of hollows in the already quite flat Fenland bedrock, to produce the flattest landscape in Southern England.

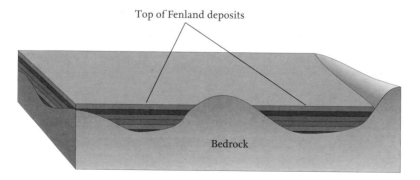

In contrast to the Silt Fens, the young soils of the Peat Fens have formed under wetland conditions that developed where the main rivers have flowed from hilly Landscape **B** into the flat Fens. Under these wetland conditions, swamps developed behind the coast and the Silt Fens, and vegetation has been preserved as black, organic-rich peats. The Peat Fens began to lose their wetland character when major engineering works began in the early seventeenth century, at which point the characteristic rectangular pattern of field boundaries, roads and drains appeared. It is typical of the Peat Fens that they lack the network of ancient roads and buildings that occur in the Silt Fens.

Figure 277 shows a typical view of the southern Peat Fens, with a sugar-beet refinery steaming away in the middle distance. The peat soils, open fields and straight drainage and road boundaries in the foreground contrast with the more ancient field-boundary pattern behind. The black soils are being lost rapidly, because their drainage and cultivation are leading to the destruction of the peat.

Before the seventeenth century, the southern Peat Fens were low-lying marshes with meandering rivers, and the few inhabitants tended to live on local 'islands'. Fen and marsh people made a living from hunting wildfowl, fishing and harvesting reed, sedge and willow. Life was not easy because of frequent flooding and the lack of well-drained land.

FIG 277. The Peat Fens, looking northwards towards Methwold (Fig. 275, **C3**). (Copyright London Aerial Photo Library)

FIG 278. Small Fenland drainage windmill, restored at Wicken Fen in the northeast of Area 13.

The major drainage work that converted much of the Fens to farmland was planned and managed by Cornelius Vermuyden (1595–1683). He was born in the Netherlands and died in London, having introduced Dutch land reclamation methods to the flatlands of England. His first major drainage projects were primarily funded by Charles I and the Earl of Bedford, along with a group of other English and Dutch investors (then known as Adventurers). His first campaign in the Fens involved the digging of the Old Bedford River (c4) and the Forty Foot Drain (c5), completed in 1637. During the Civil War, Parliament ordered the dykes to be broken in order to hinder the royalist advance. After the war, work continued, using the labour of prisoners of war, and the New Bedford Level was cut by 1652, completing the remarkably long and straight dual-river stretch of the Great Ouse that is so obvious on maps.

Vermuyden's strategy was to straighten the large rivers in order to speed up the water flow, resulting in the rapid passing of floods and avoiding the plugging of the channels by silt. In more recent times, attention has also been paid to widening and deepening rivers for navigation, and gates have been installed to help control river depth and flooding.

Water was initially lifted from low-lying areas by large numbers of windmills (Fig. 278). Later more efficient drainage was achieved by a succession of different types of drainage engines, firstly powered by steam, then diesel and now electricity. The Fens have rapidly become the most engineered landscape in Britain. This increasingly vigorous drainage of the Fenland fields has caused the surface blanket to shrink and its surface to be lowered. Intensive ploughing of the land has also caused lowering of the surface due to oxidation of carbon-rich peats (generating carbon dioxide), and the removal of the dry soil by the wind during storms.

Because of this general lowering of the ground surface, Fenland rivers now run between flood embankments that are generally much higher than the river surface. This may often be several metres above the level of the surrounding fields, which may lie well below sea level. Rainwater on the fields seeps downwards into their drains. The water is then pumped up into rivers, and the water of these is eventually released into the sea at low tide (Fig. 279).

After disastrous flooding of the Fens in 1947, it was decided to construct yet more components that would improve the major drainage scheme. Part of this involved digging the Flood Relief Channel, the larger and straighter of the channels shown in Figure 280. This greatly increased the floodwater storage capacity in this area, which had previously consisted only of the tidal Great Ouse channel (seen to the left of the Relief Channel in the photograph, winding its way towards King's Lynn and the sea). Through the last 50 years, the engineering

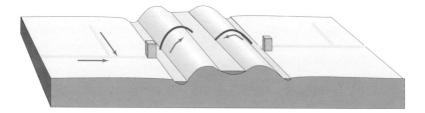

FIG 279. Drainage from low-lying Fenland fields is pumped into a Fenland river.

FIG 280. The Great Ouse (left) and Flood Relief Channel (right) at Downham Market (Fig. 275, **c6**). (Copyright Aerofilms)

of the Fen rivers has successfully avoided any serious flooding. There are current proposals to carry out more engineering work on this river system, and one of these is to allow better recreational navigation between the Fenland rivers and those of the Thames and the Midlands.

The engineering of the Fenland rivers has changed the river pattern completely. Before the drainage work there was a complicated network of winding rivers with many branches, reflecting the freedom of the flooding rivers to change their courses over the very flat landscape. This has now been changed to a network of straight, restrained rivers (Fig. 281).

But traces of the old network remain. In Figure 282 the Little Ouse rodden shows up beautifully as a ribbon of pale silt meandering across fields of darker peat soils. Many smaller silt-filled ancient channels are also visible, depending on the state of ploughing and crop-growth in the fields. The straight course of the A1102 road, running between Littleport and Shippea Hill, can be seen

FIG 281. Natural river courses of the Fens, contrasted with the present engineered straight courses.

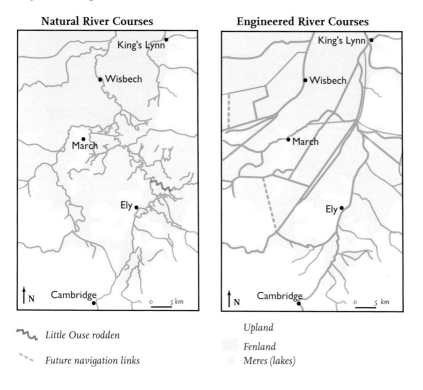

FIG 282. The Little Ouse rodden (Fig. 275, c7), a silt-filled ancient channel.
(Copyright reserved Cambridge University Collection of Air Photographs)

crossing the winding rodden, which is marked in red on the natural rivers map in Figure 281. Houses have been built where the road crosses the rodden, to take advantage of the silt, which makes for better foundations than the shrinking and wasting peat soils. This rodden is clearly shown on Ordnance Survey *Landranger* Sheet 143 (Ely and Wisbech).

Before their general drainage, the Fens contained not only numerous winding rivers, but also many lakes, often called *meres*. The conversion of the Fen wetlands to the valuable arable 'prairies' that exist today means that all of these meres are now dry and often generally forgotten. Some of the best known were those at Soham (see Area 13, Fig. 243), Ramsay and Whittlesey.

Whittlesey Mere (**c8**) was not drained until 1851. Before that, it was some 4 km across and was claimed to be the second largest lake in England, after Windermere. It was famous for its fishing, for its recreational sailing, and for the size of waves that would form on its surface under stormy conditions. It was also known for the exploits of the speed skaters who competed there under the fierce freezing winter conditions common in the eighteenth and nineteenth centuries.

The limestone blocks shown in Figure 283, the smallest weighing over a tonne, provide unusual evidence for the former presence of Whittlesey Mere. They are thought to have arrived here when the mere was open water, as they were being transported on a raft which foundered during stormy weather. They appear to have originated in one of the Middle Jurassic limestone quarries in the west, and had been destined for a building site – probably one of the religious settlements on the Fenland 'islands' to the east. They were marked out as a navigational hazard before the mere was drained and they again became visible.

FIG 283. Engine Farm limestone blocks (Fig. 275, **c8**), 9 km southeast of Peterborough.

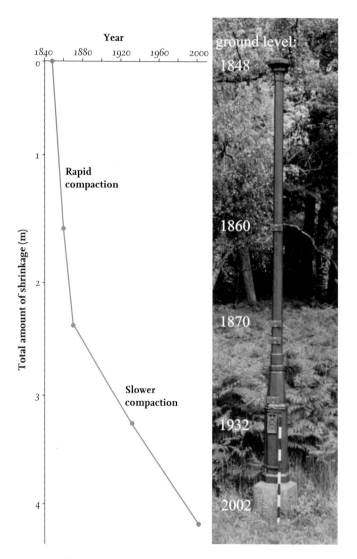

FIG 284. The Holme Post (Fig. 275, **c8**), 9 km
south of Peterborough. The red and white rule is
1 m in length. (Copyright British
Geological Survey)

FIG 285. Woodwalton Fen.

The shrinking and wasting away of the Fenland soils has been mentioned above. The Holme Post (Fig. 284) provides an impressive indication of the lowering of the surface since the draining of Whittlesey Mere. This post was buried in 1848 in a vertical shaft dug into the ground not far from the edge of the mere. When it was buried, the base of the post was fixed into the underlying mudstone bedrock, and its top was fixed level with the ground surface. The soil (much of it peaty) has shrunk 4 m in just over 150 years (almost 3 cm/year), leaving the post projecting by that amount into the air. It is interesting to see that the shrinkage was greatest in the early years, when the ground was drying out particularly rapidly after the drainage of the mere in 1851.

At Woodwalton, Wicken and Lakenheath Fens, campaigns are being directed towards preserving relics of the early Fen wetland environment (Fig. 285). This has been made more difficult by the recent drainage of the surrounding landscapes, but it now looks as if the trend towards ever more efficient drainage is being reversed. The increasing concern to protect threatened wildlife and provide people with recreational space is encouraging long-term plans to re-flood and greatly extend the wetlands in these preserved areas. The Fen wetland nature reserves are generally designed to be maintained with a high water table, in contrast to the drained fens elsewhere. This favours a range of different ecological environments, controlled by the degree of drainage. Reed and sedge form at the edge of open water, followed by a scrub of willow and alder as drainage becomes better.

FIG 286. 'Bog oak' at Wicken Fen.

The Peat Fens have often yielded large pieces of timber on ploughing, and heaps of this material can sometimes be seen at the edges of fields (Fig. 286). This timber reflects a period when the Fens were drained well enough to allow the growth of woodland with trees of this size.

Landscape D: Early Cretaceous Fenland foothills

Bedrock of Early Cretaceous age rests upon Late Jurassic bedrock along the eastern margin of Area 15 (Fig. 268), where it is sometimes covered with a surface blanket of Fenland deposits. This Landscape is more fully developed in Area 16, but it is logical to consider some aspects of the development of King's Lynn at this point.

King's Lynn (**d1**) has a long history as a transfer point between sea-borne ships and smaller, river-borne craft. The waterfront in King's Lynn shows the remarkably preserved pattern of medieval warehouses and unloading quays constructed on the tidal margin of the Great Ouse (Figs 287 and 288). Because of the presence of a number of side creeks at right angles to the waterfront, the medieval centre of King's Lynn was divided to an unusual degree.

Its position on the banks of the Great Ouse has obviously governed the growth of King's Lynn. So also has the presence of a number of drainage channels rising in the nearby hills, which form the eastern margin to the Fens, and draining westwards into the Great Ouse. These channels bring water from the Early Cretaceous hills (Carstone and Sandringham Sands), but also provide excellent sheltered channel mouths which have been developed for the unloading, loading and repair of shipping.

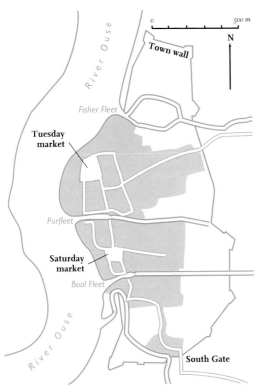

FIG 287. Part of the King's Lynn waterfront (Fig. 275, **d1**). At the left-hand margin is the large Tuesday market place, with numerous stalls. To the right of the obvious Purfleet channel, near the right-hand margin, is the Saturday market place. (Copyright Norfolk Museums and Archaeology Service & Derek A. Edwards)

FIG 288. Simple sketch map of medieval King's Lynn.

AREA 16: NORFOLK

Although Norfolk was famously described by Noel Coward in *Private Lives* as 'very flat', it generally has a much more varied topography than, for example, the Fenland of Area 15 to the west. It is true that the hills barely exceed 100 m in height, but there are open valleys between the hills, and undulating plateaus are extensive.

The only part of Area 16 (Figs 289 and 290) that approaches the extensive flatness of the Fens is the Broads area of east Norfolk, and both of these landscapes result directly from the recent (Flandrian) rise of sea level that has followed the melting of ice since the last (Devensian) cold episode of the Ice Age.

The most obviously recent landscape changes are those we can see taking place in the coastal zone, arbitrarily defined here as ground less than 20 m above sea level. These changes have been taking place over the last 6,000 years, since the rising Flandrian sea reached approximately its present level. This general map of areas of recent landscape change picks out the extent of the coastal zone, and also shows the general pathways of the main present-day rivers, where the change of inland landscape tends to be concentrated (Fig. 291).

FIG 289. Location map for Area 16.

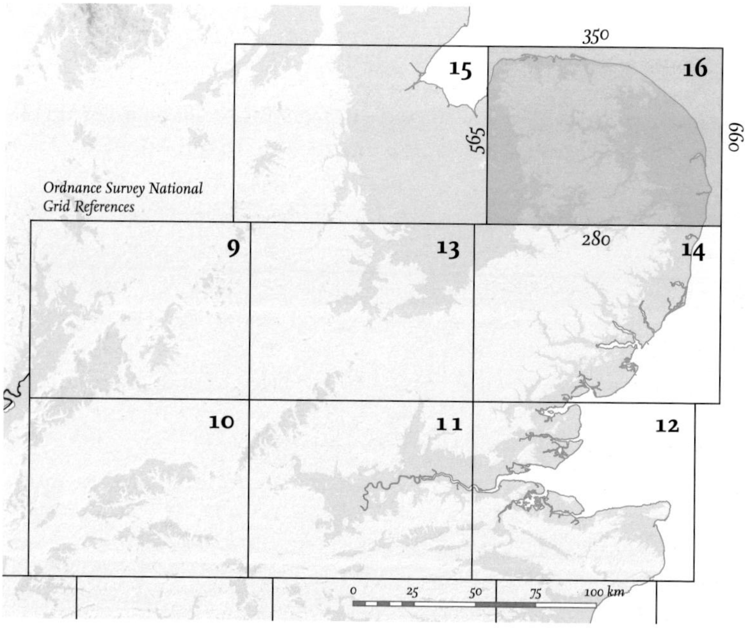

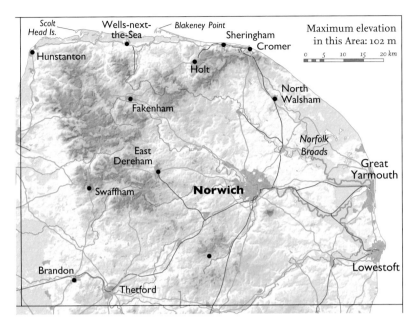

FIG 290. Natural and man-made features of Area 16.

The drainage of the Norfolk landscape depends on low-gradient rivers in open valleys draining to the west, north and east from the Chalk high ground of west Norfolk. The main westerly rivers flow into the Fens over relatively short courses, and are comparatively small. They are, from south to north, the Little Ouse (3.0 m³/s), Wissey (1.8 m³/s) and Nar (1.2 m³/s), where the mean flow figures have been measured at the stations shown in Figure 291. In contrast, the main rivers flowing to the east coast are distinctly longer, although water extraction leaves some of them with low mean flows. From south to north, mean flow figures measured at the stations shown are: Waveney, 0.6 m³/s; Yare, 1.4 m³/s; Wensum, 4.0 m³/s and Bure, 2.2 m³/s. The overall drainage divide within the Chalk hills runs from the northwestern part of the Area, inland from Hunstanton, in a southeasterly direction to the Lopham Gap, between the Little Ouse and the Waveney. Here, remarkably, the divide between the westerly-flowing Little Ouse and the easterly-flowing Waveney is less than 25 m above sea level.

Some of the examples of recent changes are so clear that they merit discussing in unusual detail below. In much earlier times, during brief periods of warmer climate and higher sea level over the last million years or so, coastal

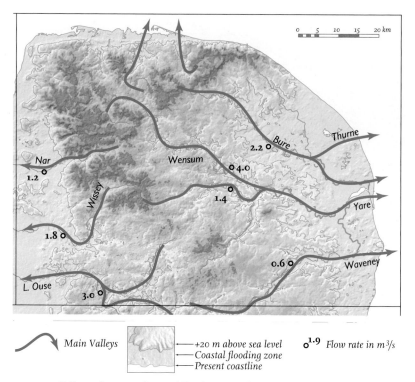

FIG 291. Valley pathways and coastal flooding zone for Area 16.

processes are likely also to have influenced the scenery along the edge of the Fens in west Norfolk.

The general introduction to East Anglia at the start of this chapter summarises the bedrock distribution (Fig. 226) and succession (Fig. 225), and this sets the scene for consideration of the Landscapes of Area 16 (Fig. 292).

The tilting of the bedrock layers to the east is very gentle, but enough to take the base of the Chalk (Late Cretaceous) from a few metres above sea level at Hunstanton to a depth of 550 m below sea level under Great Yarmouth, 80 km to the east. This amounts to an overall slope downwards to the east of less than 1 degree. The gentle tilting took place during the Tertiary period, and can be regarded as part of the general lowering of the Earth's surface that has caused great thicknesses of sediment to accumulate in the area now covered by the southern North Sea. The tilting may also have been linked to the volcanic activity and uplift of western Britain that occurred during earliest Tertiary

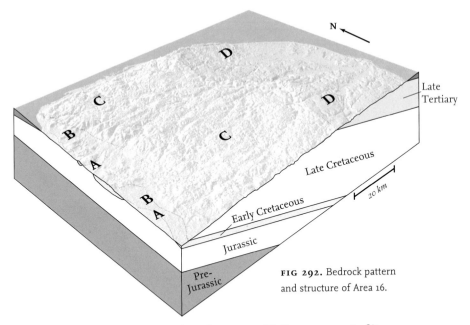

FIG 292. Bedrock pattern and structure of Area 16.

times, as the Atlantic Ocean continued to open with the movement of its underlying plates.

The hilly landscape created by the Late Cretaceous Chalk and Late Tertiary Crag contrasts markedly with the flat landscape to the west, underlain by Jurassic mudstones (Area 15).

The gentle bedrock tilt to the east that is the main feature of the structure of Norfolk is visible in the Hunstanton cliffs (Fig. 293), where the contact between the white Chalk and the underlying brown Carstone slopes down to the left in the cliff line. These cliffs are shown in more detail in Figure 297.

I have divided Area 16 into four Landscapes, labelled **A** to **D** in Figures 292 and 294, basing the division on the bedrock that underlies the surface blanket. In general the Landscapes recognised in this book, though based on bedrock differences, are similar to the character areas recognised by the Countryside Agency, which are based largely on land-use patterns.

Landscape A: Late Jurassic mudstones of the Fens

There are only very small parts of Area 16 where the surface blanket is underlain by the Late Jurassic mudstones of the Kimmeridge Clay. These occur along the western edge of Area 16 and, in topographic terms, they form part of the main Fenland that is discussed under Area 15.

FIG 293. Looking northeastwards over the Hunstanton cliffs.
(Copyright Norfolk Museums and Archaeology Service & Derek A. Edwards)

FIG 294. Area 16, showing Landscapes **A** to **D** and localities (**b1, b2** etc.)
mentioned in the text.

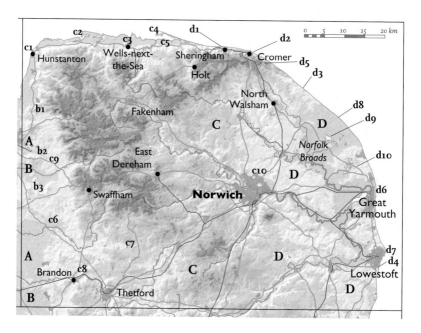

Landscape B: Early Cretaceous foothills

The Early Cretaceous bedrock succession that underlies the surface blanket in west Norfolk consists largely of Gault mudstones in the south of Area 16. However, to the north, in the areas east of Downham Market and King's Lynn, increasing thicknesses of sand are present, forming the Sandringham Sands and the Carstone. Through much of this northern area, the Carstone has been used as a distinctive local building stone: a red, brown or orange sandstone looking rather like gingerbread. The slabs or blocks are irregular, and have generally been used to face walls, requiring brick or limestone piers or frames to give strength and form to windows and doors. The photograph (Fig. 295) is of a new wall in Hunstanton.

The sandstone materials of the Early Cretaceous have resisted landscape erosion more than the underlying Late Jurassic mudstones of Landscape **A**, producing low hills often covered with acid-soil heathland vegetation. Bracken and mixed forestry, particularly extensive around the royal Sandringham estate (**b1**), have been developed for countryside shooting activity. East of King's Lynn, around Leziate (**b2**) and Roydon Heath, this heathland also contains an array of sand-pits, where the Sandringham Sands have been quarried as a source of pure quartz sand.

The variety of deposits in the Nar Valley (**b3**) shows how valley pathways have been used repeatedly as the landscape has evolved. The earliest surface-blanket deposits are of Anglian ice-laid material, some 450,000 years old. These are followed by Hoxnian deposits (about 400,000 years old) that include evidence of flooding by the sea up to a level 25 m above the present sea level. The next episode recorded in the sequence represents the deposition of gravels, sands and muds in a river delta that built outwards into a lake. It seems that the Nar Valley was dammed at this time by Wolstonian ice sheets (180,000 years old), which must have entered the Fenland basin from the northwest, creating a lake.

A final dramatic episode in the history of this Landscape is marked by the Hunstanton ice-laid till, which was deposited just inland of the present coast of northwest Norfolk during late Devensian times, about 20,000 years ago. The topography of the landscape in these recent times must have been quite similar to that of today, because the Devensian ice sheets that spread across the North Sea basin were stopped by slopes similar to those that currently face the Fenland Basin and the North Sea.

Landscape C: North Norfolk coast and the Late Cretaceous Chalk hills

The Chalk hills of Norfolk form more than half of the land area of Area 16, forming a broad belt trending roughly north–south, with the chalk strata tilted to the east by less than 1 degree. Most of the Landscape is covered by a thick

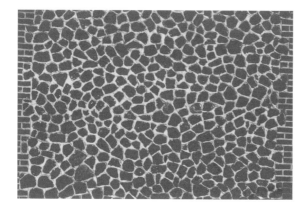

FIG 295. Wall faced with blocks of ginger-bread Carstone bedrock.

FIG 296. Flint nodules in Chalk at West Runton, 2 km east of Sheringham.

surface blanket, so the easiest way of looking at samples of the Chalk is to look at the local buildings that are made from it. White Chalk is often used as a building stone and is generally quarried from the particularly resistant layers known as 'clunch'. Flints from the Chalk (Fig. 296) are also commonly used as a facing material.

Flints are a common feature in the upper layers of the Chalk, and are the major component of the river and beach gravels of Norfolk. They have been abundantly used in the building of many walls and houses. The flints formed in the first place by mineral growth within the soft muddy sediment that was later to become the Chalk. They grew when silica was precipitated from the water in the minute spaces and cracks that are always present in young sediment, replacing the calcium carbonate that was present before. In areas close to the coast, flint walls often show the flints with their rounded, sometimes white exterior crusts, whereas elsewhere flint walls consist of 'knapped' flints with a flatter, black face outwards, created by cracking open the flint before mounting it in the wall.

The scenery of the coastal zone of northwest Norfolk is much younger than the valleys and slopes visible inland. This is because the sea has only arrived at its present position within the last few thousand years, since the general melting of the Earth's ice cover that took place at the end of the Devensian, about 20,000 years ago (see Chapter 2).

Hunstanton (c1) is the only place in the whole of East Anglia where tough, overhanging sea cliffs occur. This is because there are no other localities where hard bedrock has become directly exposed to the attack of storm waves.

Hunstanton is also famous for the three differently coloured layers of bedrock in its cliffs: a layer of Late Cretaceous white Chalk overlies an Early Cretaceous layer of brown sandstone (Carstone), with a thin layer of red Chalk between them (Fig. 297). The detached and fallen blocks of white chalk at the base of the cliff show that the cliffs are collapsing and moving inland all the time. The regular rows of weed-covered Carstone blocks in the lower part of the beach show how the storm waves have created a wave-cut platform with a regular system of *joints* (cracks). These joints were formed during an early and widespread phase of stressing of the bedrock.

East of Hunstanton the coastline is characterised by spits, beach ridges and barriers, often with salt marshes divided up by the tidal channels that are typical of this coastal stretch. The Burnham Flats are an offshore area of unusually shallow sea, north of Scolt Head (c2), that produce the special coastal scenery of this area. The Flats extend some 25 km out to sea before the depth at low tide becomes greater than 10 m. This means that when the sea level was rising due to melting of the Devensian ice, the sea must have flooded over this area of land

FIG 297. The sea cliffs at Hunstanton (Fig. 294, **c1**). (Copyright London Aerial Photo Library)

extremely rapidly. More importantly, the flatness and shallowness of the Burnham Flats has allowed vigorous attack on the sea bed by storm waves, moving considerable quantities of sediment and constructing beach barriers with their associated salt marshes.

Scolt Head Island (Fig. 298) is a beautiful example of a beach barrier island: 'beach' because it is made of sand and gravel pushed into place by storm waves, and 'barrier' because it protects the land behind it from these waves. The beach barrier forms the north rim of the island, and protected back-barrier features have formed behind it. At the western end of the island (the foreground in Figure 298), advancing storm waves have curved around as they moved up the deep tidal channel in the right of the picture. This has, in turn, curved the beaches that form the end of the island. A number of old curved beaches are visible in the foreground of the photograph, where successive storms over recent centuries have added more sand and gravel to the island.

FIG 298. Looking eastwards along Scolt Head Island (Fig. 294, **c2**). (Copyright London Aerial Photo Library)

Since the Flandrian sea-level rise, global sea level has changed relatively little over the last 6,000 years, and the Norfolk coastline itself has stayed in more or less the same position. However, the plentiful supply of gravel, sand and mud moved around by sea storms means that beach barriers such as Scolt Head Island are continually changing their shape. People who revisit stretches of the coast are always spotting year-to-year changes in the barrier's shape, the positions of the tidal channels and the build-up of mud in sheltered areas.

Wells-next-the-Sea (**c3**) is the only settlement on the north Norfolk coast that is still used by commercial shipping. For about 1 km north of Wells, the construction of a sea wall west of the main tidal channel has allowed drainage of the western back-barrier areas. A road running behind this sea wall provides easy car, pedestrian and railway access to a wide range of beach-barrier and shore environments (Figs 299 and 300).

In Figure 300, the tidal channel is the straight, light-coloured feature running inland towards Wells-next-the-Sea. The channel has been straightened by the building of a sea wall along the near side of it. The large, dark, tree-covered ridge directly behind the beach in the foreground is the main storm-built barrier, stabilised in the 1850s by planting pine trees on its wind-blown dunes. The beach

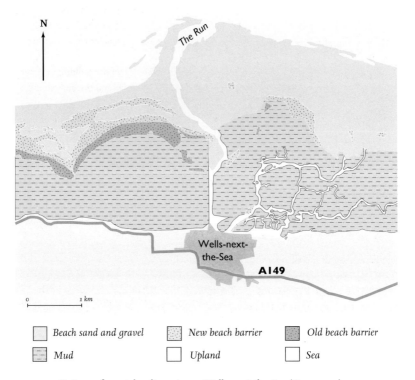

N

The Run

Wells-next-
the-Sea

A149

0   1 km

☐ Beach sand and gravel   ▦ New beach barrier   ▦ Old beach barrier

▦ Mud   ☐ Upland   ☐ Sea

FIG 299. Pattern of coastal sediment near Wells-next-the-Sea (Fig. 294, **c3**).

itself shows at least four distinct, slightly sinuous ridges of sand, more or less parallel to the tree-covered barrier. These ridges tend to be driven landwards during storms and may eventually be added to the barrier. The ridge closest to the tree-covered barrier is the lightest in colour because it has been capped by dry, wind-blown dunes formed within the last 20 years. Behind the main barrier, Wells Caravan Site can be seen, built upon meadows formed by draining ground that was previously salt marsh. These drained meadows were flooded when the sea wall was breached during a storm in 1978. This whole array of coastal features has been constructed and altered during the last 6,000 years, since the sea rose and flooded the land up to its current level.

Figure 301 shows the large barrier feature of Blakeney Spit (**c4**) in the far distance, along with a number of smaller barrier ridges forming a discontinuous, sandy strip in the middle distance, on the seaward side. Behind these barriers, in

FIG 300. Looking southeastwards across the tidal channel that leads into Wells-next-the-Sea (Fig. 294, **c3**), whose buildings cluster round the quay in the middle distance at the right-hand edge of the photograph. (Copyright reserved Cambridge University Collection of Air Photographs)

the centre of the photograph, is a large area of back-barrier salt marsh, completely covered by the highest tides and supplied with sea water and sediment by a complex network of channels. The sharp southern edge of the coastal strip (on the right-hand side of the picture) is marked by a clear, straight line that truncates fields on the hilly ground to the south. This edge is thought to mark an old cliff line formed during the Ipswichian (about 130,000 years ago), when the sea was at a slightly higher level than it is today. Between the Ipswichian warm episode and today, the sea retreated for hundreds of kilometres as ice advanced into this area. When the ice melted, the sea advanced back to its present position.

The photograph in Figure 302 was taken when the gravel barrier ridge was under attack from a severe winter storm in February 1996. A light powdering of snow has fallen on the brown winter landscape. The storm has sent waves over the top of the barrier, flooding the low-lying marshes behind and creating small gravel fans from the barrier material in this temporary lagoon.

An even more severe storm in 1953 caused loss of life in the village of Salthouse, on the left side of the flooded marshes in Figure 302. This area has been chosen for an engineering programme of 'managed retreat', where the present barrier will be left to be modified by future storms, and a new barrier will be built further inland as a second line of defence.

The presence of ripples as large as those shown in Figures 303 and 304 is evidence of high flow speeds in the tidal channels, providing enough energy and turbulence to form these remarkable and distinctive shapes. Walking over

FIG 301. Looking eastwards over the young coastal sediment from a point 1 km east of the Wells tidal channel. (Copyright Norfolk Museums and Archaeology Service & Derek A. Edwards)

beaches, you will often see much smaller ripples (20–30 cm between crests) that have been formed in the same way, but under less rapid flows in minor channels. Similar – but more symmetrical – small ripples can also be formed by the to-and-fro action of waves, as opposed to one-directional flows.

Figure 305 shows the flow patterns that create such ripples and lead to their migration. If water speed is increasing over a flat bed, turbulent eddies will come and go, always varying in size, speed and direction, but tending to form at regular intervals in a mass of flowing water. Eddies can also be initiated as water flows over an irregular surface and, once set up, they often scour the bed, having enough energy to pick up loose material. In this way, sand grains can be picked up by the flow of water and carried along the bed into ridges or ripples, separated by hollows scoured out by the eddies. Since pockets of turbulence tend to occur at regular intervals, regularly spaced ridges soon form in the sandy bed. These ridges take on the shape of ripples, with gentle upstream and steep downstream faces, and they start to migrate downstream. Eddies now become amplified in the troughs between ridges, excavating sand which is then pushed

FIG 302. Looking west over the eastern stem of Blakeney Spit (Fig. 294, **C4**). (Copyright Norfolk Museums and Archaeology Service & Derek A. Edwards)

FIG 303. Large ripples (5–15 m from crest to crest) on a sand bar in the tidal channel behind Blakeney Spit, near the village of Morston (Fig. 294, **C5**). (Copyright London Aerial Photo Library)

up the upstream side of the next ridge, before avalanching down the downstream face. This transfer of material, from the upstream side of the ripple to the downstream side, allows the ripple to be continuously rebuilt in a downstream direction whilst maintaining its size and shape.

The inland parts of Landscape **C** have a surface blanket of river and ice-laid material, often producing a gently undulating plateau surface. Much of this material is Anglian in age, so the open and gentle valleys that have been eroded in the cover of this inland plateau have largely formed over the last half-million years. The details of the Anglian events, and of earlier episodes in the Pleistocene, are the subject of much interest and research at the moment. This will be reviewed briefly in the section on Landscape **D** that follows this.

Since the Anglian cold phase, the Earth has experienced four more major cold episodes, the last of which was drawing to a close only about 18,000 years ago. During this last (Devensian) cold episode, ice from the north extended as far south as the position of the present north Norfolk coast. Most of the land to the south, though probably not covered by ice since the Anglian glaciation, had for much of the time been subjected to viciously cold temperatures, which created a

FIG 304. Sandbank in the tidal channel at Wells-next-the-Sea (Fig. 294, **c3**). The large ripples have a wavelength of about 10 m and become active only when covered by a tide high enough to flow outwards (to the left) at speeds greater than ~0.6 m/s (~2.1 km/h).

layer of ice within the ground. The northern latitudes of Canada and Russia provide vivid present-day examples of ground-freezing processes, and of the ways in which freezing in winter and thawing in summer can cause damage to the foundations of buildings and roads. East Anglia contains many examples of processes of this sort, preserved since this last cold episode.

The field shown in Figure 306 has been photographed under ideal conditions of crop growth to show a regular honeycomb pattern in the ground. Similar patterned effects are often to be seen in the present-day Arctic (see Chapter 2, Fig. 17), where areas of ground are subjected to alternations of fierce winter freezing and summer melting. When the ground freezes, the first ice tends to form at a large number of ice nucleation points scattered below the soil surface. Once some ice crystals have formed it is easier for more to grow on these than to grow on their own, so small pockets of frozen ground form and grow outwards until they meet neighbouring pockets. Here they push against each other, creating straight edges. Another important effect is that when the water in the ground freezes it expands, shifting the soil outwards slightly. Where they meet, neighbouring pockets of frozen ground cannot shift the soil outwards and so

FIG 305. Movement patterns during the migration of ripples. Movement at three levels in the water (blue) becomes increasingly marked by eddies as the floor of sand (yellow) is approached. On the surface of the sandy bed, sand is carried up the upstream side of the ripples and deposited on the downstream side, building downstream-dipping layers in the sand. As these movements continue, the ripples will migrate downstream, and this may be a steady movement if the water continues to flow in a steady way.

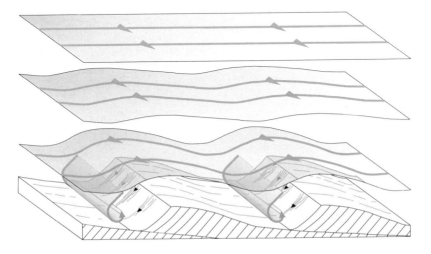

force it upwards to the surface, forming ridges which define the edges of the pockets and producing the honeycomb pattern.

The name *pingo* has been borrowed from northern native ('Eskimo') languages and applied to hillocks typical of some Arctic areas, formed when lenses of ice grow within the soil. These lenses may grow until the ice core breaks through to the surface, forming a hollow like the crater of a volcano which may contain water during the summer. At Thompson Common (**c7**), on the A1075 between Thetford and East Dereham, a Pingo Trail has been arranged, where visitors can see irregular hillocks and hollows with ponds, believed to have been formed in this way during Devensian cold episodes. These features, also seen at East Walton (**c9**; Fig. 307), are further examples of the effects of soil movements generated by ice growth and melting.

Over the southwestern part of this Landscape the surface blanket contains light sandy soils, in contrast to the heavy clay soils on the thicker ice-laid material further east. The name Breckland is used for this area of light soils, which tend to dry out quickly and lack the nutrients needed to produce good

FIG 306. Patterned ground, 2 km northwest of Oxburgh Hall (Fig. 294, **c6**), very like the present-day Arctic pattern shown in Figure 17. (Copyright Norfolk Museums and Archaeology Service & Derek A. Edwards)

FIG 307. Pingo remains near East Walton (Fig. 294, **C9**), 10 km east of King's Lynn. (Copyright Norfolk Museums and Archaeology Service & Derek A. Edwards)

crops. The area has never been valued for farming and has, even in recent historical times, resembled an arid desert, subject to widespread dust storms and removal of soil and seeds by the wind.

The photograph of the Grimes Graves area (Fig. 308) shows, in the background, the forest cover now typical of much of the Breckland. In the foreground, large numbers of craters are the relicts of the Neolithic flint mining for which Grimes Graves is famous. English Heritage provides access to some of these small mines, where the flints can be examined in the position in which they originally grew in the Chalk. The flints were used by Neolithic people to make knives, axe heads and spear heads by careful chipping ('knapping'). At Grimes Graves there are about 500 mines spread over an area of 6 hectares, many of them reaching a special seam of flints in the Chalk where the miners cut horizontal galleries from the main vertical shafts. Deer antlers were used to hammer, lever and rake the flints from the rock, before hauling them to the surface in baskets. Flint knapping is still carried out today by a few experts and there is still a small demand for flint chips for reproduction flint-lock firearms.

Much of the forestry in the Breckland was planted by the Forestry Commission in the 1920s to add value to the ground and to limit soil erosion by the wind. Parts of Thetford Forest have also been used for many years for military training. In earlier times, this empty country was used for hunting by royalty, and today it is once again becoming popular for recreation: Center Parcs is just one of the many tourist developments of recent years.

FIG 308. Grimes Graves (Fig. 294, c8), 4 km northeast of Brandon. (Copyright Skyscan Balloon Photography, English Heritage Photo Library)

A gravel quarry near Lynford (**c8**) has revealed, in recent years, a vivid picture of life some 60,000 years ago on the floodplain of the ancestral River Wissey. At that time the Devensian cold episode of the Ice Age was in full force, and local January/February temperatures are estimated to have averaged −10 °C or lower. Neanderthal man lived in the area and it appears that they used an abandoned river channel loop as a location for shepherding, trapping and butchering of mammoths, woolly rhinos, horses and bison.

Thetford has grown around a crossing of the westward-flowing Little Ouse, just below the point where it is joined by the River Thet. An ancient road here, known as the Icknield Way, followed a belt of open country marking the western edge of the Chalk bedrock and our Landscape **C**. Thetford embarked on a programme of major expansion in the 1960s, with the construction of large areas of housing and industrial development, often in conjunction with London housing authorities.

The Wensum and Yare form the longest river in the Norfolk area (Fig. 291). It is probably the latest version of a much longer easterly-flowing river that developed when the bedrock of the area first began to tilt eastwards. Near Fakenham, the headwaters of the Wensum lie in an area of very gentle hills ranging in elevation between 50 and 80 m above sea level. Much of this rather flat area is underlain by ice-laid material, and the Wensum has cut a small, open valley into this with only a narrow floodplain and a limited valley floor. Beside the river are patches of gravel moved from the local slopes when spring floods were more vigorous, probably during and immediately after the Devensian glacial.

Further downstream towards Norwich (**c10**) the river increases in size as it gathers water from its branches and gradually drops in altitude. The locality map (Fig. 294) shows how it develops a series of meanders downstream of Norwich, approximately 2–3 km from bend to bend. Gravel pits close to the Yare provide further evidence that the river carried much coarser materials under the vigorous flooding conditions following the Devensian glacial. In this area the whole shape of the valley (slopes and floor) has a meandering form cut into Anglian ice-laid material, Late Tertiary Crag and Late Cretaceous Chalk. This tells us that since the Anglian cold spell, the river has firstly formed meanders by side-cutting and only later cut downwards to produce its valley.

Although much redeveloped, it is still possible to see many features of medieval Norwich in Figure 309. To the left, the River Wensum flows generally southeast, and its first large meander became the site of the cathedral (with the spire) and the castle (on the obvious mound to the right). The River Wensum formed the early northern boundary of the city, which was surrounded on the other three sides by curtain walls that still exist in some areas.

FIG 309. Medieval centre of Norwich (Fig. 294, **C10**). (Copyright Aerofilms)

The location of Norwich represents a balance between the relative ease of bridging rivers where they are smaller above a confluence, and the advantage of being able to bring cargo further up a river when it is still tidal.

Norwich Castle and museum perch above the medieval city centre, and when the shopping centre was built nearby the excavations penetrated deeply into the Chalk. Elsewhere under Norwich, tunnels have been dug to extract chalk (for lime) and flint (also for building), as well as to create storage. These tunnels are prone to collapse and, in one incident a few years ago, trapped a double-decker bus.

Early work on Norwich Cathedral was began late in the eleventh century. It is situated lower than the castle, close to the valley floor but on a terrace of old gravels. The lack of good building stone in the north and east of East Anglia means that the stone for the cathedral was brought over from Caen in France. Barges carried the blocks via the English Channel and the North Sea to Great Yarmouth, then up the rivers Yare and Wensum to a short length of canal that ran to the cathedral.

For most of their courses, the rivers of Norwich have wide valleys with sides that are relatively low (often less than 20 m) and gentle. One exception is the slope where Mousehole Heath has been cut into by the Wensum, immediately northeast of the city-centre bend. Mousehole Heath is underlain by an extensive sheet of gravel and sand that seems to have been left there by northward-flowing rivers draining from a tongue of ice that existed to the south at some time during the Anglian cold spell. Ice-laid material to the south of Norwich, particularly near Poringland, reaches an elevation of 75 m, which is high for this area.

Landscape D: Late Tertiary Crag hills and the Broads

This Landscape is defined by the presence of Late Tertiary bedrock, generally known as the Crag, resting upon the Late Cretaceous Chalk. Chalk is exposed on the shore at West Runton near Sheringham (**d1**), but the Late Tertiary Crag is exposed above this over most of eastern Norfolk and Suffolk. Of special interest are coastal exposures of the Cromer Forest Bed, which forms a very important and remarkably extensive layer sporadically visible for more than 60 km from Cromer (**d2**) in the north to Happisburgh (**d3**) and as far south as Pakefield (**d4**). The Cromer Forest Bed consists of a variety of mudstones and sandstones, often carbonate-rich and full of fossil remains. The fossils represent temperate climatic conditions and are overlain by distinctive glacial deposits representing a return to a much colder climate. Understandably, great interest has followed the recent discovery of flint artefacts, convincingly made by early people, both at Happisburgh and at Pakefield. These are thought by some to represent the oldest evidence of early humans so far found in lands north of the Alps. However, the

Cromer Forest Bed deposits and the overlying glacial deposits are complicated, involving many local episodes, and their dating is still open to doubt and expert disagreement. Some workers believe that the glacial deposits represent a pre-Anglian glaciation, and that the flint implements beneath them must therefore be some 700,000 years old. Others feel that the glacial deposits are of Anglian age and that the flint implements are more likely to be ~500,000 years old, an age more consistent with the currently accepted date of settlement at these latitudes.

The cliffs in the foreground of Figure 310 are actively collapsing by land-slipping under the attack of North Sea winter storms. They provide a cross-section through the Cromer Ridge, one of the highest hill features in Norfolk, reaching 90 m above sea level just inland of Sheringham (**d1**), and extending more than 10 km towards the southwest. The ridge is thought to have been deposited by ice sheets and contains gravel and sand, along with contorted blocks of mixed sediment tens of metres across. Much of this appears to have been dumped, folded and fractured by ice sheets of the Anglian cold episode, which came from a northerly direction some 450,000 years ago (see Chapter 2). The deformation of the material suggests that the ice margin repeatedly advanced and retreated, scraping up and bulldozing its earlier deposits in front of it. In this respect, and because the material forms such a clear ridge, it may be that the Cromer Ridge is the remains of a moraine similar to those found at the fronts of many present-day glaciers and ice sheets.

The coastal scenery of northeast Norfolk consists of a narrow beach backed by cliffs, varying in height from a few metres in some places to over 70 m just east of Cromer. The cliffs are made of soft, clayey sediments, consisting sometimes of ice-laid material and sometimes of Late Tertiary Crag sands, muds and gravels.

When attacked by waves, these soft cliffs slump and slide down onto the beach before being washed away by storms. This contrasts with the much older and harder bedrock cliffs seen at Hunstanton, which collapse as large, hard blocks. More dramatic, however, is the contrast between these soft cliffs and the landscape of wide beaches, beach-barriers and salt marshes of the northern coast. The beach-barriers are continually being built up with new material brought in by the sea, whereas the cliffs of the northeast undergo a general regime of erosion and removal (Fig. 311).

Why is there this important change in the type of coastline around Norfolk? It may be that the facing direction of the northeast coast exposes it to more vigorous storm waves, or perhaps the shallowness of the offshore area of northern Norfolk removes energy from the waves, reducing their erosive power.

FIG 310. Looking northwestwards towards Overstrand (Fig. 294, **d5**) and Cromer (**d2**). (Copyright reserved Cambridge University Collection of Air Photographs)

The east-facing coastline of south Norfolk and north Suffolk has a continuous, narrow beach zone along its length which is locally backed by cliffs. These cliffs, though made of the same ice-laid material as those in the northeast of Norfolk, are rarely greater than 10 m in height. This stretch of coastline is under a general regime of erosion by the sea, similar to that of northeast Norfolk. In this case, however, the sea has not only removed sand and gravel material from the coastline but it has then churned it up and dumped it back on the land to produce local exceptions to the regime, where sediment has built up.

Great Yarmouth (**d6**) and Lowestoft (**d7**) have grown where important rivers flow into the sea. In each case, former river valleys have been plugged by coastal sediment over the last 6,000 years. Further north, at Sea Palling (**d8**), a successful attempt to locally combat the erosive action of the sea involved the construction of nine offshore sea-defence islands, spaced along 3 km of coast. These islands have helped to trap sediment that would otherwise have been washed along the shore by waves, resulting in a build-up of the beach in this area over the last 20 years.

In Lowestoft (Fig. 312), the muddy water of Oulton Broad (in the foreground) and the blue water of Lake Lothing (nearer the sea) make up an eastward-extending waterway around which the town has grown. Lake Lothing,

FIG 311. Happisburgh coastline (Fig. 294, **d3**) photographed in 2004. The red line marks the position of the cliff in 1994. (Copyright Mike Page/www.mike-page.co.uk)

FIG 312. Lowestoft (Fig. 294, **d7**), looking east over the town towards the North Sea. (Copyright Aerofilms)

surrounded by large buildings, leads to the sea and the harbour and quay of Lowestoft – the easternmost point of mainland England. To the northwest, Oulton Broad is linked to the River Waveney system, which drains a large lowland area further inland. It seems clear that the River Waveney originally entered the sea down this waterway. However, at times when this route was blocked by coastal sand and gravel, the main flow of the Waveney would drain to the sea near Great Yarmouth, some 20 km to the north.

The Norfolk Broads authority is responsible for the Wensum and the Yare from Norwich downstream almost as far as Great Yarmouth and Lowestoft, and also for some way up the northern tributaries of the Bure and Ant. The Broads are England's largest low-lying area of undrained wetlands and are home to many rare species of plants and animals.

The Broads contain many shallow lakes, providing marvellous habitats for wildlife and a great deal of boating pleasure for a large number of human visitors. Until the 1960s most people believed that the lakes were natural, on account of their size, but in fact the Broads are largely man-made. They are the result of medieval diggings for peat which formed in this swampy ground on the ancient river floodplains. The peat became an important fuel as an increasing scarcity of firewood coincided with growing demands for cooking, heating and evaporating sea water to produce salt for food preservation.

The peat diggings were usually 2–3 m deep. Deeper diggings were more likely to have flooding problems, but the peat cut at greater depths was usually more compact and, when dried out, provided a more efficient fuel. During the thirteenth and fourteenth centuries, flooding of the peat diggings became an increasing problem, perhaps due to climate change and rising sea level. The year 1287 saw particularly severe flooding, and the Broads were largely abandoned as sources of peat, becoming more important as sources of fish, wildfowl and reeds for thatching.

FIG 313. Looking southeastward towards Heigham Sound from a point above Hickling Broad (Fig. 294, **d9**). (Copyright Robert Harding Picture Library Ltd)

FIG 314. Looking north-westward over Hickling Broad (Fig. 294, **d9**). (Copyright London Aerial Photo Library)

FIG 315. Looking southeastwards across the Halvergate Marshes (Fig. 294, **d10**) towards Great Yarmouth on the coast. (Copyright Norfolk Museums and Archaeology Service & Derek A. Edwards)

Figures 313 and 314 show the typical pattern of lakes and channels, most of which have been created and/or modified by excavations. Particularly characteristic are the long, narrow islands that were left as the margins of some of the excavations. These Broads are the result of excavating a swamped wetland area on one side of the River Thurne, which terminates in the young beach deposits and the present-day coastline only 5 km away.

The straightness of the railway and road in Figure 315 contrasts strongly with the meandering form of the River Bure. The flatness of the Halvergate Marshes and the position of the coastline both reflect the level reached by the sea during its last Flandrian rise.

Surrounding the very flat valley floors occupied by the Broads are large areas of slightly higher ground with soils that are particularly productive. The 'island' of Flegg (**d10**), just north of Great Yarmouth, is very largely within our definition of the coastal flooding zone, and must certainly have been an island at former times of high sea level.

CHAPTER 9

The Making of Southern England

OUR SURVEY BY REGIONS AND AREAS is now complete, so we can conclude the journey by contemplating the broader patterns across Southern England as a whole, and why it has its present form and location.

In Chapters 1 to 3 I developed the idea that all landscapes are the result of a variety of processes, operating, sometimes spasmodically, over long periods of time. I also concluded that two distinctive groups of processes can be involved:

1. **Surface modification**, largely caused by moving water (rivers, mudflows, waves, tides and sometimes ice). All of these water-based processes are strongly influenced by climatic variations in temperature, rainfall and storm intensity.

2. **Solid Earth movement**, resulting from processes originating and operating within the Earth, rather than on its surface. Although most solid Earth movement is difficult to detect, except where earthquakes or volcanoes are involved, it is likely that such movement plays a key role in landscape development. Without movement of this sort, surface modification would, over millions of years, turn hilly landscapes into flat plains.

In this final chapter we shall examine a time-sequence of three major episodes that have resulted in many of the distinctive landscape features of Southern England, both locally and regionally. We start with the Variscan mountain-building episode, an example of solid Earth movement, and end with river erosion and the Flandrian rise of sea level, a remarkable example of surface modification.

EPISODE 1: THE VARISCAN MOUNTAIN BUILDING

The Variscan mountain building occurred over many millions of years, but was particularly active between 400 and 300 million years ago. It was the result of Earth movement between a tectonic plate that included the crust of northern Europe (from central Wales northward) and a southern plate, or plates. The movement and detailed shape of the plates is not clear, and there were probably a number of small plates involved in the generally convergent boundary. However, the convergence must have had a major component of north–south shortening, because there is much evidence of folding and fracturing of the bedrock that is consistent with this shortening direction.

Northern Europe, including most of Scandinavia, is made of large (100–1,000 km scale) areas of bedrock that were last intensively moved during mountain-building episodes older than the Variscan. In contrast, the bedrock of central Europe was intensively moved in Variscan times, and then developed a very

FIG 316. Southern England and surroundings, showing fold trends in the Variscan mountain belt, and the position of its northern Front.

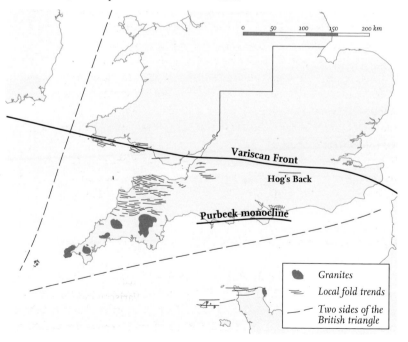

0   50   100   150   200 km

Variscan Front

Hog's Back

Purbeck monocline

Granites
Local fold trends
Two sides of the British triangle

different movement pattern involving local rising uplands and intervening subsiding basins. The Southwest Region of Southern England is typical of one of the uplands, and others are visible in northern France, Belgium and Germany. These uplands were separated from each other by areas that subsided, filling with sediments, and the Southeast England Basin is one of these.

In Southern England, the Southwest Region bedrock was given a pronounced 'grain' by its Variscan folding and fracturing. Our Area-by-Area review has picked out many cases where variations in bedrock resistance to erosion have produced local landscape features with this orientation. There are also local changes in this orientation, suggesting that the convergent movement was not consistent, and that local resistant crustal blocks, or small plates, may have been present. We have noted the great importance of the major zone of late Variscan granites that dominate some Areas in the Southwest. The northern margin of the broad Variscan belt is recognisable in south Wales, southern Ireland and the Bristol area, where the west-to-east grain in the bedrock has strongly influenced the local landscapes (Fig. 316).

East of the Southwest Region, Southern England is covered by younger bedrock that formed in the Southeast England Basin, and the effects of this on the landscapes are discussed in the next section. Here it is important to note that the Variscan bedrock, with its west-to-east grain, is present at depth below this cover. The obvious sign of this is the presence of various often rather isolated fold and fracture belts, now visible at the surface of the cover. Spectacular examples of these are the Purbeck–Isle of Wight fold monocline, and the Hog's Back structure near Guildford, but there are many other localised structures with a similar trend. Although the structures have moved sediments of Late Cretaceous and younger ages, they appear to have been localised by older Variscan structures, deeper in the crust, that became active again when later crustal forces were sufficient.

In terms of the making of Southern England, it can be claimed that the convergent movements of the Variscan mountain building have given local and regional features of the Southwest and South Coast their orientation.

EPISODE 2: THE SOUTHEAST ENGLAND BASIN

The Variscan mountain-building episode was followed by an episode, almost 300 million years long, in which the crust of southeast England subsided, and sediments accumulated in the resulting basin. For this overview, I pick out three levels in the Permian, Mesozoic and Tertiary sedimentary succession. Each of these

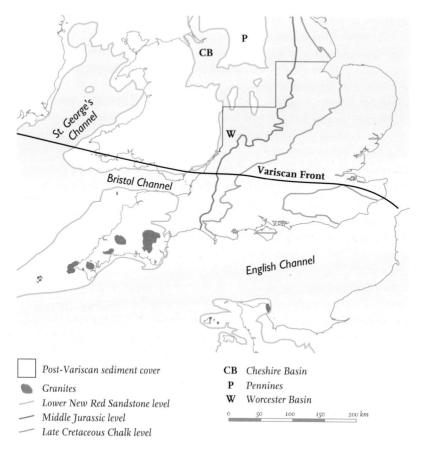

Post-Variscan sediment cover

Granites

Lower New Red Sandstone level

Middle Jurassic level

Late Cretaceous Chalk level

CB   Cheshire Basin
P   Pennines
W   Worcester Basin

0   50   100   150   200 km

FIG 317. Southern England and surroundings, showing the cover of sediment (Permian, Mesozoic and Tertiary in age) formed during Episode 2. On land, the outcrop locations of the three levels in this bedrock cover are mapped: (A) lower New Red Sandstone; (B) Middle Jurassic; (C) Late Cretaceous Chalk.

levels (Fig. 317) contains particularly resistant bedrock, so has tended to produce hills of regional landscape importance. Each level has also acted as an indicator of the net extent of earth movement since it formed as a relatively flat layer.

Although this selection of the three levels picks out erosion-resistant, hill-forming sediments in the succession, it is important to realise that the Southeast England basin-fill consists predominantly of mudstones that are easily eroded. This is one reason why the present-day landscapes are generally so low and gentle.

A: Lower New Red Sandstone level

We have already explored numerous local situations, particularly in Areas 2, 3, 8 and 9, where the contact between the Variscan-deformed Devonian and Carboniferous rocks and the overlying New Red Sandstone is very distinctive. This contact provides vivid evidence of the transition from erosional hills and valleys, at the margin of the Variscan uplands, to the basins of sediment deposition further east. Much local evidence shows that the post-Variscan landscapes contained features oriented by variations in resistance to erosion of the Variscan bedrock.

Close to places where this important surface can be examined today, the level low in the New Red Sandstone often contains gravels and sands that, on subsequent burial and cementing, have become strong enough to resist later erosion at the surface. There are, therefore, many hills today resulting from the presence of strong New Red Sandstone sediments. These hills mimic the New Red Sandstone alluvial fans that earlier extended into the basin.

Looking more widely around and across Southern England, the mapping of this level allows us to pick out some broader features of the landscape not seen before. Along the south coast of the Southwest this level has been traced below the sea, closely following the present coastline, and then, in East Devon and Somerset, the general trend of the surface turns abruptly northwards until it turns again to run westerly, forming the floor of the Bristol Channel Basin. Subsiding movements represented by this level show therefore that the Southwest Region was becoming a distinct upland in early New Red Sandstone times.

Further north, the position of the basal New Red Sandstone level shows that subsiding movements were already starting to define not only the Bristol Channel but also St George's Channel, the Worcester and Cheshire Basins and the uplifting Pennines ridge, with the South Staffordshire and Warwickshire upfolds at its southern end (Fig. 316). This pattern makes it clear that the east–west trends south of the Variscan Front are replaced by a very different movement pattern in the north.

Further east, in the East Anglian and Thames Valley Regions, the New Red Sandstone level is present below the surface, and helps to define the Midlands–London platform below the later Mesozoic and Tertiary cover. The fact that the platform surface is flat-lying, and generally at depths of only hundreds of metres, demonstrates the lack of major vertical movements in this eastern part of Southern England since Permian and Triassic times.

B: Middle Jurassic level

This is a very different sort of level, selected because it marks a widespread change to limestone-accumulating conditions (most famously producing sediments that became the Inferior Oolite) on the floor of the Middle Jurassic sea. This is important, in present-day landscape terms, because the limestones form one of the main escarpment features across the Southeast England Basin, particularly in the Severn Valley Region, where they form the Cotswolds, and in the west of the East Anglian Region.

The gentleness of the tilt of this level across Southern England, away from the localised belts of remobilisation of deep Variscan structures, is evidence of the gentleness of later deep Earth movements. The gentleness of the tilt also means that the scarp created by its surface modification, mainly by rivers, will have resulted in important migration of the scarp, down-slope, as the generalised topography was lowered.

C: Late Cretaceous Chalk level

This level marks the very widespread change in conditions that resulted in the deposition of the Late Cretaceous Chalk. The important role of the resistant Chalk bedrock in giving the landscapes of Southern England their high downlands and Chalk cliffs has been stressed in most of the chapters of this book.

The Chalk also serves as a remarkable marker for movement patterns since the Late Cretaceous, when it was formed. The mapped distribution of the outcrop of this level picks out major structures such as the London Basin downfold and the Weald uplift, as well as many more local features that have resulted from the remobilisation of deep Variscan structures. The very gentle eastward tilt of the Chalk also records downward movements that have occurred in the southern North Sea area, possibly linked to the uplift of western Britain at this time. This western uplift is believed to be due to volcanic activity and molten rock emplacement at depth related to the opening of the Atlantic Ocean.

EPISODE 3: RIVER EROSION, FREEZING CLIMATES AND SEA-LEVEL MOVEMENTS

From mid-Tertiary times (around 20–30 million years ago), two elements of the shape of Southern England started to emerge as distinct land areas. The southern element, formed by the strong Variscan convergent plate movements, was covered by the Southeast England Basin. The northern element was covered by other basins, principally centred on the North Sea and Irish Sea areas and separated by an upward-moving region along the Pennine axis. This sets the scene for the surface modification by rivers, ice and sea-level change that has resulted in the final episode of the making of Southern England. Figure 318 shows a simplified version of the pattern of rivers that have been eroding Southern England since at least mid-Tertiary times. I have extended these below present sea level to indicate broadly where they must have run during the long periods when sea level was much lower than it is today. It is clear that the shape of the coastline, particularly the drowning of valleys, is a direct result of sea-level rise.

It is also clear that the orientation and location of the coastal zones and the submarine topography must reflect the erosional activity of these rivers. The way that the southern coast runs slightly oblique to the east–west Variscan trend must reflect this erosional history. The erosion of the Bristol Channel, Severn Estuary and Severn Valley appears to be related to the river erosion of the soft

FIG 318. Southern England and surroundings, showing main river valleys and approximate continuations at times of low sea level.

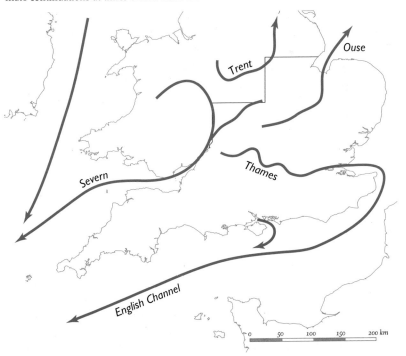

sediments of the Bristol Channel and Worcester Basin, and may have caused late-stage uplift of the Cotswolds. In the east, the coastline of the Thames Estuary and the other associated estuaries must reflect stages in this river's erosion, probably localised, to an extent, by the downward movement of the London downfold. Its form is very different from that of the Wash on the other side of East Anglia, which is likely to reflect a combination of the stability of the Midlands Platform and erosion by the Great Ouse and other Midlands rivers.

THE SHAPE, FORM AND LOCATION OF SOUTHERN ENGLAND

What has given Southern England its 100-km-scale inland landscape features?

The presence of the resistant and deformed Variscan bedrock in the Southwest Region has given it many distinctive landscape features, including the deformed killas slates, the major granite bodies and the Lizard Complex, that were all formed during Episode 1 (the Variscan mountain building). However, on the 100 km scale, the present-day shape and form of the western part of Southern England was defined during Episode 2, and it is marked particularly by the pattern of basins defined by the Lower New Red Sandstone level.

I have to admit to having no real explanation for this pattern, except that it must have formed as a movement response to the very varied patterns of materials in the Earth's crust at this point. The second, the Middle Jurassic level, has given rise to a relatively simple scarp pattern extending from the north to the south coast, and the third, Late Cretaceous Chalk level, has been eroded into the Chalk Downs, which have since been gently folded and locally faulted by Earth movements.

We began this book by wondering why it is that Southern England has such gentle and generally rather low-lying landscapes. The answer seems to be that relatively little Earth movement has taken place since the end of the Variscan plate convergence and the onset of the New Red Sandstone pattern of movements. There has been gentle uplift in the west, probably linked in part to the divergence of the American and European plates, and the growth of the Atlantic Ocean, but also probably linked to the growth and sinking of the North Sea basin. But another important factor has been that much of the sediment accumulating in the Southeast England Basin turned into soft mudstones that have been relatively efficiently eroded by river action, with the exception of the resistant levels of sandstone or limestone. These same mudstones have also been particularly prone to erosion by slope movement during the long cold episodes of the Ice Age, when much of Southern England, though not glaciated, became frozen ground.

What has given the coastline of Southern England its 100-km-scale location and shape?

We have seen how the coastline has retreated actively over the last 20,000 years as sea level has risen due to the melting of the ice of the last cold episode of the Ice Age. The shape of the present coastline depends primarily on the shape of the topography invaded by this rising sea, although in many places significant erosion by the arrival of storm waves has caused further retreat.

The pattern of river valleys (Fig. 318) has been responsible for the major features of the invaded topography. These valleys include the English Channel and the Irish Channel/Bristol Channel valleys that had earlier been eroded from the Atlantic Ocean side, and the southern North Sea (Dogger Hills) valleys eroded from the North Sea side. The shape of these valleys was already apparent in the pattern of downward Earth movements that started in Permian and Triassic times when the movement patterns of the convergent Variscan deformed belt, changed into the pattern of basins and uplands of New Red Sandstone times (Fig. 317).

The existence of the Variscan deformed belt near the surface in the Southwest Region, and its continuation under our South Coast Region, has provided a persistent west-to-east element of erosionally resistant bedrock that has given the coastline its greatest extent, north of which the British coastlines tend to converge to give Great Britain its triangular form (Fig. 316).

Why is Southern England where it is?

Southern England has been reduced in size and changed in local detail by surface modification. But its location depends on the solid Earth movements that have influenced this area of the Earth's lithosphere. The lithosphere plate movements that were responsible for the growth of a convergent boundary through this area in Variscan times produced the land of Southern England, attaching it also to crustal material further north with a very different history. Later movements, initiated in New Red Sandstone times, started to form other elements that are recognisable in the western and eastern margins of Southern England.

As we saw in Chapter 3, the Earth's surface is made up of lithosphere plates that have been continuously moving and changing their configuration for 2–4 billion years. By focusing on Southern England we have examined in detail the surface history of one small area of the Earth's crust. Although small relative to most plates, it has nonetheless seen an episode (1) of plate margin activity, followed by an episode (2) of basin movement unrelated to a plate margin, and then finally an episode (3) of surface modification, strongly influenced by climate change. During these episodes, Southern England moved from equatorial latitudes to its present northern position, as shown by measurements of rock magnetism.

Research on deep crustal and mantle structure is developing all the time, and is now starting to detect the presence of rock volumes possessing distinctive physical properties at these considerable depths. So the onion-skin model (as shown in Fig. 30) is likely to be a gross oversimplification. Some of the distinctive deep rock volumes appear to have a similar lateral extent to Southern England or the British Isles, and it is likely to be at these great depths within the Earth that the reason for the existence of such features of the Earth's natural landscape must be sought.

Further Reading

The material that I have used in this book ranges very widely. It includes leaflets and local guides available at visitor centres, general accounts for a wide readership, systematic scientific reviews and technical original research papers. I have arranged suggestions for further reading in sections that follow the order of the chapters of this book, starting with the general introduction (Chapters 1–3), proceeding through the regional accounts (Chapters 4–8) and ending with the overview (Chapter 9).

Internet search engines will also provide valuable leads on almost all the topics raised in this book.

SOURCES (REGIONAL GUIDES, LOCAL GUIDES, BOOKS AND MAPS)

British Geological Survey Sales Desk, Keyworth, Nottingham NG12 5GG
  (0115 936 3241), sales@bgs.ac.uk, shop.bgs.ac.uk.
BGS London Information Office,
  Natural History Museum, Earth Galleries, Exhibition Road, London SW7 2DE
  (020 7589 4090), bgslondon@bgs.ac.uk.
Geo Supplies Ltd, 49 Station Road, Chapeltown, Sheffield S35 2XE
  (0114 245 5746), www.geosupplies.co.uk.

CHAPTERS 1–3, GENERAL INTRODUCTION

Allen, P. A. (1997) *Earth Surface Processes.* Blackwell, Oxford.

French, H. M. (2007) *The Periglacial Environment,* 3rd edn. John Wiley and Sons.

Gradstein, F. M., Ogg, J. G. and Smith, A. G., eds (2004) *A Geologic Timescale 2004.* Cambridge University Press, Cambridge. (Timescales generally on the International Commission on Stratigraphy website at www.stratigraphy.org.)

Holmes, A. and Duff, D. (1994) *Holmes' Principles of Physical Geology,* 4th edn. Chapman and Hall, London.

Leeder, M. R. (1999) *Sedimentology and Sedimentary Basins: from Turbulence to Tectonics.* Blackwell, Oxford.

Office for National Statistics. *Population Statistics.* www.statistics.gov.uk.

Press, F. and Siever, R. (1986) *Earth,* 4th edn: Freeman, New York.

Rackham, O. (1986) *The History of the Countryside.* London, Dent.

Rackham, O. (2006) *Woodlands.* New Naturalist 100. Collins, London.

Skinner, B. J., Porter, S. C. and Park, J. (2004) *Dynamic Earth: an Introduction to Physical Geology,* 5th edn. Wiley, Cichester.

Stringer, C. (2006) *Homo Britannicus: the Incredible story of Human Life in Britain.* Allen Lane, London.

Van Andel, T. H. (1994) *New Views on an Old Planet: a History of Global Change,* 2nd edn. Cambridge University Press, Cambridge.

General coverage of Southern England

Ballantyne, C. K. and Harris, C. (1994) *The Periglaciation of Great Britain.* Cambridge University Press, Cambridge.

Brenchley, P. J. and Rawson, P. F., eds (2006) *The Geology of England and Wales,* 2nd edn. Geological Society of London.

Centre for Ecology and Hydrology: the National River Flow Archive, including river flow data and maps of the UK Gauging Station Network, is at www.ceh.ac.uk/data/nrfa.

Countryside Agency: the Character Area reports produced by this agency provide valuable summaries of local geology, geomorphology and historical development. This function of the Agency has been the responsibility of Natural England since October 2006. Most of the reports are available as downloads from www.naturalengland.org.uk or enquiries@naturalengland.org.uk.

Fortey, R .A. (1993) *The Hidden Landscape: a Journey into the Geological Past.* Cape, London.

Gibbard, P. L. and Lewin, J. (2001) Climate and related controls on interglacial fluvial sedimentation in lowland Britain. *Sedimentary Geology* **15**: 187–210.

Gibbard, P. L. and Lewin, J. (2003) The history of the major rivers of southern Britain during the Tertiary. *Journal of the Geological Society of London* **160**: 829–45.

Jones, D. C. K. (1981) *The Geomorphology of the British Isles: Southeast and Southern England.* Methuen, London.

Miller, T. G. (1953) *Geology and Scenery in Britain.* Batsford, London.

Rose, J. (1994) Major river systems of central and southern Britain during the Early and Middle Pleistocene. *Terra Nova* **6**: 435–43.

Stamp, L. D. (1949) *Britain's Structure and Scenery,* 3rd edn. New Naturalist 4. Collins, London.

Straw, A. and Clayton, K.C. (1979) *The Geomorphology of the British Isles: Eastern and Central England.* Methuen, London.

Toghill, P. (2000) *The Geology of Britain: an Introduction.* Swan Hill Press, Shrewsbury.

West, R. G. (1977) *Pleistocene Geology and Biology, with Especial Reference to the British Isles,* 2nd edn. Longman, London.

Winchester, S. (2001) *The Map that Changed the World: the Tale of William Smith and the Birth of a Science.* Viking, London.

Woodcock, N. H. and Strachan, R., eds (2000) *Geological History of Britain and Ireland.* Blackwell, Oxford.

Geological maps

British Geological Survey detailed maps are available for the whole of Southern England, which is covered by approximately 170 sheets (of which 33 are currently out of print). The currently available sheets are on the 1 : 50,000 scale.

British Geological Survey (2007) *Bedrock Geology of the UK: South Map.* 1 : 625,000 scale.

British Geological Survey (2007) *Bedrock Geology of the UK: South Booklet.*

British Geological Survey (1977) *Quaternary Geology Map of the UK: South Sheet.* 1 : 625,000 scale.

British Geological Survey (1991) *Geology of the United Kingdom, Ireland and Continental Shelf: South Sheet.* 1 : 1,000,000 solid (bedrock) geology.

British Geological Survey (1996) *Tectonic Map of Britain, Ireland and Adjacent Areas.* 1 : 1,500,000 scale.

Detailed stratigraphic reviews across Southern England
The Geological Society of London has published Special Reports dealing with
the correlation (time and layering relationships) as follows:
Permian, No. 5.
Triassic, No. 13.
Jurassic, Nos 14 and 15.
Cretaceous, No. 9.
Tertiary, No. 12.
Quaternary, revised edition, No. 23.

British Geological Survey Regional Guides
These guides systematically survey in detail the geological foundations of their
regions. Seven of the series cover Southern England, and details of the relevant
guide are given under each region, below.

CHAPTER 4, THE SOUTHWEST REGION

Durrance, E. M. and Laming, D. J. C., eds (1982) *The Geology of Devon*.
   University of Exeter Press, Exeter.
Edmonds, E. A., McKeown, M. C. and Williams, M. (1975) *British Regional Geology:
   South-West England*, 4th edn. British Geological Survey, London.
Keene, P. (1996) *Classic Landforms of the North Devon Coast*, 2nd edn.
   Geographical Association, Sheffield.
Mottershead, D. (1997) *Classic Landforms of the South Devon Coast*, 2nd edn.
   Geographical Association, Sheffield.
Parslow, R. (2007) *The Isles of Scilly*. New Naturalist 103. Collins, London.
Selwood, E. B., Durrance, E. M. and Bristow, C. M., eds (1998) *The Geology of
   Cornwall and the Isles of Scilly*. University of Exeter Press, Exeter.

CHAPTER 5, THE SOUTH COAST REGION

Brunsden, D., ed. (2003) *The Official Guide to the Jurassic Coast: Dorset and East
Devon's World Heritage Coast*. Coastal Publishing, Wareham.
Bird, E. C. F. (1995) *Geology and Scenery of Dorset*. Ex Libris Press, Bradford on Avon.
Ensom, P. (1998) *Discover Dorset: Geology*. Dovecote Press, Wimborne.
Gallois, R. W. (1965) *British Regional Geology: the Wealden District*, 4th edn.
   British Geological Survey, London.

Gibbons, W. (1981) *The Weald*. Unwin, London.
Melville, R. V. and Freshney, E. C. (1982) *British Regional Geology: the Hampshire Basin and Adjoining Areas*, 4th edn. Institute of Geological Sciences [now British Geological Survey], London.
Preece, R. C. and Bridgeland, D. R. (1999) Holywell Coombe, Folkestone: a 13,000 year history of an English chalkland valley. *Quaternary Science Reviews* 18: 1075–125.

CHAPTER 6, THE SEVERN VALLEY REGION

Goudie, A. and Parker, A. (1996) *The Geomorphology of the Cotswolds*. Cotteswold Naturalists' Field Club, Oxford.
Green, G. W. (1992) *British Regional Geology: Bristol and Gloucester Region*, 3rd edn. British Geological Survey, London.
Hains, B. A. and Horton, A. (1969) *British Regional Geology: Central England*, 3rd edn. British Geological Survey, London.
Lane, N. F., Watts, A. B. and Farrant, A. R. (2008) An analysis of Cotswold topography: insight into the landscape response to denudational isostasy. *Journal of the Geological Society of London* 165: 85–104.
Smurthwaite, D. (1993) *Complete Guide to the Battlefields of Britain, with Ordnance Survey Maps*, new edn. Mermaid, London.
Watts, A. B., McKerrow, W. S. and Richards, K. (2005) Localized Quaternary uplift of south–central England. *Journal of the Geological Society of London*, 162: 13–24.
Watts, A. B., McKerrow, W. S. and Fielding, E. (2000) Lithospheric flexure, uplift, and landscape evolution in south–central England. *Journal of the Geological Society of London* 157: 1169–77.
Williams, G. D. and Chapman, T. J. (1986) The Bristol–Mendip foreland thrust belt. *Journal of the Geological Society of London* 143: 63–73.

CHAPTER 7, LONDON AND THE THAMES VALLEY REGION

Essex RIGS Group / Essex Wildlife Trust. *The Geology of Essex*. www.essexwt.org.uk/Geology/geology.htm.
Lucy, G. (1999) *Essex Rock: a Look Beneath the Essex Landscape*. Essex Rock and Mineral Society.
Powell, P. (2005) *The Geology of Oxfordshire*. Dovecote Press, Wimborne.

Selley, R. C. (2004) *The Winelands of Britain: Past, Present and Prospective.* Petravin, Dorking.

Sumbler, M. G. (1996) *British Regional Geology: London and Thames Valley,* 4th edn. British Geological Survey, London.

CHAPTER 8, THE EAST ANGLIA REGION

Brand, D., Booth, S. J. and Rose, J. (2002) Late Devensian glaciation, ice-dammed lake and river diversion, Stiffkey, north Norfolk, England. *Proceedings of the Yorkshire Geological Society* **54**: 35–46.

Chatwin, C. P. (1961) *British Regional Geology: East Anglia and Adjoining Areas,* 4th edn. British Geological Survey, London.

Essex RIGS Group / Essex Wildlife Trust. *The Geology of Essex.* www.essexwt.org.uk/Geology/geology.htm.

Hains, B. A. and Horton, A. (1969) *British Regional Geology: Central England,* 3rd edn. British Geological Survey, London.

Jermyn, S. T. (1974) *Flora of Essex.* Essex Naturalists' Trust, Colchester.

Lucy, G. (1999) *Essex Rock: a Look Beneath the Essex Landscape.* Essex Rock and Mineral Society.

Reed, F. R. C. (1897) *A Handbook to the Geology of Cambridgeshire.* Cambridge University Press, Cambridge.

Rose, J., Lee, J. R., Candy, I. and Lewis, S. G. (1999) Early and Middle Pleistocene river systems in eastern England: evidence from Leet Hill, southern Norfolk. *Journal of Quaternary Science* **14**: 347–60.

CHAPTER 9, THE MAKING OF SOUTHERN ENGLAND

Shaw-Champion, M., White, N. J., Jones, S. and Priestley, K. F. (2006) Crustal velocity structure of the British Isles: a comparison of receiver functions and wide-angle data. *Geophysical Journal International* **166**: 795–813.

Jackson, J., McKenzie, D., Priestley, K. and Emmerson, B. (2008) New views on the structure and rheology of the lithosphere. *Journal of the Geological Society of London* **165**: 453–66.

Index

The New Naturalist Library